19th-century American women's novels

Cambridge Studies in American Literature and Culture

Editor

Albert Gelpi, Stanford University

Advisory board
Nina Baym, *University of Illinois, Champaign-Urbana*
Sacvan Bercovitch, *Harvard University*
David Levin, *University of Virginia*
Joel Porte, *Cornell University*
Eric Sundquist, *University of California, Berkeley*
Mike Weaver, *Oxford University*

Other books in the series
Robert Zaller, *The Cliffs of Solitude*
Peter Conn, *The Divided Mind*
Patricia Caldwell, *The Puritan Conversion Narrative*
Stephen Fredman, *Poet's Prose*
Charles Altieri, *Self and Sensibility in Contemporary American Poetry*
John McWilliams, *Hawthorne, Melville, and the American Character*
Mitchell Breitwieser, *Cotton Mather and Benjamin Franklin*
Barton St. Armand, *Emily Dickinson and Her Culture*
Elizabeth McKinsey, *Niagra Falls*
Albert J. von Frank, *The Sacred Game*
Marjorie Perloff, *The Dance of the Intellect*
Albert Gelpi, ed., *Wallace Stevens*
Ann Kibbey, *The Interpretation of Material Shapes in Puritanism*
Sacvan Bercovitch and Myra Jehlen, *Ideology and Classic American Literature*
Karen Rowe, *Saint and Singer*
Lawrence Buell, *New England Literary Culture*
David Wyatt, *The Fall into Eden*
Paul Giles, *Hart Crane*
Richard Grey, *Writing the South*
Steven Axelrod and Helen Deese, *Robert Lowell*
Jerome Loving, *Emily Dickinson*
Brenda Murphy, *American Realism and American Drama, 1880–1940*
George Dekker, *The American Historical Romance*
Lynn Keller, *Re-making It New*
Warren Motley, *The American Abraham*
Brook Thomas, *Cross-Examinations of Law and Literature*
Margaret Holley, *The Poetry of Marianne Moore*
Lother Hönnighausen, *William Faulkner*
Tony Tanner, *Scenes of Nature, Signs of Men*
Robert Levine, *Conspiracy and Romance*
David Halliburton, *The Color of the Sky*
Eric Sigg, *The American T.S. Eliot*
Charles Altieri, *Infinite Incantations of Ourselves*
Alfred Habegger, *Henry James and the "Woman Business"*
Michael Davidson, *The San Francisco Renaissance*
John Limon, *The Space of Fiction in the Time of Science*

19TH-CENTURY AMERICAN WOMEN'S NOVELS

Interpretative strategies

SUSAN K. HARRIS

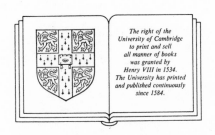

The right of the
University of Cambridge
to print and sell
all manner of books
was granted by
Henry VIII in 1534.
The University has printed
and published continuously
since 1584.

CAMBRIDGE UNIVERSITY PRESS

CAMBRIDGE

NEW YORK   PORT CHESTER   MELBOURNE   SYDNEY

Published by the Press Syndicate of the University of Cambridge
The Pitt Building, Trumpington Street, Cambridge CB2 1RP
40 West 20th Street, New York, NY 10011, USA
10 Stamford Road, Oakleigh, Melbourne 3166, Australia

First published 1990

Printed in the United States of America

Library of Congress Cataloging-in-Publication Data
Harris, Susan K., 1945–
19th-century American women's novels : interpretative strategies /
Susan K. Harris.
p.   cm.
ISBN 0–521–38288–2
1. American fiction – 19th century – History and
criticism.   2. American fiction – Women authors – History and
criticism.   3. Women and literature – United States – History –
19th century.   4. Women – United States – Books and reading –
History – 19th century.   5. Women in literature.   I. Title.
II. Title: Nineteenth-century American women's novels.
PS374.W6H37   1990
813'.3099287–dc20   89–23936
                                                                    CIP

British Library Cataloguing in Publication Data
Harris, Susan K., *1945 –*
19th-century American women's novels : interpretative strategies.
I. Fiction in English.   American women writers, 1800–1900 –
Critical studies.
I. Title
813'.3'099287

ISBN–0–521–38288–2 hard covers

To Kate
now a reading woman herself

CONTENTS

ACKNOWLEDGMENTS

Academics produce books deeply indebted to the people and institutions that nurtured their creators. My debts are numerous. First I wish to thank the Radcliffe Research Scholars Support Awards, which gave me a "babysitting grant" enabling me to work in the Arthur and Elizabeth Schlesinger Library on the History of Women in America in 1983 when I, a new mother, accompanied my husband to Cambridge during his fellowship year. Subsequently my own institution, the City University of New York, granted me Professional Staff Congress–Board of Higher Education (PSC–BHE) awards in 1984–5, 1987–8, and 1988–9, which gave me travel and support money during summer vacations. The English Department at Queens granted me a course reduction during the fall semester of 1987; and the CUNY Faculty Development Program admitted me to a course on Computing in the Humanities and Social Sciences in 1985–6, which taught me to use a computer and consequently accelerated production of this book by at least a year. To all these support programs, I am deeply grateful.

As always, libraries and their staffs figure prominently among the institutions and people integral to this kind of project. While researching this book I learned to value the New-York Historical Society's Manuscripts Division and its Curator, Mr. Duning; The American Antiquarian Society and its staff, especially Barbara Trippel Simmons and Keith Arbour; the New York Public Library; the Stowe-Day Foundation; the Arthur and Elizabeth Schlesinger Library on the History of Women in America at Radcliffe College, especially its Director, Patricia King; the Antiochiana Archives and its Director, Nina Myatt; the Rare Books and Manuscripts Library of Columbia University's Butler Library; and the Long Island (now Brooklyn) Historical Society.

Early versions of three chapters of this book were published in scholarly journals: Chapter 6, on Elizabeth Drew Stoddard's *The Morgesons,* in *ESQ: A Journal of the American Renaissance,* Volume 31, 1st Quarter, 1985;

Chapter 5, on E.D.E.N. Southworth's *The Deserted Wife*, in *Legacy: A Journal of Nineteenth-Century American Women Writers*, Volume 4, Number 2 (Fall, 1987); and Chapter 4, on Fanny Fern's *Ruth Hall*, in *Style*, Volume 22, Number 4 (Winter, 1988).

Many friends and colleagues aided and encouraged me as this book slowly evolved. Joanne Dobson, Janice Radway, Jane Tompkins, Glenna Matthews, David Richter, Cathy Davidson, Mary Kelley, Don Stone, Lawrence Buell, and Fred Kaplan all read early versions of proposals and/or chapters and gave me invaluable advice. Joanne Dobson and Jane Tompkins, especially, helped me sort out my ideas during long conversations. I also want to thank my undergraduate students in English 152 and 351, and my graduate students, all of whom listened, questioned, and challenged me as I began to question and challenge the very concepts and authors I was teaching them. Cambridge University Press readers urged this book to its final version; I thank them for their kind, but incisive, readings. Albert Gelpi, the Editor for the Cambridge Studies in American Literature and Culture series, deserves my gratitude for his decisiveness and promptness, as does Andrew Brown, Publications Director for the Humanities, for his encouragement.

But most of all I want to thank my husband, Billy Joe, helpmate and wise counselor always; my daughter, Kate, who has shown me that even very little women question their inscription in texts; and my babysitter, Myrtle Levy, without whom this book surely would never have been written.

PART I

INTRODUCTION

I have been reading *Ruth Hall* and I must say I enjoyed it a good deal. The woman writes as if the devil was in her; and that is the only condition under which a woman ever writes anything worth reading. . . . Can you tell me anything about this Fanny Fern? If you meet her, I wish you would let her know how much I admire her.

(Nathaniel Hawthorne to William Ticknor, his publisher, 1855)[1]

"Hell has no fury like a woman scorned," and one may add, no fight is so relentless as a family row. [Fanny Fern] threw her grievances into the novel *Ruth Hall,* a book characterized by Beers as a "caricature." In it, he says, she "washed a deal of family linen in public". . . . Doubtless Hawthorne, totally unaware of the family feud and the rage of the scorned author, attributed the intense atmosphere of the novel and its over-done picturings of the effects of extreme poverty upon a struggling feminine soul for genius, and had commended it.

(Fred Lewis Pattee, *The Feminine Fifties,* 1936)[2]

How do we make sense of a book? Or, more specifically, what are the conditions under which nineteenth-century American women's novels have had meaning for twentieth-century critics? The passages quoted above reveal radically different constitutive conventions: For Hawthorne, writing in the 1850s, anger and passion lend merit to *Ruth Hall* regardless of the author's identity; the text has meaning *within* his associations with passion and anger and *outside* his associations with the general run of women's writing. In contrast, for Fred Lewis Pattee, writing in the 1930s, the text can only be interpreted in terms of what he sees as wom-

1

en's innate vindictiveness. Here, passion and anger are seen only in the context of the circumstances that fueled them; unlike Hawthorne, who processes the book first, then seeks information about its author, Pattee does not separate the text, the artifact, from the matrix originating it.

This chapter is designed to help us reconsider twentieth-century readings of mid–nineteenth-century American women's novels, and to suggest means for expanding our own reading strategies. Section 1 surveys those major twentieth-century critical works that focus on the American women novelists of the 1850s and 1860s, tracing the constitutive conventions that these critics (all working within the assumptions of traditional Anglo-American literary criticism) have brought to their subjects, and tracking shifts over time. Section 2 presents the responses of some nineteenth-century readers to what they read, and proposes a multileveled hermeneutic for nineteenth-century women's texts. Section 3 presents alternative reading strategies that help us retrieve some of those novels' possible meanings. In addition, the final section provides the context for (and in the process shows the indebtedness of) my work in relation to the work of all those critics who have also struggled with this literature and with the means they have had for interpreting it.

THE NINETEENTH-CENTURY WOMEN'S TEXT AND THE TWENTIETH-CENTURY ACADEMIC READER: STUDIES IN CONSTITUTIVE CONVENTIONS

It may not be fair to start a review of twentieth-century critical approaches to women's novels of the preceding century with Pattee's *The Feminine Fifties* – it is an easy book to shoot down – but the text occupies an important place in the critical history because it so crudely exhibits assumptions guiding many subsequent critics' evaluations. In his survey of nineteenth-century women's novels, Pattee demonstrates a methodology commonly applied to those texts by twentieth-century critics writing before 1978: a critical strategy that starts with assumptions about the author's sex, moves out to her autobiography, and proceeds to examine her work as an extension of her biological structure and life experiences. In addition, until recently most critical assessments of nineteenth-century American women's novels assumed the primacy of authorial intent and then criticized nineteenth-century women writers' intentions for being either pernicious, confused, or escapist. Consciously or not, these studies have acted in complicity with the cultural assumption that women's writing – with women's oral discourse – was testimony to female irrationality and emotionalism and to American women's struggle to emasculate the American male.

A man who bridged the centuries (he was born in 1863 and died in 1950), Pattee produced many literary histories that helped introduce

American writers to an academic audience still uneasy with the idea that American literature could be academically respectable. On the whole, his work is measured, informed, and fair. *The First Century of American Literature, 1770–1870* (1935), for instance, has an excellent chapter on annuals and gift-books, two genres important for the study of women's literature that have generally been either ignored or maligned. In addition, Pattee's chapter on women's literature of the 1850s is generally favorable to writers like Sarah Josepha Hale, Harriet Beecher Stowe, and Alice and Phoebe Cary. But when he came to expand that chapter (also titled "The Feminine Fifties") into a book, his entire focus shifted.

Interestingly, it is not clear whether Pattee actually read many of the novels about which he writes in *The Feminine Fifties*. Judith Fetterley has already noted how Pattee quotes reviewers and parodists of women's fiction rather than the novels themselves.[3] Pattee's insistence that the novels' themes functioned only to pander to women's hysterical tendencies – an extraordinary feat of interpretive blindness for anyone who has even casually perused them – fuels suspicions. Pattee's remarks are relentlessly invidious. If we can interpret authorial bias through key words and syntactical patternings – and I think we can – Pattee's vocabulary quickly reveals that he is repelled by emotional display. In this text Pattee characterizes the 1850s in terms of excess, especially emotional excess, and he does not like it: Using words like "flush," "fervid," "intense," "emotionalism," and "explosion," he sneers at "the effeminate early Tennyson" (27) and declares that Dickens's influence on American writers was "unquestionably . . . bad. . . . In an overemotional age he added emotion" (72). For Pattee, women were both the cause and the representatives of this excess: irrational, unreasonable, and – excessive; spilling over with feeling and, worse, expressing it verbally. Claiming that the decade was "a feminine period, undoubtedly," (11) Pattee introduces his chapter on agitation for women's rights by noting that "During the 1850s, American women had reached a point where they were handed everything a woman could dream of possessing with one single exception – their 'Rights,' and for these the sex arose in a rebellion that made the decade a battlefield – of words" (92). Pattee's syntactical patterning exploits cultural associations of women with irrationality and verbosity: In his initial clause he suggests that women's demands for the franchise were unreasonable, first, by implying that women were spoiled (they already "were handed everything a woman could dream of possessing") and second, by belittling the concept of civil rights through enclosing the word *rights* in quotation marks, thus signaling the reader to alter his or her reception of that generally revered American sign. In the final clause of the sentence, Pattee continues undermining the women's rights movement by provoking associations of women with excessive speech.[4] Later in the same chapter, he employs a brief syntactical construction to provoke yet another invidious association with women: Commenting on a dispute over the naming of Vassar College, he declares "But a woman always wins her fight" (105). Both through careful manipulation of syntax and wording and through overt statements, Pattee shows that his approach to the literature he is to analyze is at least in part motivated by bias against emotional display and the women who, to him, represent it. Consequently the constitutive conventions he employs in reference to the novels can only make sense of them *as* contributions to that excess.

The Feminine Fifties was the first full-scale twentieth-century study to focus exclusively on American women writers of the preceding century, and it is an important text for us to examine because it appears in subsequent bibliographies and exhibits constitutive conventions that appear – generally more subtly – in subsequent texts. As part of the "critical background" its interpretive conventions became part of the consciousness of succeeding critics, influencing their own approaches to nineteenth-century women's novels. Herbert Ross Brown's *The Sentimental Novel in America, 1789–1860* (1940)[5] demonstrates that legacy by extending the onus against feeling into an attack on the novels' ahistoricism. If women's novels only had meaning for Pattee through their contribution to emotional excess, their major meaning for Brown came through their contribution to emotional "escapism." Following Van Wyck Brooks's indictment of "much of our literature" for catering to "a national mind sealed from experience," in *The Sentimental Novel in America* Brown extends this to the female sentimentalists: "His [Brooks's] indictment applies with peculiar force to the writings of the sentimental novelists. They were escapists, artfully evading the experiences of their own day. . . . They fed the national complacency by shrouding the actualities of American life in the flattering mists of sentimental optimism" (360). Generalizing remarks like these are telling: Coming, as these do, after lengthy chapters demonstrating these same novelists' thematic absorption in the national debates over temperance, slavery, and theological shifts; in the cult of domesticity that formed the secular humanism of the day; and in the "isms" (phrenology, Spiritualism, Transcendentalism, etc.) that absorbed both elite and popular cultures, it is clear that some criteria other than textual evidence is guiding Brown's evaluation. Clues to those criteria perhaps lie in sentences such as "authentic artists like Nathaniel Hawthorne might well ask about the mysterious appeal of these popular books which found their way into the hearts of so many readers and sold by the hundred thousand" (322) or "The enlarged heart of sentimentality is a disease to which those who readily respond to the appeal of human nature are peculiarly susceptible. It is the excess of a virtue, the perversion of an ideal" (369).

As with Pattee, though with far less venom, these remarks suggest that what is at fault is an excess of feeling; key words here are "excess," "heart," and – used in contrast to them – "authentic." Writing in a decade dominated by Dos Passos, Farrell, Wolfe, and Steinbeck, Pattee and Brown reflect 1930s' writers' concern for the meaning of American life – a meaning threatened by the failures of the Depression. They saw sentimental literature – and women – as irrelevant because they could not see that women's literature, too, engaged in the national dialogue about the American Dream; that women's novels emphasized feeling did not, within their historical context, preclude their engagement with American history or American ideals. Assuming that Hawthorne's writing did not appeal to the heart (an assumption not supported by contemporary readers, who tended to share diarist Mary Ann Parker's opinion that ". . . Hawthorne has so many bright and happy thoughts – It is pleasant to read his writings aloud and hear the electric current at the same moment strike another mind"[6]), Brown takes his assessment of Hawthorne's work from other twentieth-century critics who devalued sentiment and valorized historical allegory; he uses Hawthorne's work as a standard for evaluating Hawthorne's contemporaries. Consequently, in Brown's usage, the word "sentiment" always has pejorative implications. Rather than exploring the nineteenth century's valuation of the heart within the context of the history of ideas – as Fred Kaplan has recently done in his study of British Victorian sentimentality[7] – Brown sees it through a twentieth-century ideology that rejects the notion that human nature contains within it the possibility of achieving the high moral plane posited by sentimental idealism.[8] Moreover, he equates "excess" and "the heart" with women. The result is, in effect, a deep-seated repulsion from the feminine, for everything that points to "excess" and the "heart" in this literature is, by definition, within that realm. Despite his *knowledge* that women's novels treated a broad range of contemporary issues, Brown's constitutive conventions only permitted him to see their contributions to a pernicious emotionalism.

Helen Waite Papashvily's 1956 *All the Happy Endings*[9] extends the contradictory critical situation Brown's text initiates. Papashvily shows an informed sense of the novels' thematic and structural movements, recognizing an intentional bifurcation in many that makes them critically intriguing and that reflects a sexual bifurcation in the society that produced them. Yet Papashvily's interpretive conventions are also predicated on her distrust of women's nature and intentions. Her own rhetorical form – the paragraph construction she uses first to summarize, then to analyze, and finally to generalize the action of any given novel – is homologous to the rhetorical forms that, as I shall argue later, rule one category of these novels themselves; she develops an idea that emerges from her reading and then tags on an evaluation that comes from her assumption that women want to emasculate men.

Papashvily views midcentury women's novels as representative of a social state in which women were striving to become the superior sex – an observation, I hasten to add, that may well be true. But Papashvily's a priori assumption is that this goal is undesirable and that the women seeking it were psychologically warped. Taking her evaluative line from Pattee and Brown, she casts the women novelists as aggressors and the male characters they create (as well as various real husbands they possessed) as victims. For instance, in her introduction she begins developing the idea that men and women read the domestic novels of the 1850s differently, a possibility that I, too, will explore in this study. But Papashvily's interpretation of the function of the literature is that, for women, the novels "were handbooks . . . [for] a pattern of feminine behavior so quietly ruthless, so subtly vicious" that it was subversive of the culture as a whole. Words like "ruthless" and "vicious" occur frequently in *All the Happy Endings;* to borrow a schema from Nina Auerbach for a moment, all Papashvily's women authors are demons. Thus she reads the convention of female moral superiority as one strategy to mutilate the male, suggesting that women portrayed female competence in practical affairs and superiority in religious ones not only in order to undermine male hegemony but also to undermine male confidence. "To maim the male, to deprive him of the privilege of slavery and the pleasure of alcohol was not, of course, enough," she begins her chapter on religion in nineteenth-century women's novels. "Female superiority at the same time had to be established and maintained" (95). Despite recognizing the social – if not the ethical – usefulness of abolitionism and prohibitionism, Papashvily is constitutionally incapable of affirming women's leadership in those areas; her ironic tone undermines any legitimacy the women reformers might have had. *All the Happy Endings* concludes with a peroration about sexual relationships among Papashvily's contemporaries, another sign that the criteria she brings to nineteenth-century novels were shaped by the sexual perceptions of her own decade – the decade of the War between the Sexes, of "The Honeymooners" and "The Bob Cummings Show," of *Peyton Place* and of Levittowns where good women devoted themselves to domesticity – in short, the decade whose repressive sexual definitions stimulated Betty Friedan to write *The Feminine Mystique* (1963). Papashvily's final lines, in which she claims that "It still takes more courage than many women can muster to love a whole man. So the emasculation process continues. . . . when at last whole men and whole women are free to love as equals, they will find the real happy ending" (211), suggest that by the conclusion of her study she was no longer sure whether she was writing literary criticism about the past or sexual criticism about her present.

Pattee, Brown, and Papashvily can be seen as an early group of critics whose general vision of women's texts is ruled by their sense of women as Monstrously Female: excessive and vicious. The majority of academic works focusing on nineteenth-century women's texts produced in recent years has rejected such assumptions, in large part because the academics writing them are women who have emerged from the consciousness raising of post-1960s feminism and who no longer see either themselves or other women as biological anomalies. One recent text, however, spans the gap between the pre- and postfeminist critics, Ann Douglas's *The Feminization of American Culture* (1977).[10] On the one hand, Douglas's study of nineteenth-century American women's literature as the formative factor in the development of modern consumerism throws the text into a new arena: part of the study of mass culture. On the other hand, Douglas brings with her many of the values implicit in the earlier works. While Pattee and Brown interpreted women's texts through their vision of women's emotionalism, and Papashvily interpreted them through her vision of women's misandry, Douglas interprets them through her vision of the deterioration of the Puritan ethic, the spread of sentimentality, and the pernicious effects of women's complicity in the development of a consumer economy.

Although it has been seen as a central text in women's literary studies since its publication, *The Feminization of American Culture* actually devotes very little of its attention to analysis of the novels and poems produced by nineteenth-century American women. Douglas's contextual/historical approach to the marketing process and its effects on readers-as-consumers places women's texts within a self-consciously "transactional" relationship between writers and readers, a fruitful line of investigation for critics interested in reader-response studies. However, Douglas forecloses such lines, choosing to project this relationship as an aspect of the shaping, and degrading, of American literary taste. Perhaps ironically, *The Feminization of American Culture* is the only book concerning nineteenth-century women's literature to have gone into an inexpensive paperback edition and to have been marketed through national chain bookstores. The materials it uncovers in its survey of the roots of mass literary culture have lent themselves to a widespread developing interest in the evolution of modern society. As part of this investigation, *The Feminization of American Culture* is a valuable book. Its conclusions and methodology are inappropriate, however, when it is viewed as a study of nineteenth-century women's literature because its exclusive focus forbids the activity of taking the novels on their own ground and subjecting them to literary critical – as opposed to historical/contextual – analysis. In other words, Douglas's focus on the development of the marketing process creates a critical worldview that prohibits other approaches to the women's novels she surveys.

Like Pattee, Douglas's underlying – even a priori – premise about the women's novels is that these are bad books, not, as with Brown and Pattee, because they show an excess of feeling, but because they contribute to a cultural phenomenon that does not meet standards of taste established by the Calvinist legacy. Her key words for acceptable literature suggest the value stance she holds – creative works are valuable if they show "mastery," "control," "history" (i.e., linearity), and "uncompromised detail." Since the literature she examines, especially given the methodology she employs, does not demonstrate these qualities, it is not treated from a literary critical point of view. Her reading of Susan Warner's *The Wide, Wide World,* for instance, presents it as an "economic handbook" that teaches its readers how to shop for writing tables and bibles; the protagonist's experience of "the world" from which she shrinks is seen as an experience of male commerce. By focusing so exclusively on her consumerist framework Douglas excludes exploration of the other definitions of "the world" the text contains – such as its insistence on the young female's powerlessness.[11] Similarly, her reading of Harriet Beecher Stowe's *We and Our Neighbors* as the record of a "parasite" who "consumes" rather than "produces" limits her appreciation of a novel that attempts to bring its author's long-standing concern for rural domestic values into the urban landscape. In fact, *The Feminization of American Culture* is not actually "about" women's literature at all because it contains no premises that admit the legitimacy of nineteenth-century women's concerns. Beginning by setting up the Calvinist clergy as a standard from which to compare and contrast the female literary establishment, *The Feminization of American Culture* ends with Margaret Fuller's and Herman Melville's "revolt" from those "self-announced refugees from history" (223) whose works are "courses in the shopping mentality" (73). For Douglas, as for Brown, nineteenth-century women refused to confront history; the difference is that Douglas's women escape into department stores instead of into tears.

Most studies of nineteenth-century American women's texts published since the mid-1970s reject assumptions about women's innate hysteria, misandry, and degraded values. Rather than beginning with the biological, most have begun with the social, examining women's writing within the context of their social status and the constraints that entailed for women seeking a voice in a culture that forbade them power in the verbal/political sphere. In addition, they have begun focusing on the texts as well as the writers, bringing traditional literary critical methods to bear on their analysis. The results of these studies have been remarkably fruitful, generating further discussion (as the earlier studies did not) and fueling the emerging field of women's studies. Working almost exclusively within the Anglo-American tradition of literary criticism, these studies have helped expand the American literary canon.

Nina Baym's *Woman's Fiction: A Guide to Novels by and about Women in America, 1820–1870*[12] (1978) is the first full study to analyze seriously mid–nineteenth-century women's novels for characterization and plot. *Woman's Fiction* is a pioneering work in more than one respect: It introduces a body of literature to a generation that had been taught to ignore its existence other than as a despicable genre; it approaches the material on its own terms; it questions the prevailing criteria for determining the "greatness" of individual texts; it brings literary criteria to bear on its analysis of the materials; and it takes nineteenth-century feminist ideologies – in all their manifestations – seriously.

Examining the works of the major women writers between 1820 and 1870, Baym identifies an "overplot" in which all the novels participate and which defines this exclusively female genre. Briefly, this overplot mandates that the heroine of any given work will be left destitute – usually financially; will struggle for physical subsistence; and, in the process, will learn to value independence. Baym sees this overplot as imposing a "formulaic restraint" on the individual works produced in the genre, and is concerned to show, primarily through plot analysis, how individual works simultaneously observe those restraints and create variations on the basic theme. While marriage terminates the adventures of nearly all nineteenth-century heroines, for instance, Baym points out how strongly the novels by women emphasize female self-reliance. Thus she says of Fanny Fern's *Ruth Hall* that the theme of "the gifted, virtuous heroine mistreated by her family" is "hardly something new"; recognizes the anger expressed in the book as a common theme in the genre (noting, for instance, that *The Lamplighter* and *The Wide, Wide World* share it though they handle it differently); and sees its triumphant denouement as in common with other women's novels that all "permitted their heroines to triumph in satisfying ways over their enemies, thereby indulging the readers' wish for revenge" (252). But Baym also highlights *Ruth Hall's* deviations, pointing out that it advocates independence over dependence for women and suggesting that its successful protagonist is best left unmarried and self-supporting.

Baym's own textual restraints necessarily limit her study. First, although she has included an extraordinary number of writers within her purview, her definition of women's writing as including only those texts that fit within the restraints created by their participation in the overplot prevents her from including others. Her own difficulties with this limitation are evident in her discussions of why she does not include the novels of Harriet Beecher Stowe in her study. Another significant writer she does not mention is Elizabeth Drew Stoddard, whose novels, unconventional by any nineteenth-century standard, do not conform to the definition of women's fiction as Baym sees it.

In addition to her own definitional restraints, Baym also exhibits an evaluative conflict arising from the contradiction between her training in canonical American literature and her interest in nineteenth-century women's novels. Like Pattee and Papashvily, in *Woman's Fiction* Baym segregates women's writing from other writing of the period. On the one hand, given her genre exclusions, this is a strategic necessity. But it also highlights the evaluative impasse that Baym shares with other American critics, a dilemma of which she is fully conscious and which is the impetus behind her later examination of American interpretive conventions in her essay "Melodramas of Beset Manhood."[13] Even in that essay, however, she questions prevailing conventions rather than attempting to reevaluate nineteenth-century American women's texts. Admitting in her introduction to *Woman's Fiction* that "I have not unearthed a forgotten Jane Austen or George Eliot, or hit upon even one novel that I would propose to set alongside *The Scarlet Letter*," (14) Baym, like the scholar/critics who preceded her, shows her entrapment in the interpretive conventions of the American academic literary establishment. The dearth of interpretive means that she rightly identifies as critics' major problem with nineteenth-century women's fiction is, finally, also her own. Despite this impasse, *Woman's Fiction* is path breaking in its attempt to escape the restraints imposed by most earlier American critics' visions of women's nature and literary intentions; its openness to the legitimacy of women's concerns broke genuinely new ground for American literary criticism.

Mary Kelley's *Private Woman, Public Stage: Literary Domesticity in Nineteenth-Century America* (1984)[14] follows Baym in approaching the novels for what they are trying to do and evaluating them on those terms. Rather than viewing her materials through a formal lens, that is, through a common structural component, as Baym does, Kelley views them through a psychosocial lens, seeing the works, and their authors, as embodying conflicts arising from the social definitions of women's place in nineteenth-century American culture. By far the most contextually layered study of mid–nineteenth-century American women's novels to date, Kelley's approach is primarily historical. It does, however, also consider the works from traditionally literary points of view.

Like *The Sentimental Novel in America* and *The Feminization of American Culture*, *Private Woman, Public Stage* is an ambitious book, casting its net widely into the cultural sea from which these novels sprang. One of the study's points of origin is publishing history, and its chapter chronicling the publication histories of the twelve novelists Kelley treats rivals the work of John Tebbel[15] and Frank Luther Mott.[16] But, in addition to the publication context, Kelley surveys the social milieu in which her subjects matured, seeing their lives and work in terms of their conflicts between the socially mandated "privacy" of the domestic sphere and the necessary "publicity" of the world of the successful novelist. Because the prevailing definitions of women's nature and "place" forbade women's existence in the world beyond the home, women who placed themselves, through their writing, in that world experienced intense conflicts that, Kelley holds, are reflected in the writing itself. Her reading of Fanny Fern's *Ruth Hall,* for instance, focuses on the protagonist's conflict between her womanly heart – especially evidenced in her concern for her children's welfare – and her economic distress, which drives her (once teaching and sewing, both approved feminine occupations, have proved inadequate) not only to write for a living but to approach editors, negotiate contracts, and drive bargains.

Kelley's focus on such dualities shapes her study. Her sense of these conflicts arises from her examination of the writers' biographies and the letters, diaries, and other literature produced by both the novelists themselves and other writers and readers of the period, making her book the first full-length study of nineteenth-century women's novels to utilize material of this kind. Like Baym, then, she lets the material itself suggest the framework in which it is to be examined; like Douglas, she reaches beyond the purely literary, to the publishing industry that had the power to catapult these retiring authors to fame; unlike any of her predecessors, she looks for evidence to support her interpretation among nonliterary materials produced at the same time as the novels. These multiple approaches result in a remarkably fruitful study of her twelve authors, their works, and the relationship of both to the society that produced them.

Baym and Kelly's full-length studies show the radical changes in the interpretive conventions recent academic readers have begun bringing to nineteenth-century American women's novels: Clearing away the misogynism of the early critics, we are beginning to focus on genuinely literary as well as autobiographical and social factors in the construction of the texts. It remains the case that no large-scale study has yet produced in-depth readings of mid–nineteenth-century American women's novels. What work has been done exists in chapters of books whose major focus is elsewhere, such as Alfred Habegger's *Gender, Fantasy, and Realism in American Literature* (1982),[17] Annette Kolodny's *The Land before Her* (1984),[18] Nina Baym's *Novels, Readers, and Reviewers* (1984),[19] Jane Tompkins's *Sensational Designs: The Cultural Work of American Fiction, 1790–1860* (1985),[20] and David S. Reynolds's *Beneath the American Renaissance* (1988).[21] Readings and contextual information also appear in forewords and afterwards to reprint series, such as Rutgers University Press's American Women Writers Series; in collections of original essays such as Elizabeth Ammons's *Critical Essays on Harriet Beecher Stowe*[22] and Eric J. Sundquist's *New Essays on* Uncle Tom's Cabin[23]; and in essays published in academic journals. For instance, Ann Douglas Woods's early essay

"The 'Scribbling Women' and Fanny Fern: Why Women Wrote"[24] anticipates Mary Kelley's book in demonstrating the social tensions manifested
in the psychic and rhetorical split in Fern's work; Jane Tompkins's essay
"Sentimental Power: *Uncle Tom's Cabin* and the Politics of Literary History"[25] asks readers to "set aside some familiar categories for evaluating
fiction . . . and to see the sentimental novel . . . as a political enterprise,
halfway between sermon and social theory, that both codifies and attempts to mold the values of its time" (126). Highly influential essays
such as Kolodny's "Dancing through the Minefield: Some Observations
on the Theory, Practice, and Politics of a Feminist Literary Criticism,"
which calls for new interpretive strategies for elucidating a women's
literary tradition, have also suggested some of the theoretical parameters
of this endeavor.[26] Together, these essays prepare the ground for subsequent literary analysis, as well as suggesting ways of conducting it; like
any other literature from an alien culture, this body of work needed
preparation in the history and sociology of the subculture that produced
it. We are beginning to see the fruits of this labor in in-depth literary
analyses, often from a feminist perspective, of individual works: articles
such as Habegger's "A Well-Hidden Hand,"[27] which raises questions
about the readership of nineteenth-century women's novels; Kolodny's
"A Map for Misreading: Or, Gender and the Interpretation of Literary
Texts," which focuses on Charlotte Perkins Gilman's "The Yellow Wallpaper" and Susan Keating Glaspell's "A Jury of Her Peers" to explore
interpretive strategies for nineteenth-century American women's fiction[28]; Joanne Dobson's "The Hidden Hand: Subversion of Cultural Ideology in Three Mid–Nineteenth-Century Women's Novels,"[29] which
demonstrates the "fracturing" of "formal imperatives" in the works
through the multiple reading levels the novels permit; and Judith Fetterley's "'Checkmate': Elizabeth Stuart Phelps's *The Silent Partner*,"[30]
which sees Phelps's novel as "essentially about language," exploring "the
sources of speech and the reasons for [women's] silence" (17). Clearly, a
new era in mid–nineteenth-century women's literary studies has begun.

THE PUBLIC TEXT AND THE PRIVATE READER: TRACE STUDIES IN GENDER-BASED READING STRATEGIES

The following study seeks to participate in this literary project by
taking advantage of recent approaches to literary analysis that emphasize
language and textual structure. I am particularly interested in applying
these to the novels of the mid–nineteenth-century – the "sentimental"
novels whose "happy endings" seem so formulaic – because I feel that
those textual restraints actually functioned as a cover – or cover-up – for a

far more radical vision of female possibilities embedded in the texts. Like Baym, I see these novels as having a common structural overplot; I am most interested, however, in the way the overplot functions to disguise multiple hermeneutic possibilities. Like Papashvily, I see these novels as being open to different interpretations by different groups of readers; unlike her, I do not see this as a strategy in a war between female demons and male victims. My "readings" of these novels, however, do assume "readers," and my discussion is predicated on the assumption that nineteenth-century readers were as capable as we – perhaps more so – of bringing more than one interpretive strategy to the texts they read. In suggesting this expansion of our interpretive strategies I do not mean to negate the work of those who have written before me. Rather, a study like this one builds on the groundwork of its predecessors. Moreover, in pointing out their blindnesses I do not mean to imply that I alone can see. In the novels I will discuss, the "reconstitution" of meaning from narrative summaries will operate differently according to the schemata brought to it, and the integration of the levels of meaning along both horizontal and vertical axes will take correspondingly different forms.[31] The goal of this study is to join the insights that modern formalist studies can make to the interpretive conventions employed by recent scholars, in order to increase our appreciation of the complexity of those schemata.

As many of *my* readers will have already remarked, my project is influenced by the investigations into textual structure and reading behavior articulated by continental criticism as well as by the insights into the novels' plots, themes, and rhetorical structures that have been my legacy from the scholars and critics in the Anglo-American tradition that I have discussed above. Certainly the overall premises of this book, (*a*) that women's novels written during the midcentury embed radical possibilities within their thematic and rhetorical frameworks, (*b*) that those "deviations" were accessible to contemporary readers and that those readers were capable of "configuring," or realizing, the texts differently than the cover story indicated, and (*c*) that these reconfigurative possibilities were ultimately reflected in the much more overt radicalism of women's texts written later in the century, are analogous to Hans Robert Jauss's contention that literature has the power to change readers' social as well as literary expectations.[32] In *Interpretive Conventions: The Reader in the Study of American Fiction*,[33] Steven Mailloux proposes a reception study based on the theoretical work of Jauss that takes into account how readers' preexistent (and therefore prescriptive) grasp of traditional literary conventions influences their evaluations of specific literary texts (169–70). He also demonstrates the process through which readers use traditional conventions to interpret incomplete texts, thus transforming the conventions into constitutive ones. Mailloux's discussions are relevant to this study in their focus on the activity of the reader in constituting, or realizing, the text.

This realization depends, of course, on the disposition of individual readers, an almost impossible task to reconstruct. Although publication and sales records of most of the novels I will discuss indicate that they had thousands – even, at times, a million – readers, few of those readers recorded their responses to them. For instance, among the many collections of contemporary readers' diaries and letters I have read, not one discusses E.D.E.N. Southworth's novels – yet every contemporary reviewer refers to Southworth as an immensely popular writer. Nor have I found many references to Susan Warner's *The Wide, Wide World,* certainly a midcentury bestseller. Two major reasons account, I suspect, for this silence. The first concerns self-consciousness. Then, as now, popular novels were held to be a lower form of literature; even private diarists were embarrassed to record their indulgence. Consequently, we must obtain our information indirectly, from readers who record, as did Julia Newberry in 1870, that "I have not read but one novel since we arrived, which I think is doing pretty well"[34] – an entry suggesting that she normally read a great many, and was trying to break herself of the habit. The second reason so few references to these novels exist concerns the kind of publicity – or lack of it – accorded women's fiction. As a writer for the *North American Review* remarks apropos of Susan Warner's *The Wide, Wide World, Queechy,* and Amy Lathrop's *Dollars and Cents,* "nobody talked very loud about these simple stories. They were found on everybody's table, and lent from house to house, but they made no great figure in the newspapers or show-bills. By and by, the deliberate people who look at title-pages, noticed the magic words, 'Tenth Thousand,' 'Twelfth Thousand,'" and so on; and as the publishing house was not one of those who think politic fibs profitable, inevitable conclusions began to be drawn as to the popularity of the books."[35] This reviewer assumes that the "simplicity," the unpretentious nature, of domestic fiction, especially those novels tending to religious piety, accounts for its lack of public notice. According to this view, consumption and its advertisement are unrelated.

Despite the dearth of specific responses to specific texts, it is clear that a community of readers did exist for these novels. Among them, a few have left letters and diaries suggesting that they could read on more than one level, could penetrate beneath the novels' "covers." I will quote from these materials later in this chapter. Before I do so, however, I want to demonstrate how this reading process might proceed by examining a work of nonfiction, a book of speeches that may have been collected, edited, and prefaced with an eye for more than one category of reader, and more than one level of interpretation.

The speaker and editor of this text is Catharine Beecher, the spokeswoman for the conservative branch of American feminism in mid–nineteenth-century America. Although Beecher had been active in women's education since the 1820s (her Hartford Female Seminary first opened in 1823), her program is succinctly summed up in a publication of 1871, *Woman Suffrage and Woman's Profession,* a collection of public addresses.[36] "An Address on Female Suffrage," delivered in Boston's Music Hall in 1870 to a primarily prosuffrage audience, is polemical, presenting "the views of that large portion of my sex who are opposed to such a change of our laws and customs as would place the responsibility of civil government on woman" (3). But, in preparation for her argument against female suffrage, Beecher first establishes "the points in which we agree, that we may more clearly appreciate those in which we differ." (4) She continues

> We agree, then, on the general principle, that woman's happiness and usefulness are equal in value to those of man's, and, consequently, that she has a right to equal advantages for securing them.
>
> We agree, also, that woman, even in our own age and country, has never been allowed such equal advantage, and that multiplied wrongs and suffering have resulted from this injustice.
>
> Finally, we agree that it is the right and the duty of every woman to employ the power of organization and agitation, in order to gain those advantages which are given to the one sex, and unjustly withheld from the other.

The remainder of this speech (expanded, in its published form, well beyond the limits of the original) is given to a critique of female education and an explication of Beecher's plan for a women's university which would not only secure each girl "as good a literary training as her brothers," but would also train her "to some profession adapted to her taste and capacity, by which she can establish a home of her own, and secure an independent income" (52). Subsequent addresses also deplore the state of women's health and advocate courses of physical and health education that would improve it. Throughout, Beecher's focus is on improving the status of women through means effected largely independently of men.

As Kathryn Kish Sklar has pointed out, Beecher's conservatism did not devalue women.[37] On the contrary, with her sister Harriet, she wanted to make American society more responsive to women's needs and reflective of women's values. Nina Baym has noted that female disclaimers of the vote often meant, to those rejecting it, rejection of a sphere of activity associated in the public mind with rudeness, corruption, drunkenness, and violence.[38] Espousing the vote also would mean espousing the idea of legislated reform, whereas American Christianity had always seen reform in intensely personal, moral terms. For conservative feminists, the right to vote was extraneous to their central goals and antithetical to their idea of femininity.

But that left a very large sphere of endeavor, the size of which may be indicated by Beecher's contentions that "it is the right and duty of every woman to employ the power of organization and agitation," that is, *disruption* of the social fabric, and that women have the right "to equal advantages for securing their happiness." It is also significant that the sphere of activity she delineates is almost entirely controlled by women. One of the addresses in *Woman Suffrage and Woman's Profession* praises the Catholic hierarchy for creating convents, where single women could recognize a "still higher ministry" than marriage and where they found "comfortable positions and honorable distinctions" (116). Beecher also faults married women for giving more money to their husband's colleges than to their own. She urges employment of women teachers and administrators and encourages women doctors. Clearly, she is not interested in creating a ghetto of feminine underprivilege.

Moreover, there is a peculiar framework to Beecher's book. Prior to the addresses, delivered to female audiences and expanded for female readership, Beecher attaches a dedication "To the Ministers of Religion in the United States." The peculiarity of this dedication justifies extensive quotation.

Dedication
To the Ministers of Religion in the United States
Fathers and Brethren:

As the daughter and sister of nine ministers of Jesus Christ you will allow me to address you by those endeared names; and also because there is an emergency that demands unusual measures.

This *woman movement* is one which is uniting by co-operating influences, all the antagonisms that are warring on the family state. Spiritualism, free-love, free divorce, the vicious indulgences consequent on unregulated civilization, the worldliness which tempts men and women to avoid *large* families, often by sinful methods, thus making the ignorant masses the chief supply of the future ruling majorities; and most powerful of all, the feeble constitution and poor health of women, causing them to dread maternity as – what it is fast becoming – an accumulation of mental and bodily tortures.

Add to this, that extreme fastidiousness which not only excludes needful instruction from the pulpit, but makes mothers shrink from learning and teaching those dangers which their daughters most need to know, and prevents medical men and even women physicians from uttering needful warnings. . . .

> It is the *women teachers of our common schools* who must be instructed to
> become lecturers on health in all our school districts and teach mothers
> how to instruct children. . . .
>
> If the clergy of this nation will give their powerful influence to pro-
> mote the aims of this work in modes they will more wisely devise than I
> can suggest, success will be ensured; and to them I appeal (as I used to
> do to a beloved father and I often do to dear brothers) to help me where
> my own strength and courage fail.
>
> With christian love and respect.
> Yours truly,
> Catharine E. Beecher
> (3–5)

This is an odd account to preface the text that follows it, not because of its
content (which offers a standard argument against the women's movement, especially as represented by radical feminists such as Victoria
Woodhull, whom Beecher and Stowe attacked more than once), but
because little in the addresses themselves follow out the line of argument
struck in the dedication. True, Beecher does call, strongly, for measures
to improve women's health. But that is not the dominant note of *Woman
Suffrage and Woman's Profession*. Rather, the call for a women's university
dominates all other concerns.

Of course Beecher may simply have been thinking most strongly of
women's health when she wrote her dedication; perhaps it was written
right after she finished her final lecture, which does report an informal
survey of the state of married women's health; certainly many of the
other essays were written at different times and reflect different moods. It
is also possible, however, that the disparity is partly deliberate, that
Beecher was using her status as the daughter and sister of ministers – her
"sanctification" in the party of the elect – to deflect attention from her
goals to strengthen the position of women. By indicating her abhorrence
of "this *woman movement,*" while simultaneously reminding the ministers
of her privileged status, and by imploring ministerial help in reaching her
goal to improve the state of women's health (thus suggesting that the
primary mission of her university would be to train teachers competent
to deal with women's bodies, a mission that, because it remains in the
realm of the private, does not threaten the status quo), Beecher guides her
male readers away from her dominant theme. The addresses themselves
follow a similar procedure: She begins by avowing disinterest in suffrage,
then proceeds to outline her goals for a women's institution, financed,
staffed, controlled, and populated by women, that would prepare women
for intellectual and financial equality with men.

But to what would such an institution lead? Clearly, much more than
Beecher bargained for. What she could not see – or did not wish to see –

or refused to admit she saw – was that women who achieved educational
and economic parity with men would soon seek political parity. The
structure of her addresses does not account for that, of course, yet the
consequences of her goals anticipate it. Looking back from the vantage
point of the late twentieth century, we can see ourselves growing out of
Catharine Beecher's dreams. Whether or not she understood what she
was doing, the substance of her book reaches beyond the limitations
claimed by her dedication.

But could nineteenth-century readers discern the "subversiveness" of
this apparently conservative text? And could they extend their perceptions into the realm of imaginative literature? Could they, to alter Rachel
Blau DuPlessis's phrase, read beyond the ending?[39] Certainly, when novelists created texts that could satisfy both public demands for women's
submission to cultural norms and subcultural needs for alternative possibilities, they seemed to acknowledge women's ability to bring a multileveled approach to their reading. Moreover, there is some indication in
readers' diaries that they could recognize the need for multiple reading
strategies. The transactional relationship between writers and readers did
exist, in other words, but in a very different form than either Helen
Papashvily or Ann Douglas has recognized.

One example of this relationship appears in a letter from a well-known
writer about a British text that was sweeping literary America. On April
17, 1848, Lydia Maria Child, aged forty-six and author of *Hobomok*
(1824), *The Rebels* (1825), *Philothea* (1836), and numerous abolitionist
essays, wrote to her friend Marianne Silsbee that

> I have read Jane Eyre before you had the kindness to send a copy. I was
> perfectly carried away with it. I sat up all night long to finish it. I do not
> at all agree with the critics who pronounce Rochester unloveable. *I
> could have loved him with my whole heart.* His very imperfections
> brought him more within the range of warm human sympathies. *Ought*
> Jane to have left him at that dreadful crisis? She was all alone in the
> world, and could do no harm to mother, sister, child, or friend, by
> taking her freedom. The tyrannical law, which bound him to a mad and
> wicked wife, seems such a mere figment! I wanted much, however, to
> make *one* change in the story. I liked Rochester all the better for the
> impetuous feeling and passion which carried him away; but I wanted
> conscience to come in and check him, like a fiery horse reined in at full
> gallop. At the *last* moment, when they were ready to go to church to be
> married, I wish he had thrown himself on her generosity. I wish he had
> said, "Jane, I *cannot* deceive you!" and so told her the painful story he
> afterward revealed. There might have been the same struggle, and the
> same result; and it would have saved the nobleness of Rochester's love
> for Jane, which has only this one blot of deception. I am glad the book
> represents Jane as refusing to trust him; for in the present disorderly

> state of the world, it would not be well for public morality to represent
> it otherwise. But my *private* opinion is, that a real living Jane Eyre,
> placed in similar circumstances, would have obeyed an *inward* law, high-
> er and better than outward conventional scruples.[40]

In this, a letter to an old and intimate friend, Child displays many of the
contradictions readers of novels faced in the middle of the nineteenth
century. On the one hand, she disagrees with contemporary reviewers
who pronounce Rochester sexually unattractive. At the same time she
shares many of their ideological premises. As Nina Baym has shown,
among the criteria nineteenth-century reviewers held for a good novel
was the stricture that it present models of order to counter what Child
refers to as "the present disorderly state of the world."[41] But Child,
writing to a friend, can be more candid than a reviewer, confessing that
her *"private"* self – the reader attuned to the emotional complexity of a
character like Jane rather than to the effect of Jane's choices on a morally
unstable readership – thinks that the "real" Jane would – and should –
have lived with Rochester out of wedlock. This *private* reader assumes
that only those acts that touch other people – be they acts of writing or
acts of sexual relationship – need conform to the restrictions called for by
the need for order. *Private* acts of disorder, acts that cannot harm "mother, sister, child or friend," that is, do not affect the social fabric in such
dire need of ordering, are not only condonable, they may be laudable,
signs of a "higher and better" *"inward* law."

This conflict between the private and public reader – the Janus face of
this consumer of popular fiction – appears, I believe, in much of the
writings (writings by authors and writings by readers), published and
unpublished, by American women in the middle of the nineteenth century. On the one hand, the writings show an intense, almost paranoid
awareness of the needs, and censures, of "the public," an entity conceived
of as easily influenced by the written word. On the other hand, they are
equally intensely aware of *other* possibilities for female protagonists than
the ones they publicly espouse. But few articulate their private opinions
as clearly as Child. Most, in fact, do not articulate them at all. They do,
however, express fascination with deviant characters, ambiguous situations, and most of all, with heroic women, both historical and fictional.
And authors of fiction develop characters, situations, and narrative
stances that, like those Child discerned in *Jane Eyre,* are open to more
than one kind of interpretation. There exists, then, a community of
expression and interpretation actively involved in examining women's
nature and possibilities – a women's community in continuous discourse
about itself. Within this context, women's novels function as a means of
testing women's possibilities for alternative modes of being – as laborato-
ry experiments, much as Zola would conceive of the Experimental Novel

in France a few years later. The women's novels' mode of presenting themselves – their formulaic covering or overplot – is a means of participating in that discourse without, at the same time, seeming to challenge social definitions of women's roles.

I suggest that the most prevalent use of formulaic covering – that is, to disguise subversive discourse – occurs in the dominant novelistic subgenre of the 1850s and 1860s, the novel type that Brown called "sentimental," Baym "women's," and Kelley "domestic," but that I prefer to call *exploratory* because it explores just such extensions beyond the realm of approved female behavior, an exploration that takes place as much on the formal level as the thematic. My objection to "sentimental," "women's," and "domestic" as genre descriptives is that the terms themselves encourage us to continue approaching women's novels of the mid–nineteenth century within a particular hermeneutic that focuses on the social/sexual context and that, consequently, restricts our access to the novels' verbal, structural, and thematic adventures. It is important to note that this form is not restricted to women's texts, even though I am only examining women's writing in this study. One parallel male text is *Moby-Dick,* which takes as its cover story a situation analogous to the female cover-plot of abandonment, adventure, and redemption: That is, Ishmael's stages of alienation, adventure, and reconciliation. Like the protagonists of women's fiction, Ishmael is redeemed for ordinary domesticity (which critics of this male text tend to refer to as the human community); that is, in Melville's words, Ishmael learns to lower his "conceit of attainable felicity," and settle for "the wife, the heart, the bed, the table, the saddle, the fire-side, the country."[42] Ishmael's story, then, is the coverplot for *Moby-Dick.* The subversive plot of course belongs to Ahab, who represents the antithesis of domesticity and who has effectively (and documentably) seduced many readers, especially young academics, over the years.

Clearly, nineteenth-century novels written both by women and by men can be read on more than one level. In this study, however, I am restricting myself to women's texts because investigation of their peculiar subversions tells us much about the evolution of nineteenth-century women's literature and ideology. For the radical difference between *Moby-Dick* and almost any women's text is that, while the cover-plot of Melville's novel assumes that Ishmael can save himself, the cover-plots of women's novels assume that women need men for protection. Never featuring a female Ahab, the radical aspect of women's texts consists of their suggestion that a woman can be an Ishmael – that she can stand alone. What is radical in women's texts, in other words, is conservative in men's: The differences between social definitions of men's and women's natures can be measured by the dreams – and the daring – of their fictional representatives. But because women's novels did not feature protagonists journeying to ontological extremities does not mean that they did not broach heretical ground. It only means that the restrictions they challenged lay closer to home. Melville's claim that he had "written a wicked book, and feel[s] spotless as a lamb" could be appropriately applied to women's exploratory novels as well: Their cover stories of female dependence are radically undermined by their underplots, which suggest, at the very least, that women can learn how to achieve physical, emotional, and financial independence. These were forbidden grounds for midcentury women; upon them the novels' middle portions encroach. Moreover, the long-term effect of these subversive "middles" appears in women's texts of the later nineteenth century, which, slowly and hesitantly at first, began to posit women's a priori capabilities for self-determination.

The chapters that follow will focus on the novels' middles and their potential for ideological disruption. Like Beecher's text, many of the exploratory novels produced by and for women in the nineteenth century have prefaces, and many of the prefaces have little relevance to the fictional themes that succeed them. As Baym has shown, most begin and end with conventional plots. Most also, however, feature events – and rhetoric – that serve to undermine those plots. Like Beecher's description of woman's sphere, the middle portions of these texts establish an area of female independence, competence, emotional complexity, and intellectual acumen that sets the stage, whether the author intended it or not, for other women to "read" a far different message than the one the novels overtly profess, just as Lydia Maria Child "read" *Jane Eyre* differently from the critics. Baym has pointed out that the tacit "bargain" struck between reviewers and writers of the period entailed the premise that

> women may write as much as they please providing they define themselves as women writing when they do so, whether by tricks of style – diffuseness, gracefulness, delicacy; by choices of subject matter – the domestic, the social, the private; or by tone – pure, lofty, moral, didactic. Where the novel, generally speaking, was defined as a field for the expression of the individual author, possibly rising to genius, it was defined in the case of the woman author as a field for the expression of the sex, in which case genius in the large sense is out of the question, since the most she can do is lose herself in gender and hence sacrifice the individuality that is the foundation of genius.[43]

This transaction by and large ignores the readers themselves; it concerns the definition of acceptable women's writing in the *public* domain. Neither all readers nor all writers agreed with the terms of this bargain. But those who ventured to express their opinions did so privately, not publicly, often in letters to other women. Harriet Beecher Stowe, for instance, recognized the individuality of one of her contemporaries; writing a letter of introduction for E.D.E.N. Southworth to Lady Byron, Stowe asserted that despite the "glaring defects" of Southworth's novels they nevertheless "have *genius* – she is almost the only instance I know of a really original, creative southern author. . . . even her faults and exaggerations [are] characteristic – they are *herself* they come from that ardent tropical exuberance of fancy and emotions which belong to our southern women and of whom as I said she is the only specimen expressed."[44] Stowe is *not* conflating self and type here; although she places Southworth within the framework of Southern writers, even Southern women writers, she singles out Southworth's work as above the rest, exhibiting those signs of genuine inspiration the nineteenth century chose to designate as "genius." Stowe, at least, conceived of women authors as individuals, not simply as representatives of their sex.

In addition, the phrase "that ardent tropical exuberance of fancy and emotions" suggests that Stowe heard a deeper note of sexual imperative in Southworth's novels than the reviewers cared to acknowledge. In 1844 Harriet Beecher Stowe had written to her absent husband, "Tho by hard endurance I have learnt a degree of self control which sometimes makes me doubt whether I have any feeling, yet there are times when the old fountain rises again, warm, fresh and full. . . . Oh this love. If we only could have enough of it. . . ."[45] Stowe thus had the appropriate emotional framework to appreciate a writer who could say of her heroine, "conjugal love was her master passion. . . . she wished to be every thing to the being who was every thing to her."[46] Although neither Stowe nor Southworth entirely condones the intensity of this passion (Stowe speaks of having learned self-control, and the plot of *The Deserted Wife,* as we shall see, involves its heroine's learning control over – but not extirpation of – her passion), nevertheless both writers recognize its existence and its value. Even Nathaniel Hawthorne, in his letter about Fanny Fern, commented that "Generally women write like emasculated men. . . . but when they throw off the restraints of decency, and come before the public stark naked, as it were – then their books are sure to possess character and value."[47] Hawthorne's metaphor is telling; he, too, senses the power lying beneath the "covers" that hid and distorted the female self.

One way to uncover subversive possibilities in nineteenth-century women's texts is by paying attention to the way women writers manipulate language, not only words but also sentences, paragraphs, and full narratives; mindful, with Roland Barthes, that, just as the sentence "being an order and not a series, cannot be reduced to the sum of the words which compose it and constitutes thereby a specific unit, [so] a piece of discourse . . . is no more than the succession of sentences composing it."[48] The "endlessly complicated" expansion of simple propositions "with duplications, paddings, embeddings," that Barthes notes[49] works on the paragraph level as well as on the sentence and, finally, on the level of the narrative itself. I suggest that in exploratory novels, these expansions serve to hide – but not obliterate – the voice that celebrates female genius.

Of course in order to "hear" the female voices in this literature readers must have the right ear, bringing to their reading what Mary Crawford and Roger Chaffin call schemata, or organizing structures that provide the frameworks necessary to understand what they have read.[50] Schemata differ according to the personal history, especially the gender history, of the reader. As Lydia Maria Child, from her history of antiestablishment ideology (her abolitionism and feminism) brought to her reading of *Jane Eyre* a schema that permitted her to disagree with the critics, responding to a different Rochester than they saw and affirming a pattern of conduct they would have interpreted as immoral; and as Stowe, bringing her own sexual and marital history to bear on her reading of Southworth's works and life, could discern Southworth's genius; so other readers, even those less socially or literarily sophisticated, can "reconstitute" the meaning of novelistic texts according to the schemata they bring to them.

Crawford and Chaffin report that preliminary investigations into reading memory indicate that understanding and memory of written material are gender determined.[51] "What is recalled, according to schema theory," they claim, "is not usually the actual sentences presented but a reconstruction based on what was understood" (5). For instance, their finding that "interpersonal verbs have different meanings for women and men" – that women rate them "as more extreme in emotional tone," and men [rate] them "as more extreme in power," supports their claim that these findings have "intriguing implications both for the interpretation of prose by female and male readers and for the potential for misunderstanding between female and male speakers" (15).

Although analysis of the mechanics of reading behavior is a peculiarly twentieth-century concern, nineteenth-century writers and readers, surrounded as they were by militant definitions of the differences between male and female intelligence, nature, and experience, would have accepted the idea that men and women read, as well as wrote, differently. If they had not, they would not have placed such emphasis on reading suited to each sex. Intuitively aware of these cognitive predispositions, writers could, consciously or not, structure their works so that male and female readers could extract different meanings from them. Thus Catharine Beecher's address to the "Ministers of Religion in the United States," prefacing a text that proposes a women's institution that would ultimately threaten the foundations of those ministers' power, assumes that male readers would bring to the text schemata enabling them to see *only* what

Beecher wanted them to see, whereas women readers, both from their own frustrations about education and their own experience of medical disabilities resulting from childbearing, would bring a different set.

Bearing Crawford and Chaffin's material in mind, it is useful to look at records left us by nineteenth-century readers who were not writers themselves. This material is difficult to find; though many nineteenth-century Americans kept records of their reading in diaries or in the memoranda sections of pocket almanacs, few did more than list the books they read. Responses like Child's – thoughtful, analytical, and frank – are rare. Among this community of readers, however, there are several consistent patterns of response indicating that women readers, consciously or not, were drawn to independent, heroic, and even deviant female characters.

One consistent pattern among women who recorded their reading is an intense interest in biographies of heroic women. For instance Hannah Davis Gale, probably between ten and fourteen years old when she studied under Margaret Fuller in 1838, kept a "memory" diary (a school requirement) in which she recorded her recollections of works read aloud in class.[52] One of the notes Gale made indicates that she had asked Miss Fuller to allow her to learn French from *Corinne*, a hint that this very young girl was attracted to stories about strong women. This is supported by another note, where she singles out Charlotte Corday's assassination of Marat as the most memorable (if "horrid") aspect of Carlyle's *History of the French Revolution*, one much more interesting to her than "Mr. Fuller's" (presumably Hiram Fuller, the headmaster) account of King Louis. In her memory compositions Hannah wrote her most detailed recollections about stories involving female heroines, especially two featuring girls who save their fathers' lives. The selective memory of this very young reader clearly highlighted women who dared to act beyond the limits prescribed for them.

Similarly, in 1870, wealthy Chicago socialite Julia Newberry listed biographies of "Mrs. Sigourney," "Theodosia Burr," and "Mad. Necker" among the books she found "interesting,"[53] and, in 1856, Ada Parker, a pious New Englander, told a friend that "an old edition of Madame Guyon's Life, written by herself, is in our hands now. It is good truly, and well worth *study*. In this way I am going over it. I hope to find much benefit from these lessons of experience."[54] Finally, in 1841, Julia Parker Dyson recorded in her diary that she had "read portions of the life of Madam De Staël. She was a most interesting woman. I love to read of the splendid qualities that made up her character. What a compliment, that Bonaparte dared not have her in his dominions by reason of her powerful influence."[55] A teacher, Dyson brought women's biographies into the classroom. After recording that she had "read from the Memoir of Margaret Davidson. Was intensely interested. Such astonishing powers of mind, developed at so early an age . . . She was, indeed, all that was lovely, as well as intellectually great. A sparkling Gem in the constellation of American literature,"[56] she noted that she had "Spent an hour this morning in the classroom relating to the young ladies some of the prominent characteristics of Margaret Davidson. They seemed much interested."[57] Although Davidson – a poet who died at the age of fifteen – did not produce literature that challenged contemporary values, the publicity accorded her work would be inspirational to young women. Dyson's attention to Davidson in the classroom gave her students one more female figure in their constellation of models of achievement.

Dyson is one of the few diarists to articulate her responses to women's texts. Writing, again, of De Staël, she records "I cannot contemplate a mind like hers without the most ardent longing to turn aside from the beaten track of life and explore. . . . Surely I would be what I am not."[58] Dyson's "longing" to participate in the exceptional explains one of the impulses motivating women to read about other women's lives: Through the reading experience they could explore what it would be like to be extraordinary – "what I am not." Similar impulses motivated them to read about the adventures of fictional women, even affecting their choice of Bible portions. Catharine Merrill, for instance, recorded in 1843 that "It was so cold I did not go to evening meeting but read aloud to Ma and the children two stories, 'Maternal Affection' and 'Elsie Grey,' and the book of 'Esther.' "[59] What is striking here is that, Biblical or fictional, Merrill's choices all concern female protagonists – there is a sense here that the story of Esther was read, not for its Sunday evening devotional content, but because it was a good exemplary woman's tale.

Hannah Davis Gale's diary illustrates this attraction to strong female models most strikingly and most consciously. Writing in 1838 that "I recited in Corinne – I find it extremely interesting," she first claims not to like the "romantic part of the – story. [because] Corinne is represented as – perfect, and Lord Nelvil is made to perform such wonderful exploits, that we readily perceive that the scenes – are far from being such as could – have been actually performed." Later in the entry, however, she changes her mind about "the romantic part," admitting that "I do like it in some respects, it renders it, to me, I must confess, more interesting. . . ."[60] Eight days later Gale notes that "I was reading the Life of Josephine. . . . I could not but compare Josephine with Corinne. Though different in many respects, their lives are to me equally – interesting. . . . In Josephine's – character, I discovered, energy, benevolence, firmness, strong maternal affection, united to a most delicate, and refined taste, and a graceful ease of manners. . . . [In trouble] the weak, effeminate – spirit of woman, shrank not, but – she shone forth brilliant, as a new risein [sic] star."[61] Young Hannah Gale, tutored by Margaret Fuller, was fully conscious of women's potential; she was drawn to women's texts that showed her just how strong women actually could become.

Women's responses to Elizabeth Barrett Browning's *Aurora Leigh* and to Charlotte Brontë's works are another indication of their attraction to literary models that deviated from domestic femininity. Women's responses to *Aurora Leigh* were universally positive. "I have been Reading *Aurora Leigh*. The divine of Mrs. Browning's nature shines out in every line" claims a typical response by Mary Willard, sister of Frances Willard, founder of the Women's Christian Temperance Union (WCTU), in 1861. And immediately afterward she queries, "When will a change come to my life?"[62] In 1856 Ada Parker asked a friend if she had "seen 'Aurora Leigh,' Elizabeth Browning's last book? . . . I long to possess her poems, – to have them by my pillow with the most precious of my books, as a personal inspiration to faith and courage. She drinks at a fountain whose waters cannot fail, and her words are full of hope and healing."[63] Similar responses to Browning's feminist text are overwhelmingly recorded in American women's fiction: A typical example is Elizabeth Stuart Phelp's character Avis, whose awakening to her vocation as an artist occurs as she is reading *Aurora Leigh*. Responses to Charlotte Brontë reveal nearly the same level of adulation. Julia Newberry lists "Jane Eyre. And all that Charlotte Bronte ever wrote" among her favorite books,[64] and poet Celia Thaxter indignantly responded to a friend's query: "To think of your asking such a question as 'Do I care about Charlotte Brontë'! As if I did not care everything I am capable of caring for anything! As if Levi and I hadn't read her books with rapture, and hadn't looked forward to the publishing of Mrs. Gaskell's book about her as one of the most interesting things that could happen! As if we didn't lament her loss to the world every year of our lives!"[65]

As Nancy Cott, Cathy Davidson, Mary Kelley,[66] and others have noted, women's desire for better educations is another hallmark of this community. Evidence of their longing to possess learning is amply recorded in women's diaries, as they list their attempts to learn classical languages, note the philosophical or historical texts they read, or simply lament the inadequacy of their educations. Typical of young women's ambitions is Julia Newberry's confession to her diary that

> My strong points are Composition, drawing, painting, French, history, dancing, and general information – I am weak as regards English grammar, and as I have not touched an Arithmetic for two years I feel uneasy. As to chemistry, astronomy, botany, and natural philosophy, I know next to nothing; this comes from being abroad so much, and travelling all the time. I hav'n't announced the fact, but *privately* I intend to study hard this Winter, and do *something*. . . . 'Be somebody, July,' Papa always used to say, and 'be somebody' I WILL. – I've always been told I

had plenty of brains, and every natural advantage; so why shouldn't I be
Somebody? ? ? *Laziness* is the bane of my existence.[67]

As we shall see, the desire for an education is one of the most common
themes evinced in nineteenth-century women's literature; throughout,
moreover, there is a sense that knowledge is power, definition; a chance
to "BE SOMEBODY."

Most significantly, but far less prevalently, some readers of this community indicate that they are aware of gender differences in the way
books are read. This is especially evident in the writings of Mary Guion,
who, writing early in the nineteenth century, reveals much about the
fusion of literature and life in her imagination. To highlight Guion's
responses, I want to quote first from a male contemporary, Samuel
Gilman. The differences between Samuel Gilman's and Mary Guion's
approaches to the material they read show us how culturally based gender
imperatives shape selective perceptions.

On February 3, 1810, Samuel Gilman, then a college student in New
England (later to be a Unitarian minister in South Carolina and husband
to the writer Caroline Howard Gilman), wrote to his sister Louisa about
Hannah More's *Coeleb in Search of a Wife* (1809). As Gilman correctly
summarizes, "The evident object of *Coelebs* [sic] is to describe the qualifi-
cations and the requisitions of a virtuous wife." He comments favorably
on the central female character, then explicates the novel's moral for his
sister:

> Oh, Louisa, endeavour with all the mental energy you are possessed of,
> to transfuse into your conduct the brilliant and excellent traits of Lu-
> cilla's character. Whether you travel through life in the solitary track of
> celibacy, [sic] or wander in the more variegated regions of matrimony,
> you will ever find those principles your support and your guide, they
> will smooth the path; they will conduct to felicity.[68]

Despite its publication in the nineteenth century, *Coeleb* is essentially an
eighteenth-century advisory tract, and Gilman, uncritically reading its
message to women, wishes to transmit it intact to his sister. In his effort,
his language falls into hortatory patterns, using conjunctive clauses and
parallel structures imitative of the advice literature itself and of the ser-
mons and public prayers from which the literature took its own rhetorical
cast.

Now, Gilman is not a naive reader. Well educated, he is increasingly
thoughtful about literature and its effects. In 1821, in a letter to the same
sister, he noted apropos of reading *Kenilworth* that ". . . I am beginning
to think there is nothing puritanical . . . in condemning this species of
reading [i.e., novels] *in toto.* . . . there is no such thing as amusement in
reading a novel. It is all *employment* from beginning to end. It engrosses

the whole being. It usurps . . . *all* our time."[69] Gilman's "condemnation" of novel reading is not entirely serious here; he loves novels, responding so vehemently to *Kenilworth* because it had "seized hold of my soul's attention."[70] Gilman understands how novels engage readers' imaginations, guiding them along paths they might not consciously wish to take. But his sophistication is about the reading process, not about the implicit assumptions of any given text.

Female readers, on the other hand, have a tendency to question their inscription in texts. For instance, early in the century Mary Guion, a voracious reader with a scanty education, brought to her reading a consciousness of the precariousness and powerlessness of being female that made her sensitive to the way women were projected in literature and even to the schema other readers brought to specific works. In July, 1801, the nineteen-year-old noted in her diary that several men

> all came here [to her parents' home] they read some in Popes works and
> discoursed upon the subject wich would a been entertaining to me but
> there was two amongst them that one might Judge from their discourse
> to be woman haters for they pick'd out all the vulgar blackguardly and
> those pieces that Despise them [i.e., women] to the last degree for fine
> pieces so I made an excuse to go after some Cider to get rid of their
> (may I not stile it) rudeness.[71]

Potentially interested in a discussion of Pope's works, Guion is nevertheless aware that her father's friends are selecting those aspects of Pope's works that bolster their own misogyny. Unwilling to confront them openly, this dutiful daughter chooses to be silent and absent rather than to encounter the men's implicit hostility.

Mary Guion also read selectively. Like her father's visitors, she focused on sections of her reading that spoke to her own dispositions. But her angle of vision is revealingly different from male readers; it shows just how intensely she brought her sense of being female to her literary engagements. In *Revolution and the Word: The Rise of the Novel in America*[72] Cathy N. Davidson suggests that, although women readers in post–Revolutionary America read for "self-improvement," they also extracted from their reading different paradigms for female behavior than those male readers perceived. And certainly the context of their reading – the personal history that constitutes part of the vertical axis of the reading process – was shaped by their gender-based experiences. When Samuel Gilman advised his sister to imitate More's heroine, he was beginning to look around for a wife for himself. During the nine years in which Mary Guion most actively kept her diary, she was in an apparently similar, but actually much different, position of choosing a husband.

As important as a fit mate was for Gilman, he had many other plans to consider, dominant among them choice of a profession. For Guion, in contrast, marriage *was* her profession; her choices lay in which suitor to accept. The place, or space, that the idea of marriage occupied in her mind was much larger than it was in Gilman's, leading her to give far more weight to the "instructive" aspect of novels and making her need for them more acute than his. While he struggled to condemn novel reading because it "paralyzes the sense of *duty*,"[73] Guion defended it because "we [she and another woman] thot people might very much improve the understanding by a serious attention to them. . . ."[74] And the understanding Mary Guion seeks not only involves the process of choosing a spouse but also the consequences of that choice.

To this end she copies into her diary passages from sources as varied as a newspaper article giving general advice to both sexes on choosing a spouse[75] to "Milton's Paradise Lost Book," where the passage that "particularly hit my fancy" is "a discourse between Adam and Eve when he was informed she had been eating the forbidden fruit."[76] This she reads first as a love story: "This piece describes in so beautiful and strikeing a manner the love of our first parents, before they were tempted to sin, and after that the mournful lamentations and Adams hatred of Eve, which I have not roat, but he soon was brot to see the folly of that, and he then bore his calamities with fortitude for her sake. . . ." She then proceeds to interpret the passage, seeing it as a model for marital behavior: "where [were] every one but as strongly atach'd to their own . . . second self, if so easily would the one pardon the failings of the other, how much more satisfaction would many families enjoy; . . . but I much fear that the people of the preasant age, thinck that rather an old fashion, it is sertainly antient but not the less good – ."[77] In other words, Guion is actively interpreting Milton's text in light of her effort to understand sexual relationships, both historical and contemporary.

Similarly, Guion reads novels as parables for her own life and, at times, as models for her own language. After a suitor tries to become too intimate, for instance, she writes that ". . . I thot several times of makeing the same speach to him as Evelina did to Clement 'Your freedom, Sir, when you are more acquainted, may perhaps be better accepted' but did not speak it."[78] She *does* speak novelistic discourse to her diary, however. Shortly after reading *Charlotte Temple,* one of the period's great novels of seduction and betrayal, she discovers that one of her suitors has lied to her about his situation. In language unlike her own, but much like the discourse of Charlotte and other unfortunate heroines, she laments "Oh! What a Villain! . . . I believe the Gentlemen thinck it an honour to them, to tell so many Fictious stories to the Ladies as their imagination can invent. . . . I must learn to suspect all, even age itself is sometimes found to be in error. Adieu! Adieu! for ever, I will endeavor never to write, speak, or even thinck of him more – ."[79] Clearly, Mary Guion not only reads for general education, she actively selects aspects of her reading that will help her make sense of, and maneuver through, her own predicaments. Like all readers, she brings her own experience and needs to the texts she reads; what is remarkable about her is her consciousness of her own gender-based imperatives.

These letters and diaries suggest that nineteenth-century women readers shared an interest in, and admiration for, outstanding women, that they desired an education that would give them what they conceived of as power in the world of ideas, and that they were intensely attracted to fictional heroines who determined to develop themselves professionally – as in *Aurora Leigh* – or who learned, painfully, emotional self-sufficiency, as in Brönte's novels. In addition, some of these readers articulated specific consciousness of gender, demonstrating that they read, as Jonathan Culler would term it, as women. In sum, the letters and diaries reveal the existence of a community of female readers who brought to their reading gender-determined schemata.

WIDENING THE SCOPE: STRATEGIES FOR MULTILEVELED READING

These schemata, or predispositions, stand in the background of my proposal that we learn to read nineteenth-century women's novels on more than one level, actively searching for the thematic alternatives available to readers who sought fictional as well as biographical models for outstanding women. Though these diarists do not discuss the popular novels they read with anything like the fluidity of their discussions of biography and canonical fiction, they nevertheless did read women's novels, often voraciously, and often in tandem with their other reading. While we cannot duplicate their hermeneutic process, I suggest that we can learn to read in a multilayered, gender-specific mode that will reveal just how vulnerable these texts are to ideological subversion and suggest how women searching for alternatives to conventional roles might perceive them as far more radical than their cover stories suggest. What Rachel Blau DuPlessis calls "writing beyond the ending," and locates in late nineteenth- and twentieth-century women's texts, begins at least back in the 1850s, in Janus-faced texts accessible to Janus-faced readers.[80] Awareness of some of the ways the reading process works helps us to see how the middle portions of these apparently conservative texts lay the grounds – that is, prepare receptive readers, till their cognitive soil – for the more overtly radical novels appearing later in the century.

One place to begin liberating ourselves from the confines of our critical past is with Roland Barthes's distinction between "readerly" and "writerly" texts, that is, between texts that unfold themselves to readers within the framework of traditional models and those that reject those conventions and therefore force readers to construct ways of making the text intelligible.[81] Readerly texts are analogous to what Jauss terms "culinary" or "entertainment art" – works that maintain little or no distance between readers' horizons of expectations (that is, the literary and social experience they bring to their reading) and the horizons of the texts. In other words, these texts confirm readers' values and fulfill their expectations.[82] In contrast, writerly texts maintain a distance between those horizons, forcing readers to alter their expectations if they are to interpret the text and achieve cognitive harmony with it.

In the literature I am examining, this demands that readers "re-read," that is, to use another of Barthes's concepts, transcend what they bring to the text.[83] According to this theory, as readers, with a wealth of reading (that is, of absorbing literary conventions) behind us, we bring to each new text only those expectations that have been created by other texts. The first reading involves having those expectations aroused and either fulfilled or disappointed, a process of trying to "place" the text, of identifying it in terms of all the other texts we have read (its intertextual context). The re-reading, however, focuses on the division within the text itself, a process of discovering that there is no such thing as a stable identity. Rather, within each text exist subversive elements that disrupt the possibility of identity.

Taking the concept of re-reading on its most literal level, that of repetition, it becomes clear that one problem twentieth-century critics have had with nineteenth-century women's texts is that they have given them (at best) only a first reading, whereas nineteenth-century readers, as inscriptions on novels' flyleaves and their generally dogeared appearances testify, read them more than once, often repeatedly. Taking the concept of re-reading on its hermeneutically more significant level, however, necessitates our awareness that any given reader's constitution of meaning will depend to some extent on her processing of words and phrases that continually defer concrete significance. For Jacques Derrida, we are mistaken to assume that literary works have a central presence, even a center; that is, we cannot assume that such a thing as a totality of the work exists for us to analyze. Rather, attention to the play of significations in texts shows that instead of integrating their elements into a coherent, mimetic whole, they "play off" one another and thereby deconstruct the totality of the text. We cannot, according to this theory, fix the "meaning" of a text because within each the play of significations will continuously defer meaning.[84] While I am not arguing that nineteenth-century women's texts continually defer meaning, Barthes's and Derrida's concepts of re-reading and *différence* are extremely useful in helping us perceive how the texts can be processed in radically different ways, often depending on how much weight individual readers assign to specific themes, images, or even phrases. And those varying weights will depend in part on gender-influenced schemata.

The following study is not deconstructionist, structuralist, reader-response, nor even reception theorist. But it does borrow from the work of all these schools and acknowledge its debts to them. With Jauss, I believe that literary texts have the power to change readers' social and literary horizons, and therefore, ultimately, to change both literature and society. With Barthes, I believe that novels can use traditional conventions – appeal to dominant cultural and symbolic codes – to point toward, to evoke, set patterns of response in their readers. I have found Barthes's ideas of *écriture*[85] especially helpful in my thinking about the conventions of the nineteenth-century American woman's novel because it has helped me transcend the limitations of my own training. Barthes defines *écriture* as writing that is rooted in institutional conventions, that depends on, is fueled by, the assumption that readers will share its values and its mode of conceptualizing its world. In *Writing Degree Zero* Barthes gives an example from Madame de LaFayette, who, writing of a man who has just learned that his wife is carrying another man's child, noted that "he thought everything that it was natural to think in such circumstances." As Culler points out, that Madame de LaFayette could construct such a sentence reveals an extraordinarily high degree of social cohesion, of shared values and worldview.[86] While Barthes's examples come from French literature of an earlier period than the one I am discussing, his analysis holds true for mid–nineteenth-century American women's novels as well. They, too, are rooted in institutional conventions and need only nod toward them for their readers to "fill in" the outline they have sketched. Since my own literary training at first only allowed me to see these structures as irredeemably "stereotyped," and "sentimental," I am deeply indebted to Barthes and his successors for helping me to understand the significance of these verbal codes or key words in understanding the texts' readership and the cultures and/or subcultures they inhabited. At the same time, I have been most interested in Gerald Prince's discussions of engaging and distancing narrators and the phenomenon of the narratee. Especially useful as a tool for studying didactic texts, both Anglo-American (Wayne Booth) and continental (Gerald Prince) approaches to narrator–reader relations tell us much about the assumptions writers could make about the nature of their audiences.[87]

With all this, I do not reject the concept of authorial intention. Rather, authorial intent is the framework, the "cover story" that is almost omnipresent in the texts discussed and that may be seen most usefully as a cultural overplot, the accepted way one told a story about women in the middle of the nineteenth century. Many of these cover stories reflect the author's own conscious values and narrative designs. Others, however, *disguise* authorial values; these writers use the "cover" to cover their subversive intentions. The concept of authorial intention is integral to the study of these novels, then, but from a rhetorical rather than a psychological point of view.

Moreover, structuralist and deconstructionist ideas are not antithetical, in practice, to critical definitions of authorial intent. What a text, employing narrative conventions and reflecting cultural codes, *thinks* it is saying (or pretends to be saying) and what it may be saying to some readers are not necessarily the same thing. In nineteenth-century women's literature, in fact, the putative authorial voice, heard through the strong narrative persona, sounds the note for the cover story, and this is the voice that most first-time readers hear. Subsequent readings reveal other voices, however, in addition to character, plot, and thematic variations, that function to undermine the narrator's authority. Lawrence's injunction to "trust the tale, not the teller" is in these cases extended to let us see how the finite field of the author/narrator – the text's overt structure – is subverted by the potentially infinite field of significances which prevent it from achieving a fixed meaning, or totality. As DuPlessis observes, in nineteenth-century American women's novels, codes often conflict, particularly those especially pertinent to women's subculture. In more traditional Anglo-American critical terminology, the novels contain thematic and structural tensions that prevent them from achieving harmonic closure.

But this only makes them more interesting from an interpretive and literary historical point of view. For in their loose narrative constructions and disjunctive codes, exploratory novels give readers far more freedom to constitute their own hermeneutic, to perceive different configurations, than they would be permitted to perceive in more tightly structured didactic texts. And, over time, exploratory novels effected a change in readers' horizons of expectations, changes that can be measured in the overt thematic radicalism of women's texts in the generation succeeding the exploratory novel. Exploratory novels were a structural watershed between two kinds of didactic texts: the early ones emphasizing women's dependence and valuing self-abnegation, the later ones emphasizing women's independence and self-realization.

The plan of this study is as follows. Chapter 1 examines two early didactic novels, Susannah Rowson's *Charlotte Temple* (1791) and Catherine Sedgwick's *A New-England Tale* (1822), in order to demonstrate how this form controls access to its themes. Here, I focus on the narrator–narratee relationship, showing how in *Charlotte Temple* the narrator restricts her readers' interpretive options through including only those details that serve her didactic intents. *A New-England Tale,* though equally didactic in intention, is less single minded in its form, making room for verbal incidentals – primarily character and landscape descriptions – that are not intrinsic to its plot. These literary "frills" lay the groundwork for the kind of verbal play that can give rise to alternative configurations in exploratory novels.

Chapter 2 introduces the exploratory novel of the 1850s and 1860s, beginning with Augusta Evans Wilson's *St. Elmo*. In this novel, the conflict between authorial intent (revealed in its conventional structure and its narrator's explicit comments) and textual values (revealed in thematic tensions and verbal inconsistencies) results in a text that can be *re-read* as subversive of its declared intentions. Wilson herself seems partly conscious of these reading possibilities; what she calls the "hasty, careless novel-reading glance" describes the consumer of the "readerly" text, the reader who sees in a novel only what she or he expects to see. Wilson tries to shame this reader into a creative engagement with her text; she fails to see, however, that to do so would encourage her reader to affirm far different values than the ones she claims to espouse.

Chapter 3 continues examining exploratory novels whose thematic and structural subtexts undermine their authorial design. Susan Warner's second novel, *Queechy,* employs a distancing narrator who tells her story through reference to a series of literary conventions. With *St. Elmo* and *A New-England Tale, Queechy* begins with an orphaned heroine and ends with her marriage to a man who rescues her from her plight. But this cover story is countered by the heroine's demonstrated competence in areas generally reserved as male preserves. In this novel, as in *St. Elmo,* authorial intent and narrative demonstration serve conflicting ends.

Chapters 4 through 6 shift the focus of examination to exploratory novels that consciously and deliberately subvert their cover stories. Chapter 4 examines Fanny Fern's *Ruth Hall* to show how that satirist indulged in just such verbal play by manipulating the conventions of "flowery" rhetoric to disguise her story of a woman's movement out of the self-obliterating silence of saintly wifehood into the self-creating speech of authorship. Juxtaposing the voice of the "teller" – the story's narrator – and the other characters who interpret the initially almost wordless protagonist to the protagonist's own eruption into speech (both oral and written) that is anything but conventional, I extend Ann Douglas Wood's earlier observations that Fanny Fern "built her work openly on the defiance her fellow authoresses labored to conceal."[88] That twentieth-century readers such as Pattee could not perceive Fern's rhetorical strategy only highlights the limitations of his interpretive criteria.

Chapters 5 and 6 look first at E.D.E.N. Southworth's *The Deserted Wife* and then at Elizabeth Drew Stoddard's *The Morgesons*. In *The Deserted Wife,* I concentrate on the structuring iconography of the text, showing how Southworth used the cultural association of women with houses to examine and finally subvert the cultural convention that valued passive women. Stoddard's *The Morgesons* differs from all the texts previously examined in that it is narrated in the first person, and the narrator's voice is notably ambiguous. The focus of this chapter is on showing how informed readers willing to fill in the conceptual gaps left in the narration will see how this seemingly domestic tale actually calls for a radical revision of female sexuality.

Finally, Chapters 7 and 8 examine texts written after the height of the exploratory novel. Focusing on Elizabeth Stuart Phelps's *The Silent Partner* (1871) and Louisa May Alcott's *Work: A Story of Experience* (1873), in Chapter 7 I show how, formally, the texts shift back to the didactic structure but thematically and overtly extend the ideological radicalism begun as rhetorically subversive elements of the exploratory strain. Chapter 8, the conclusion, briefly surveys the effects of these thematic and ideological changes in women's texts written later in the nineteenth century and on into the twentieth, including Phelps's *The Story of Avis* (1877), Sara Orne Jewett's *A Country Doctor* (1884), Kate Chopin's *The Awakening* (1899), and Willa Cather's *O Pioneers!* (1913).

This study could not have been undertaken without all the work of earlier scholar/critics – even the ones I have so strongly criticized – that laid its foundations. I am indebted to Papashvily for the observation that women did not necessarily read like men; to Baym for her analysis of the overplot in much of this fiction; to Douglas for the notion of transactions between writers and readers. Historians Barbara Welter, Nancy Cott, Mary Kelley, and others were among the first to investigate the nineteenth-century's "cult" of true womanhood and its effects on women writers and readers, and without their spadework in the historical–social context I could not have produced the much more narrow literary focus of this study. In turn, I hope my study will generate others, each taking us closer to an honest reevaluation of our literature and the methods we bring to reading it.

PART II

NARRATIVE DESIGNS AND TEXTUAL REBELLIONS

1

PRELUDES: THE EARLY DIDACTIC NOVEL. NARRATIVE CONTROL IN CHARLOTTE TEMPLE AND A NEW-ENGLAND TALE

. . . It appears to me now, that I stand upon a precipice, and if I attempt to move, shall sertainly alter my situation very much but I find my courage hardly sufficient for the undertakeing, there appears on every side so many different scenerys for my eyes to survey, I hardly know which path to chuse, some of them, at their entrance, appear delightsome they are spread with roses, almost without a thorn, but by observing it a little further I perceived some scattering brambles to intrude, and at no greater distance than my eye could disern, the pleasant walck is greatly contrasted and ends in a thicket, wich often becomes a snare for the inocent and unsuspecting who were alured by the pleasantness of the entrance – and again there are other walcks quite the reverse of the former, whose entrance is nothing but a labrinth and appears almost imposible to pass through, a plase that has so many obstructions in the way, but after you have seen a little of the confusion, differences and discords of human life represented in this garden, you will at last break through the maze which ends in pleasant walcks and delightful landscape – I know the lofty house and gilded Chariot attracts the eyes of all, and perhaps the envy of some, but real happiness I believe as often resides in more inferior stations, and I am lead to believe as often takes its original from the hut as out of Palaces.[1]

When Mary Guion wrote this diary entry late in 1804, she was trying to decide which of several suitors to marry. Uppermost in her mind the night she projected life as a maze was the thought that one of her sisters had made a poor choice, even though her parents had fully approved it. Mary Guion does not want to repeat her sister's mistake; during the entire year of 1804 she agonizes over her decision, writing down her thoughts within the conceptual frameworks provided by her reading. One of those frameworks was the literary allegory. In the above entry Guion conflates the image of an eighteenth-century garden maze with ideas about the journey through life common to familiar texts like *Pil-*

grim's Progress. As she did with advice tracts and "Milton's Paradise Lost Book," Guion is again turning to literature for ways to conceptualize her life.

Women in the early nineteenth century read not just for information about the world but also for instruction about their lives, finding in imaginative literature models for their own conduct.[2] And the novels they read were designed to address their needs, reaching out to them through their narrative structures and instructing them not only through allegory but also through direct narrative exhortation. Novels about women in early nineteenth-century America featured narrators who sought the counterparts they inscribed in their texts, that is, their narratees, engaging them openly in a dialogue intended to teach them how – and how not – to live. Whereas exploratory novels foreground their plots, didactic novels foreground their themes, differing from their successors not only in the kinds of heroines they present but also in the kinds of reading processes they permit. As we shall see in *St. Elmo,* exploratory novels create a reading environment that tolerates a high degree of ambiguity and employs distancing rather than engaging narrators, thus creating the possibility for multiple readings. Didactic novels, in contrast, *exclude* such readings, guiding their narratees through the hermeneutic process and severely limiting the interpretations they permit. I will be dealing extensively with narrator–narratee contracts in my analysis of these texts, first, because such contracts inform us about the issues the authors deem important to their readers, and second, because they illustrate how tightly didactic texts control readers' interpretations. Narrator–narratee contracts are the ontological bedrock of didactic literature; as such, they tell us much about the subjects, audiences, and modes of presentation peculiar to the periods in which they were written. This is not to confuse narratees with actual readers – the flesh-and-blood people who read books and occasionally leave records of their responses. It is, however, to bring an appropriate analytical tool to a subgenre that explicitly acknowledges its communicative purpose. As we see in the similarities between the problems articulated in Mary Guion's diary and the problems addressed in *Charlotte Temple,* aspects of the worlds of the actual readers and the worlds of the novels' narratees intersect; this study focuses on the areas defined by those common concerns.

I begin this study by examining the narrator–narratee relationship in two early didactic novels, both in order to exhibit the acknowledged areas of common interest between women's fiction and its readers – actual and fictional – and to show the formal structures that elements of exploratory novels will undermine. The differences between didactic and exploratory novels is evident in the chapter, paragraph, and sentence levels, in their differing casts of characters, and in the degree of presence and control their narrators exhibit. Almost invariably, didactic novels tend to be shorter, with limited casts and pointed dialogue and narration. Because their overt intention is to persuade rather than to explore, their writers tend to employ classical strategies for argumentation more often than do writers of exploratory novels. Like exploratory novels, they are essentially teleological; unlike exploratory novels, however, their middles as well as their ends are predetermined.[3] As a result, didactic novels often display a marked self-consciousness; their language is carefully structured, tending to the oratorical in narrative passages, and their character portrayal leans toward the exemplary. In these formal aspects, they remain essentially the same throughout the nineteenth century. Ideologically, however, they undergo a radical shift. In this chapter, I will begin studying didactic novels by looking closely at two early ones, *Charlotte Temple* (1791) and *A New-England Tale* (1822). *Charlotte Temple* is a seduction novel that twentieth-century readers have generally examined in the light of *Clarissa*[4]; it is useful for this study less for its trans-Atlantic context than for its formal design, which illustrates a structural and narratological pattern that American didactic novels exhibit throughout the period I am examining. Published nearly thirty years later, *A New-England Tale* also exhibits these forms. With these early texts as models, we will be in a better position to understand both the formal differences emerging in exploratory texts and the ideological differences occurring in the later didactic ones.

Although Susannah Rowson's *Charlotte Temple (A Tale of Truth)* (1791)[5] was published well before most of the other novels I will be discussing, I want to examine it in detail because it is one of the first novels by an American woman and because it exhibits structural and rhetorical forms common to nearly all subsequent didactic works. Like most didactic novels, it is short: thirty-five chapters, mostly brief, in an edition of less than 200 fairly large-print pages. The cast of characters is limited, comprising only those figures needed to tell the story twice; and the omniscient narrator, standing closely behind the events and personalities of the story, continually monitors her narratee's interpretation of events, personalities, and choices.

The major area of concern in most nineteenth-century women's novels is, of course, marriage, with all its attendant dangers and delights. One place, consequently, to examine the intersection of fictional concerns and the concerns of readers is in the way they treat marriage, other forms of mating, and reproduction. *Charlotte Temple* is a cautionary tale warning young women not to give in to sexual impulse; it intersects with Mary Guion's diary in their mutual concern that unmarried women not be taken advantage of by men. In *Charlotte Temple* the basic plot of attempted seduction is told twice, a strategy that reinforces the novel's didactic intent.[6] While the levels of repetition reiterate the central message, the binary opposites functioning on each level (that is, the presentation of both positive and negative apprenticeships) permit the narrator to draw her narratee's attention to specific choices to be made and errors to be avoided on her journey to responsible adulthood.[7] The problem of *Charlotte Temple* poses the tension between immediate and deferred gratification, recast here into the tension between the female protagonists gratifying their own immediate sexual desires or allowing parental authority to dictate sexual (and therefore all other) aspects of their lives. In this novel, the levels of repetition are structured generationally. In the first generation of the Temple family, an unscrupulous seducer has the father of a virtuous girl (Lucy Eldridge) thrown into debtor's prison after the father refuses to give him his daughter for a mistress. The determination of the heroine's virtue turns on her candor: When queried by her parents as to her affections regarding the young man (Lewis) who has insinuated himself into their family, the father reports, "She was unaffectedly artless; and when, as I suspected, Lewis made professions of love, she confided in her parents, and assured us that her heart was perfectly unbiased in his favor, and she would cheerfully submit to our direction" (16). Because she turns to her parents for advice rather than consulting her own wishes – she turns to them before she even is *aware* of her own wishes – Lucy is presented as a positive exemplary heroine. She and her father are ultimately rescued, and she proceeds to marry their rescuer, Henry Temple, and to become Charlotte's mother. Achieving a good husband, a happy home, and a lovely daughter, she provides a vicarious experience of the rewards of filial obedience and deferred gratification for the narratee, an example, that is, of a positive apprenticeship.

Readers were affected by such examples of filial obedience, even if they did not follow exactly the same paths themselves. Writing about the conflict she felt between "love and duty" when her parents gently indicated their preference in her "choice of a husband," Mary Guion noted that "My Parents wishes so well for their children that I often thinck it would grieve me worse to displease or cause them the least unnecessary trouble, than it would to suffer the same myself."[8] Nevertheless Guion did not lay bare her heart to her parents, nor turn over the decision to them: "Mother the other day said to me she thought Father would rather I should marry Ben Smith than any one that had ever been to see me. I almost wish I could thinck so too, said I – but thought I, that will never be the case so long as his amiable Cousin thincks me worthy his attention. . . ."[9] Unlike the fictional Lucy Eldridge, the historical Mary Guion reserves her thoughts – and decisions – for herself, ultimately marrying yet another suitor, Samuel Brown, after making him wait over two years. It was a good marriage (the diary continues into Guion's sixty-sixth year) that vindicated her care in making her choice. But her story might not have ended so happily. A girl less well read in the "history" – fictional or true – of courtship and marriage might well have fallen for the blandishments of one of her less sincere suitors, for, as Guion herself meditates: "Can an inocent female account for the meaning of so much discimulation in the other sex – my answer is no – and I am of the opinion it would off't times puzzle their own brain to give an account of it themselves."[10]

We can see the intersection of Guion's and Rowson's concerns in their mutual mistrust of men's designs on women. Soon after writing the above entry, Mary Guion read *Charlotte Temple*. "I road home alone – brot with me Charlotte Temple, a Novel, I borrowed of Miss Dann wich I sat reading in the Parlour," she notes.[11] Since the narrator of *Charlotte Temple* is most conscious of the narratee who is vulnerable to "the disci-mulation of the other sex," Guion was reading a text designed to address her needs. In fact, Lucy's story sets the pattern for a positive heroine within a context of sexual threat; the first narratee the narrator addresses is the young woman who is sexually vulnerable and the first issues she takes pains to establish are the dangers of sexual license to women and to those about whom they care. Addressing her preface to "the young and thoughtless of the fair sex," the narrator urges them to consider her story as "reality" with "a slight veil of fiction . . . thrown over the whole" (5). The young man who has Lucy's father thrown into prison is her first negative example of one who allows his sexuality to rule his reason; though he does not pay the penalty for his passions, he does cause suffer-ing among people with whom the narratee is encouraged to identify, an innocent young woman and her honorable father.

The close control the narrator maintains over her narratee's interpretive process is designed to teach readers like Mary Guion that "the discimula-tion of the other sex" is so pernicious that young women should not trust their own instincts at all. The dual temporal frames and binary charac-terizations with which the novel opens succintly introduce this theme. *Charlotte Temple* does not actually open with the story of the positive apprenticeship; the tale of Lucy and her father is a flashback, begun in the second chapter. The novel actually opens by introducing Montraville, the man who will destroy Charlotte, a thematic descendant of the villain who destroyed Lucy's family. Although Davidson is right in noting that Montraville is not projected as irredeemable[12] (he does agonize over his perfidy even as he commits it), he is characterized by a vanity that blinds him to his real designs (10), especially his intentions regarding Charlotte. Certainly his debased friend Belcour "knew that Montraville did not design to marry her" (59). Moreover, whatever his confused intentions, it is Montraville who, in this first chapter, articulates the idea against which the book will argue: "I never think of the future," he proclaims, "but am determined to make the most of the present . . . " (10). These words spell the end of young Charlotte's innocence; Montraville's goal – which he achieves – is to convince Charlotte to run away with him. Bribing Charlotte's companion, La Rue (a French teacher at her boarding school), into arranging meetings between him and her protegée, Montraville acts in bad faith, even if he deludes himself into believing that his intentions are honorable.

By introducing first Montraville (and his designs) and then flashing back to the positive-apprenticeship story of Lucy and her father, the narrator constructs a series of contrasts off of which she will play the subsequent events. Charlotte, less wise than her mother, takes the treacherous La Rue as her confidante instead of her parents. Although she understands her filial duties, she allows herself to be persuaded to elope to America. Her story is a negative apprenticeship because she, like her seducer, puts "inclination" above "discretion," short-term desires before long-term goals. "Indeed, I do repent," she remarks even before the elopement has actually occurred, "from my soul; but while discretion points out the impropriety of my conduct inclination urges me on to ruin" (44). Here, inclination signals both the present (evoking Montraville) and sexual desire, whereas discretion signals both the future and filial obedience. Knowing that she will "wound the hearts of those dear parents who make my happiness the whole study of their lives" (46), she nevertheless allows herself to be persuaded to run away. As a consequence she reaps the harvest she has sown: pregnancy, poverty, desertion, and an early death in New York.

Certainly one way to examine this novel is from an economic point of view: By valuing deferred gratification over immediate pleasure, and by encouraging emotional and mental reliance on external authority, the novel inculcates an ideology central to the bourgeois work ethic. But it is also important to note the sexual ideologies that exist as subtexts to the political–economic ones. First, there are threats inherent in Charlotte's story that could not exist in any comparable story of a young man's negative apprenticeship – one biological, the other cultural. Because Charlotte can become pregnant (the biological threat) and because she is incapable of supporting herself (the cultural threat) she is predestined to failure if she attempts to gratify her immediate sexual desires before she has ensured that she will receive economic support (i.e., before she is married). And, unlike male protagonists, her failure will be permanent – at least in her mortal life – because her child's presence will ensure that she never erases her past. Second, the terms in which women are presented positively imply that they must surrender all personal desires as well as all immediate gratifications. The exemplary heroine is passive, an empty vessel; Lucy is a positive protagonist because she never formulates a wish for herself. Seen always in self-abnegating postures (bent over ailing or dying relatives, or quietly painting in her father's prison cell to earn money to pay off his debts), her reward for emptying herself of all personal desire is to be filled with "content" – good man, good home. The narrator highlights this image in her chapter-length homily to her narratees, urging them to refrain from seeking "pleasure": "Ye giddy flutterers in the fantastic round of dissipation, who eagerly seek pleasure . . . tell me, thoughtless daughters of folly, have you ever found the phantom you have . . . sought? . . . Pleasure is a vain illusion. . . ." Instead, she urges them to accept the decisions of others and presents their rewards in classical imagery: "Look, my dear friends, at yonder lovely virgin arrayed in a white robe. . . . her name is Content; she holds in her hand the cup of true felicity. . . ." (34). Content and content here both signal a willingness to permit others to define world, self, and duty; the narratees here are envisioned as young women who, tempted to seek their own pleasure, to define self and world for themselves, must be shown the folly of straying from their parents' benevolent authority; like "the cup of true felicity" [elsewhere referred to as "the cup of life" (17)], good women are filled – provided with content – from external sources.

Having established her themes, her values, and her positive and negative characters within the first five chapters, the narrator of *Charlotte Temple* proceeds to tell her story. Unlike exploratory novels, in which the narrator often withdraws from direct mediation between the narratee and the story – away, that is, from continuous monitoring of the narratee's interpretive process – in early American didactic novels such as *Charlotte Temple* the narrator always makes her presence felt, addressing a female consciousness she perceives as extremely susceptible to whatever error her tale is designed to prevent. In these novels, the narratee is representative, standing for a class of readers susceptible to similar error, and the narrator's mission in telling her tale is surgical: By correcting the problem – cutting out the ulcer – in the narratee (who, because she is essentially defined by the problem addressed in the text, is especially receptive to the narrator's admonitions), the narrator will prevent its eruption in the body of those readers who stand beyond the text. It is important to note, however, that the auditor's role shifts in late didactic texts; while the early narratee (and the class she represents) is projected as passive, the later auditor is seen as active, able not only to change herself, but her society. While the narrator in early didactic novels sees herself as a surgeon, then, the narrator in later ones sees herself as a gestalt psychologist, helping her patient reconfigure her own life and the lives of those around her.

In *Charlotte Temple* the narrator employs two major modes of making her presence felt: by directly confronting the narratee with her own weaknesses and by commenting on characters and events as she tells the story. Both modes are dialogized; this narrator is constantly arguing. She even names her auditors. While her predominant narratee is the impressionable young girl, she is also conscious – almost paranoically so – of another auditor, the girl's mother, projected as the stern censor of her daughter's reading, a woman who is as wary of the world as her putative child is not. To this Personage the narrator strives to make her intentions clear. Addressing her as "my dear, sober matron," for instance, she hastens to assure her that the text's apparently favorable description of men in military apparel is meant to be taken ironically, "to ridicule those girls who foolishly imagine a red coat and a silver epaulet constitute the fine gentleman" (28). Aware that novels can be interpreted in more ways than one, that ironies can be missed, satires unappreciated, sympathies misconstrued, the narrator does not want her "matrons" to misinterpret the story and so keep it from their daughters. She also wants to remind them that they, too, are not perfect, and to use their consciousness of their own faults to solicit their sympathies. "My dear madam, contract not your brow into a frown of disapprobation," she protests as she begs sympathy for Charlotte. "I mean not to extenuate the faults of those unhappy women who fall victims of guilt and folly; but surely, when we reflect how many errors we ourselves are subject to, how many secret faults lie hidden in the recesses of our hearts, . . . I say, my dear madam, when we consider this, we surely may pity the faults of others" (67). In gently reminding "madam" of her own secret sins, the narrator can appeal to her Christian conscience and enlist her aid in teaching young women to avoid "guilt and folly."

More often, the narrator of *Charlotte Temple* addresses "My young, volatile reader" (98), "the mind of youth" that "catches at promised pleasure" and "thinks not of the dangers lurking beneath [it]" (27). These she admonishes relentlessly, soliciting their belief through the testimony of her own emotional responses. To this end she beseeches them to "trust me, my heart aches while I write it; but certain I am that when once a woman has stifled the sense of shame in her bosom . . . she grows hardened in guilt" (32); or, she informs them that "the burning blush of indignation and shame tinges my cheek" as she records Belcour's perfidy (98). And the belief she solicits is in the truth of her claim that young women should not trust their own inclinations in sexual matters but rather let their elders decide for them. "Oh, my dear girls – for to such only I am writing – listen not to the voice of love, unless sanctioned by paternal approbation. . . . resist the impulse of natural inclination, when it runs counter to the precepts of religion and virtue" (29).

In addition, this engaging narrator monitors her narratee's interpretations by commenting on events and characters as she tells the story and by presenting dialogue that admits no interpretive ambiguity. The following is typical narrative commentary used to bridge dialogue:

> Charlotte had taken one step in the ways of imprudence, and when that is once done there are always innumerable obstacles to prevent the erring person returning to the path of rectitude; yet these obstacles, however forcible they may appear in general, exist chiefly in the imagination (36).

Here, although she does not directly address her narratee, the narrator assumes that her auditor, like Charlotte, also believes that first steps in error, once taken, cannot be retraced, and that the sinner must inevitably pursue the road to ruin. The narrator wants to assure her that she can choose to be chastised and save herself. Like Mary Guion, Charlotte stands upon "the brink of a precipice," at the bottom of which, for the fictional character, lies only "the dark abyss of ruin, shame, and remorse" (46). For the narratee, however, there is time to retreat. Again, within the framework of the novel's major point – that future content outweighs present desire – the narrator makes clear that a woman has two choices. Here "present" is signaled by Charlotte's choice to obey the dictates of her pride rather than the admonitions of her good sense. The two possibilities point in opposite directions: pride, to a fall; good sense, to salvation. Unlike in exploratory novels, at no point in *Charlotte Temple* does the narrator suggest that other options may exist – that a fall, for instance, might lead Charlotte to self-knowledge, and from there to mature adulthood. Rather, responsible adulthood here is defined in terms of obedience to authority, of emptying the self of personal desire, of happiness as the reward for settling for a state of being – for having been defined by external authority – rather than a state of becoming – of struggling to create an internal authority that will define the self for itself.

While narrative commentary is dialogic, always arguing with the narratee, in *Charlotte Temple* dialogue is monologic, illustrating the ideological stances characters represent. For instance during one of Charlotte's periods of temptation, four words convey the author's evaluation of the character's "friend":

> ". . . I thought [Charlotte says to La Rue, her female betrayer] the gentlemen were very free in their manner; I wonder you would suffer them to behave as they did."
> "Prithee, don't be such a foolish little prude," said the artful woman, affecting anger. "I invited you to go in hopes it would divert you and be an agreeable change of scene; however, if your delicacy was hurt by the behavior of the gentlemen, you need not go again; so there let it rest" (30).

By playing on Charlotte's fears, inclinations, and pride, in short, by capitalizing on the fifteen-year-old's foolish naïveté, La Rue leads her to her ruin. Here, the narrative description framing La Rue's speech projects her as a temptress; the phrase "the artful woman, affecting anger" succinctly conveys La Rue as artificial (as opposed to the culturally sanctioned "naturalness" of virtuous women, especially Charlotte), insincere, and designing. Moreover the alliteration marks this phrase as narratively significant. The dialogue itself directly exhibits the characteristics that the narrator has already proclaimed: Charlotte's conveys her sexual innocence and her virtuous instincts; La Rue's, her intentions to manipulate her unsuspecting prey. Few other types of communication are portrayed in the novel: There is no filler, fleshing out the characters' lives for the readers; no casual conversations, no moments of ease in which complex personalities can be developed. Communication between characters is so devised as only to drive home the narrator's idée fixe; it is interchange, not conversation, dialogue created to illustrate a single point, not to explore the manifold directions human relationships can take.

Throughout *Charlotte Temple,* then, narrative commentary, dialogue, and the narrator's direct addresses reiterate the prefacing declaration that this novel was written "with a mind anxious for the happiness of that sex whose morals and conduct have so powerful an influence on mankind in general" (6). And the authorial message is twofold: The best course to follow is that set by Lucy, to serve and to obey; the only recourse for those who do not is to sincerely repent and hope for the "deferred gratification" of forgiveness by God and acceptance in heaven.

> Remember the endeavors of the wicked are often suffered to prosper that in the end their fall may be attended with more bitterness of heart; while the cup of affliction is poured out for wise and salutary ends, and they who are compelled to drain it even to the bitter dregs often find comfort at the bottom; the tear of penitence blots their offense from the book of fate and they rise from the heavy, painful trial, purified and fit for a mansion in the kingdom of eternity (99).

Unlike apparently similar sentiments we shall see expressed in *St. Elmo,* this narrative moralizing contains no ambiguities, no suggestions that the divine plan might be fallible or even a fraud. In addition, no loose ends remain in the plot; all the characters are meted out their just rewards. As Charlotte dies, "a sudden beam of joy passed across her languid features: she raised her eyes to heaven – and then closed them forever" (116). Clearly, the sin of self-gratification can be forgiven (though not on this earth) if the woman committing it admits her guilt. For self-gratification, rather than unchastity, has constituted Charlotte's real transgression, and the narrator never lets her narratee forget that fact. The other characters decline or fall according to their standing on this moral scale: Belcour and

La Rue meet miserable ends; Montraville lives a life of bitter remorse. Most significant, perhaps, Charlotte's baby becomes a reincarnation of virtuous womanhood, a throwback to her grandmother, showing no signs of her mother's rebellion. Named Lucy, she is in effect her grandmother's clone. Thematically as well as rhetorically, *Charlotte Temple* leaves no room for heretical speculation. To Mary Guion's question whether "an inocent female" can "account for the meaning of so much discimulation in the other sex," *Charlotte Temple* answers that the female need not account for it at all, rather that her duty – and her safety – lies in avoiding all men and all decisions other than those to which her parents direct her.

Relentlessly didactic, *Charlotte Temple's* characterization, description, dialogue, and narrator–reader contracts all contribute to the fulfillment of its narrative design. Similar ideologies, narrative mediation, redundancies, and contracts with readers mark most early didactic novels, making it clear that their authors write with specific audiences in mind and with specific messages to communicate. Catherine Sedgwick's *A New-England Tale* (1822), dedicated to the English novelist Maria Edgeworth "As A Slight Expression of the Writer's sense of her eminent services in the Great Cause of Human Virtue and Improvement,"[13] was, according to the 1822 preface, intended as "a very short and simple moral tale."[14] That is not necessarily the way it was received; one of the first notices taken of it came in a footnote to a lengthy review of Cooper's *The Spy,* where the reviewer expressed his appreciation of Sedgwick's character sketches, putting her – as he was busily putting Cooper – within the context of a burgeoning native American literature. This reviewer describes the novel as "a beautiful little picture of native scenery and manner, composed with exquisite delicacy of taste, and great strength of talent. . . . If rumor has rightly attributed this excellent production to a female pen, we may with far greater confidence boast of a *religious* Edgeworth in our land, than of a wonder-working Scott."[15] While Sedgwick conceived of her book in moral terms, then, the *North American* reviewer conceived of it in nationalistic ones. Charles Henry Dana, Senior, disagreed with both. Writing about the review to his friend Gulian Verplanck, Dana complains

> How the Reviewer should have come to such a very tolerable conception of [Cooper's] work, and yet *tag* on such an absurd note about the New England Tale, is past my finding out. Its *delicacy* is the least thing I should think of praising it for, "Wormy children" – and then the Quaker gentleman 11 years in advance of the girl, whom we are made to feel is a sort of adopted child of his, and then see snugly and warmly bedded with him. And then the *first* wife's miniature is very ingeniously put to quite a delicate and novel use at the love declaration. Yet the book

has some good things in it, taken from what, I understand, the authoress had seen. It certainly shows a considerable talent, and is a great deal cleverer than any woman I know of here about, could write. Pray don't tell what I say, for I should reap the *benefit* of it for years to come amongst her friends.[16]

Whereas the reviewer, preoccupied with the creation of a national literature, foregrounds Sedgwick's local color detail, Dana foregrounds the novel's moral singularities, both intentional (the "wormy children") and unintentional (the marriage). Like Lydia Maria Child, when Dana wrote a private letter he felt under less pressure to see all products of female pens in terms of their "delicacy" (within the context of the letter, the word's appearance suggests sarcasm). Consequently he picks out the indelicate (and perhaps more interesting) aspects of Sedgwick's tale.

Although enough readers apparently saw *A New-England Tale* as an attack on the New England character to elicit a defense of her moral concerns in the author's preface to the 1852 edition, the novel's original didactic intent is clear.[17] Like *Charlotte Temple, A New-England Tale* concerns the relationship between parents and children and the ability to discriminate between justified and unjustified external authorities. But where *Charlotte Temple*'s dominant narratee is the vulnerable young woman, *A New-England Tale*'s is the unjust parent, the older generation whose debased Calvinism has undermined the legitimacy of New England religion. Moreover, *A New-England Tale* is also a more complex and subtle novel than *Charlotte Temple,* directly addressing its narratee less frequently, distributing its message among a varied cast of minor characters, and posing its major problem in terms of the differences between words and deeds as signs of false (selfish) and true (benevolent) Christianity.

The basic plot of *A New-England Tale* is a New England version of the Cinderella story; its protagonist an orphaned girl reluctantly taken in by a tyrannical and hypocritical Calvinist aunt who uses and abuses her. Jane Elton, the heroine, has learned Christian fortitude and generosity from her weak but religious mother (in this she is the forerunner of many American heroines, especially those in Susan Warner's novels), and though her aunt makes her do the servants' work and even accuses her of thievery, Jane's religious strength and generous character carry her through her trials until she marries Mr. Lloyd, a Quaker whose character and religious principles are similar to her own. In the six years (covering ages twelve through eighteen) of her life treated in the novel, Jane also eagerly pursues an academic education. In addition she contracts an engagement with an unworthy young man that she ultimately realizes was a mistake, and subsequently breaks. Jane Elton cannot quite be described as having grown during this period; like Lucy Eldridge, she is a positive exemplary heroine whose function is to illustrate the best characteristics of young womanhood. But she does receive an education, both academic and social, that strengthens her religious faith, helps her discriminate between true and false Christians, and demonstrates the value of obedience to justified authority.

Juxtaposed to Jane's positive example is the negative example of her tyrannical aunt, Mrs. Wilson, whose portrait is drawn to warn mature readers against the dangers of parental tyranny and all readers against the abuses of Calvinist doctrine. It is her children whom Dana characterized as "wormy"; living under the eye of a woman who, in Jane's final summation, "deceived herself by her clamorous profession" of piety, they have learned to use their mother's self-deception for their own ends. As her cousin Elvira warns Jane when the latter refuses to deceive her aunt, "Pooh, Jane, you have brought your deaconist nonsense to a poor market. It was easy enough to get along with the truth with your mother, because she would let you have your own way on all occasions; but I can tell you, disguises are the only wear in our camp!" (58). These children are all eventually brought to ruin; with their mother, they are examples of how not to live.

> If Mrs. Wilson had not been blinded by self-love, she might have learnt an invaluable lesson from the melancholy results of her own mal-government. But she preferred incurring every evil, to the relinquishment of one of the perogatives of power. Her children, denied the appropriate pleasures of youth, were driven to sins of a much deeper dye, than those which Mrs. Wilson sought to avoid could have had even in her eyes; for surely the very worst effects that ever were attributed to dancing, or to romance-reading, cannot equal the secret dislike of a parent's authority, the risings of the heart against a parent's tyranny, and the falsehood and meanness that weakness will always employ in the evasion of power; and than which nothing will more certainly taint every thing that is pure in the character (72).

While no less determined to ensure the correct reading of her narrative, in *A New-England Tale* the narrator's voice is less admonitory than interpretive; that is, compared to *Charlotte Temple,* there are fewer passages that directly address the narratee but more that direct the attention to the necessary discriminations called for by the text's ideology. Like the narrator of *Charlotte Temple,* this narrator is assuming more than one kind of reader, but unlike the speaker in the earlier novel, she speaks more often to her older auditor than to her younger. She is, in fact, not quite sure she *has* a young audience – in one of her rare references to a specific audience, she speaks of "our fair young readers (if any of that class condescend to read this unromantic tale)" (183). But speaking *of* is not the same as speaking *to;* in this novel the narrative glance at the young reader is far more often to the side than in the eye. Nor is this narrator so anxious to record her own responses to the events she relates; she projects herself far less flamboyantly. Nevertheless, she has an equally serious, and fairly complicated, message to communicate, and her occasional use of the first-person plural "We fear" is as cautionary as the earlier narrator's references to her own aching heart. Apparently less worried about being misunderstood, she uses irony more frequently than does the narrator of *Charlotte Temple*. In one of her initial descriptions of Jane's aunt, for instance, the narrator characterizes Mrs. Wilson as a woman who

> had fancied herself one of the subjects of an awakening at an early period of her life; had passed through the ordeal of a church-examination with great credit, having depicted in glowing colors the opposition of her natural heart to the decrees, and her subsequent joy in the doctrine of election. She thus assumed the form of godliness without feeling its power. We fear that in those times of excitement, during which many pass from indifference to holiness, and many are converted from sin to righteousness, there are also many who, like Mrs. Wilson, delude themselves and others with vain forms of words, and professions of faith (31).

Although the first sentence of this passage paraphrases Mrs. Wilson's opinion of herself (Bakhtin would call it an example of character zoning, the refraction of the character's voice in the narrator's language),[18] the word "fancied," which connotes whim, conceit, and imagination (not concepts conducive to true religious feeling) is a direct interpolation by the narrator intended to warn the reader not to take Mrs. Wilson's evaluation of herself seriously. Had the phrase "fancied herself" been replaced by "been," readers would be less prone to grasp the narrator's irony. However, just in case a dull auditor misses it, the narrator drops the ironic mode after her first sentence and, in one crisp sentence, summarizes the situation from her interpretive position. Finally, in the third sentence she assumes a personality, suggesting through her "fear" that she is telling this story in order to caution readers about committing similar errors. In fact the "we" of this narrative voice assumes more authority than the "I" of *Charlotte Temple's* narrator; rather than projecting a discrete individual – one who, in her defensiveness, demonstrates that she is aware that she is isolated – the representative voice suggests a diffused personality that speaks for the authority of a changing New England culture. In focusing on Mrs. Wilson's misunderstood Calvinism as a vehicle for her attack on misplaced parental authority, Sedgwick, who became a Unitarian before she wrote *A New-England Tale,* demonstrates her grasp of the crisis in contemporary New England theology, when Calvinism was reluctantly giving way to Unitarianism. Certainly this is the basis for those readers who saw *A New-England Tale* as an attack on New England culture; the

THE EARLY DIDACTIC NOVEL

narrative voice sides with the new religious spirit and speaks with an authority that assumes that her (their) position is the only rational one possible.

Throughout *A New-England Tale* the narrator maintains a caustic attitude toward Mrs. Wilson and the Calvinist hypocrites she represents. Whenever her story touches on the difference between speaking words, especially religious words, and understanding them, the narrator accentuates the issue, pointedly holding up Mrs. Wilson as a negative exemplar. For instance, she actively, even sharply, emphasizes how poor a grasp Mrs. Wilson has of the spirit behind religious doctrines: "Mrs. Wilson should have remembered that God does give the increase to those that rightly plant, and faithfully water. But Mrs. Wilson's tongue was familiar with many texts that had never entered her understanding, or influenced her heart" (16). Throughout, the narrator's concern is for the parent who abuses her power; her intention here is to encourage parents to monitor their own use of authority. While *Charlotte Temple*'s primary narratee was the daughter, and its primary intent was to teach her filial obedience, *A New-England Tale*'s primary narratee is the mother, and its intent is to teach her to wield her power correctly, that is, to use it in the service of others – benevolently – rather than for her own aggrandizement.

Consequently, parents are held up as models for conduct throughout *A New-England Tale*. Not only does Mrs. Wilson come under such censure, but also both of Jane Elton's parents. Mrs. Elton is especially censured for having joined her husband in a charade to hide their economic embarrassments from their friends:

> It may seem strange, perhaps incredible, that Mrs. Elton, possessing the virtues we have attributed to her, and being a religious woman, should be accessory to such deception, and (for we will call "things by their right names") dishonesty. But the wonder will cease if we look around upon the circle of our acquaintance, and observe how few there are among those whom we believe to be Christians, who govern their daily conduct by Christian principles, and regulate their temporal duties by the strict Christian rule. Truly, narrow is the way of perfect integrity, and few there are that walk therein (8).

Here, the narrative begins with Mrs. Elton, who has previously been described in largely positive terms, then expands to include the narrator's "acquaintance" – and by implication, the auditor herself – and ends with an appropriate admonitory reference to the Bible. Rather than devote entire passages of admonition directly to her narratee, this narrator conceals them in examples, always probing and suggesting, but rarely accusing outright. That this charade undermines Mrs. Elton's parental virtues – and ultimate authority – is evident later, when a former servant, now destitute, reveals that Jane's parents had never paid her the last $100 they owed her. The daughter, deeply shamed, repays the debt, but her respect for her dead parents is weakened. The crime exhibited here is twofold: As in loco parentis to the young servant, Jane's parents failed in their duty to their employee; as models for right conduct for their daughter, they failed to leave an honorable legacy. For the mature narratee, the story incorporates a warning against economic deception that carries the penalty of losing her children's respect.

A New-England Tale introduces its characters gradually, bringing them one by one to the village where the action will take place. As each is introduced, her or his virtues or vices are developed through extended character sketches. Unlike in *Charlotte Temple, A New-England Tale* features many minor characters whose tales are not integral to the central plot (which by itself, is very slender) but that are integral to the central theme: the valuation of benevolence and its definition as an emptying of self in the interests of others. Many of these stories are fitted into the larger narrative to provide contrasts to the major characters and to exhibit shades of difference in manners, morals, and religious understanding. Mary Oakley, Crazy Bet, and Old John have the most extended minor tales: Mary, who lets herself be seduced by Mrs. Wilson's scoundrel son, is, like Charlotte Temple, a warning against filial impiety; Crazy Bet, gone mad after the death of her fiancé, functions both as a voice of Christian benevolence and as a warning against emotional excess; Old John, whose house is destroyed by the young owners of his land, functions at once as an example of Christian benevolence (he and his wife take in Mary Oakley and her child), of doctrinal reason [unlike Mrs. Wilson, he insists that "the great thing is how we live, not how we die," (15)], and of necessary truth telling (he lets Jane know that her fiancé, a lawyer, has defended the young louts who destroyed his house). Through all these characters, especially when they interpret each other (as John, or Jane's fiancé, or Polly Harris, to whom Jane's adored parents owed money), Jane (and the narratee) learn not only the fine shadings of Christian virtue, but also how to apply those shadings to the evaluation of characters whom they would like to trust but who, seen "objectively" (that is, from the point of view of the text's standard of benevolence), are proved to be inadequate. With other minor characters these function to increase textual coherence; unlike in *Charlotte Temple,* however, in this text most repetitions accumulate on the same temporal plane as the central action.

While most minor characters are described briefly, one, Rebecca Lloyd, who dies soon after she is introduced, is described extensively, nearly a whole chapter given to her before ending with her death. In fact her death is recorded twice in this chapter, first in the second paragraph, then again at the end, after a flashback devoted to her life and marriage that covers the years prior to the time set by her death at the chapter's inception. The centrality accorded her suggests that her life – and death – are integral to the central theme, and in fact Rebecca is the exemplary woman who sets the standard against which all the other women in the text will be measured, the godly, virtuous good wife who stands, in this novel, where Lucy Eldridge stands in *Charlotte Temple*.

The narrator devotes more attention to describing Rebecca than her status as a character would seem to warrant because her status as an archetype rules the rest of the tale and because the Lloyds's marriage is the model for spousal relationships. Rebecca is gentle, educated, reflective, soft-spoken, loving toward her husband, and enamored of her God. First cousins, both orphaned (Rebecca twice; by her own parents and her adoptive parents, her aunt and uncle), Robert and Rebecca Lloyd's relationship exhibits the generosity, the reaching out of the self toward others, that marks this narrative's highest value.

> Three years glided on in uninterrupted felicity. Excepting when they were called to feel for others' woes, their happiness was not darkened by a single shadow; nor did it degenerate into selfish indulgence, but, constantly enlarging its circle, embraced within its compass all that could be benefitted by their active efforts and heavenly example (37–8).

Rebecca is held up not only as a model in her spousal relationship, she is also projected as closely in touch with nature and nature's God. I shall be discussing the intertextual significance of the nineteenth-century association of good women with nature more thoroughly in my chapters on *St. Elmo* and *Queechy;* here, it is useful to note that Rebecca's love of nature is a sign that she is one of those virtuous women already inscribed in the culture through a complex of associations. Rebecca and Robert's conversations as they drive through the countryside exhibit Rebecca's affinity for nature and amplify the narrator's affirmation of her piety.

> Whenever [Rebecca] felt herself a little better, she would pass a part of the day in riding. Never did any one, in the full flush of health, enjoy more than she, from communion with her Heavenly Father, through the visible creation. She read with understanding the revelations of his goodness, in the varied expressions of nature's beautiful face.
>
> "Do you know," said she to her husband, "that I prefer the narrow vales of the Housatonic, to the broader lands of the Connecticut? It certainly matters little where our dust is laid, if it be consecrated by Him who is the 'resurrection and the life;' but I derive a pleasure which I could not have conceived of, from the expectation of having my body repose in this still valley, under the shadow of that beautiful hill."
>
> "I, too, prefer this scenery," said Mr. Lloyd, seeking to turn the conversation, for he could not yet but contemplate with dread, what his courageous wife spoke of with a tone of cheerfulness. "I prefer it, because it has a more domestic aspect. There is, too, a more perfect and

intimate union of the sublime and beautiful. These mountains that surround us, and are so near to us on every side, seem to me like natural
barriers, by which the Father has secured for His children the gardens
He has planted for them by the river's side" (48).

This conversation ends with Robert's pledge to rear their child in the
country, "far from the stormy waves of the rude world – far from its
'vanities and vexation of spirit' " (49). While the discourse on aesthetics
serves to flesh out the Lloyds's personalities, developing their thoughtful
piety (in implicit contrast to Mrs. Wilson's ignorant bigotry), the pledge
provides the rationale for Robert Lloyd's remaining in the neighborhood.
Though a minor character, Rebecca Lloyd is integral to the novel's theme.
The proliferation of descriptive incidents and dialogue concerning her
sets the stage for later thematic developments.

Jane's eventual marriage to Mr. Lloyd should be seen within this context. Charles Henry Dana, Senior, was right to notice the odd fusion of
the sexual and the paternal here; to be disturbed by the ease with which a
male who has acted as a young female's protector becomes her sexual
partner. Yet Lloyd's transformation from father to husband is no more
startling than Jane Elton's transformation from daughter to wife. In both
instances, a marked loss of individuality occurs that precisely illustrates
the exemplary function of characters in didactic novels. In the scene Dana
(probably sarcastically) called both "ingenious" and "delicate," the miniature of Rebecca serves to fuse the women. Mr. Lloyd wears the miniature around his neck; in the scene to which Dana refers, Lloyd's daughter, little Rebecca, draws it out.

> Little Rebecca was sitting on her father's knee; she took from his bosom
> a miniature of her mother, which he always wore there, and seemed
> intently studying the face which the artist had delineated with masterly
> power. "Do the angels look like my mother?" she asked.
> "Why, my child?"
> "I thought, father, they might look like her, she looks so bright and
> good." She kissed the picture, and after a moment's pause, added "Jane
> looks like mother, all but the cap; dost not thee think, father, Jane would
> look pretty in a quaker cap?" (262)

Since Mr. Lloyd is about to propose marriage to Jane, the remark comes
at an appropriate time for the exigencies of the plot. But it has been
prepared for thematically throughout the novel. References to Rebecca's
angelic nature have occurred since her entrance into the tale: After Robert
Lloyd had donated money to a crippled mountaineer's building fund, for
instance, the man had remarked to his wife that

> ". . . if the days of miracles weren't quite entirely gone by, I should
> think we had 'entertained angels unawares.' "
> "I think you might better say," replied the good woman, "that the

angels have entertained us; any how, that sick lady will be an angel before long; she looks as good, and as beautiful, as one now" (47).

Jane, too, has always been viewed as angelic. Even as a child

> Little Jane had nursed her mother with fidelity and tenderness, and performed services for her, that her years had seemed hardly adequate to, with an efficiency and exactness that surprised all who were prepared to find her a delicately bred and indulged child. She seemed to have inherited nothing from her father but his active mind; from her mother she had derived a pure and gentle spirit . . ." (10).

Her friend Mary Hull regards her as "so different" that she "need not go by the common rules" (266). Even Edward Erskine, Jane's rejected suitor, "felt the value, the surpassing excellence of the blessing he had forfeited. . . . 'Oh, Jane,' he said, 'you are an angel; forget my follies, and think of me with kindness'"(215).

Like Rebecca, Jane is pious, graceful, loyal, and good, the female icon celebrated in nineteenth-century art and literature. As such, she is Rebecca's double, fit to take the senior woman's place. All she needs, as young Rebecca remarks, is the Quaker cap, and that she promptly dons, having "been early led to inquire into the particular modification of religion professed by her benefactor" (268) and realizing that it, rather than the religion of her own family, agreed with "the preference she always gave to the spirit over the letter, to the practice over the profession" (269). This doubling of female characters is compounded by young Rebecca, who, like Jane earlier, has been reared by godly Mary Hull, and is as gentle and as pious as her mother and Jane before her. Like the two Lucys in *Charlotte Temple,* all the good women in *A New-England Tale* are in effect imaged as one, with names, faces, circumstances, and virtues overlapping and finally merging.

Mr. Lloyd's movement from foster father to husband is one more aspect of this fusion. Moving into Jane's father's house, he takes her father's "place" – literally as well as figuratively. Even before the first Rebecca dies, the stage is set for Mr. Lloyd's assumption of the fatherly role in Jane's life. "He had passed [the deserted Elton house] with Rebecca, and they had together admired its secluded and picturesque situation. The house stood at a little distance from the road, more than half hid by two patriarchal elms. . . ." The back lawn slopes to the river, and on the other side a tree-covered mountain rises, "tree surmounting tree, and the images of all sent back by the clear mirror below" (50). Like the mirrored and proliferated trees, the favored female characters in this tale are mirrored and proliferated, each one imaged in the other. When Mr. Lloyd "purchased the place and furniture, precisely as it had been left on the morning of the sale" he moves into Jane's house as the restored – and redeemed – father. When Jane marries him and returns "home," then, she becomes not only the first Rebecca, but also her own mother, while young Rebecca takes Jane's own place as the daughter.

Once Jane's former fiancé and the Wilson family have left the village – through either death or desertion – balance is restored to the fictional world Sedgwick has created. With the benevolent Mr. Lloyd serving as father, lover, and even Christ within the framework of Jane's journey, the village becomes a quasi heaven, where benevolence and obedience replace tyranny and rebellion. And if Mr. Lloyd represents the best of patriarchs, Jane represents the best of wives, mothers, daughters, and even nieces – the image of the good woman, able to discriminate between just and unjust authorities and willing to follow the rule of righteousness.

But obedience to external authority is still that rule. The last judgment of Mrs. Wilson is spoken by Mr. Lloyd, and it focuses on her disobedience.

> I have no doubt thy aunt has suffered some natural compunctions for her gross failure in the performance of her duties, but she felt safe in a sound faith. . . . Professions and declarations have crept in among the protestants, to take the place of the mortifications and penances of the ancient church; so prone are men to find some easier way to heaven than the toilsome path of obedience (259).

Mrs. Wilson's lapse was from obedience to her God, who, in the author's view, values benevolence over doctrine. But benevolence here is defined as giving up the self, the giving over to God and other people that made both Rebecca and Jane qualify as "angels." In refusing to recognize the needs of others – in interpreting her God's commands in the light of her own need for power – Mrs. Wilson has broken the most primary law in the system of values promulgated in this novel's world. Exploratory novels, while professing to censure similar female appropriations of power, will also be fascinated by them, exploring their ramifications for the development of female hegemony before returning their fictional universes to culturally sanctioned, male-dominated balance. E.D.E.N. Southworth's *The Mother-in-Law; or, Married in Haste* (1851) for instance, features a mother whose lust for power makes her compelling as well as repelling. Early didactic novels, however, do not embark on such adventures. Neither the narrator's remarks, the story's plot or theme, nor the novel's structural or rhetorical levels suggest that Mrs. Wilson's conduct has either mitigating or engaging factors. Rather, all aspects of the text indicate that in seeking power she has broken a primary law. In contrast, Jane has always obeyed, even her aunt – "It is my duty to subdue, not rouse my spirit," she declares (117), and she is deemed fortunate because she "had the rare habit of putting *self* aside: of deferring her own inclinations to the will, and interests, and inclinations, of others" (182). Like Lucy Eldridge and Rebecca Lloyd, willing to empty herself of herself for others, Jane Elton, too, earns the right to be filled with "content" through her marriage to a just – but nonetheless dominating – man.

Charlotte Temple and *A New-England Tale* certainly do not exhaust the varieties of plot or theme, or all the relationships between narrators and their narratees, existing in didactic women's novels in early nineteenth-century America. Nevertheless, they do show the predominant forms: engaging narrators, exemplary characters, a high incidence of doubling and other repetitions, a consistently admonitory tone, and a reluctance to venture into skeptical inquiry. They also show the predominant values: obedience to legitimate external authority, female passivity, and self-denial. Exploratory novels may begin with these values, but because of their propensity to expand rhetorically, to proliferate and, in the process, to reshape and ultimately redefine their ideas, they are open to far greater hermeneutic possibilities than didactic texts. Their formal structures are part and parcel of their shifting ideological makeup. In the next chapter I will begin examining exploratory texts, starting with Augusta Evans Wilson's *St. Elmo,* a novel in which the elaborate prose disguises rhetorical and thematic subversions that the author did not intend but that are nevertheless accessible to readers.

2

INTRODUCTION TO THE
EXPLORATORY TEXT:
SUBVERSIONS OF THE
NARRATIVE DESIGN IN
ST. ELMO

Although Augusta Evans Wilson's *St. Elmo* sold 1 million copies within four months of its publication in 1866,[1] and had at least one play and one movie based on it early in the twentieth century,[2] it appears to late twentieth-century readers as a work that is grossly, even ludicrously, overwritten. Some contemporary readers also saw it that way: Charles Henry ("John Paul") Webb, a humorist perhaps best known today for having edited and published Mark Twain's first book, parodied *St. Elmo* with a book titled *St. Twel'mo, or the Cuneiform Cyclopedist of Chattanooga* (1867). What, then, appealed to those who bought it? Contemporary reviewers cited its sentimental idealism, while later critics focused on the sexual attraction of its male protagonist or on the way the novel fulfilled Victorians' love for classical culture.[3] But *St. Elmo's* verbal density and multiple mythological and classical references would have precluded full comprehension from most readers. Moreover the story – which features an orphaned protagonist and her bitter, Byronic lover, was standard enough to be readily available in other, less inaccessible, novels. Part of the answer must lie in what readers drew from the other configurations the text permits. These configurations are not, it should be noted, deliberate on Wilson's part. Rather, they arise in spite of her overt projections. But exploratory novels are not all intended to challenge the status quo; in many, subversion arises from complications of verbal, structural, and thematic developments. *St. Elmo* is exactly that kind of text.

While most critics and reviewers have viewed *St. Elmo* – both favorably and unfavorably – in terms of its linguistic opulence, its Christian sentiment, or its Byronic hero,[4] a few have also remarked on Wilson's "picturesqueness of abstract statements, [and] her deep love of scholarship."[5] That authorial fascination with erudition can be dismissed for its pretentiousness, or it can be examined for its appeal to readers attracted to educated women. When Julia Dyson wistfully told her diary "Would that I were the favored child of knowledge, placed in the midst of her

60

treasures, initiated into her deep mysteries. Surely I would be what I am not,"[6] she was expressing a longing for education and for the wisdom and power it is supposed to impart that many of her contemporaries shared. The "deep hunger for culture" that William Fidler noted as the basis for *St. Elmo's* popularity in Victorian America[7] also marked the "romantic schoolgirls" Fred Pattee claims read the novel only for the sake of its Byronic hero[8]; Julia Newberry was not the only teenager who vowed to "BE SOMEBODY," who pursued an independent course of instructional reading and who, when she indulged in a novel, chose one that featured female heroes. In *St. Elmo*, the heroine's development into a productive scholar and an influential writer reflects these women's hunger, and challenges the prevailing assumption that classical learning was a male prerogative. This chapter will argue that the novel's stress on female education and its resultant power was as important a factor for women readers as was the sexual tension created by the Byronic lover.

Briefly, the plot of *St. Elmo* is as follows. Edna Earl, the heroine, is orphaned early in the novel. Deeply angered by what she perceives as a divine plot against her, at age thirteen she leaves her home in the Tennessee mountains, taking a train for Georgia, where she plans to work in the factories at Columbus while pursuing an education. The train wrecks, and Edna is gravely injured. She is taken in by Mrs. Murray, a wealthy woman who eventually offers her a home, an event that makes her repent her anger and reconcile her heart to God. At this juncture, however, Mrs. Murray's son, St. Elmo, enters the scene. St. Elmo is a proud, bitter, cruel man whose moral character was blighted when his best friend and his fiancée betrayed him in his youth. Having shot his friend, and later deliberately brought on the premature death of his friend's sister, he has compounded his alienation through murder, and leads an angry life wandering about the world, collecting esoterica and wreaking his revenge on women.

St. Elmo at first believes Edna is a schemer, but later comes to trust her, as her religious piety seems to be manifested in her honest and loyal character. When she is seventeen, he proposes to her, declaring that "with your dear little hand in mind to lead me, I will make amends for the ruin and suffering I have wrought, and my Edna – my own wife, shall save me!"[9] (278). Edna, however, declines, responding to his demand that she "give your pure, sinless life to purify mine" (278) by declaring that "I am no viceregent of an outraged and insulted God! . . . Go yonder to Jesus. He alone can save and purify you" (279). Shortly after, Edna goes to New York, where she takes a position as governess in a wealthy family and plunges into the city's intellectual life (Edna's intellectual life is the major subplot, which I will next discuss). While in Georgia, she had refused proposals by two men, St. Elmo and Gordon Leigh, a gentle young lawyer; in New York she refuses two more, Douglas Manning, the editor of the learned magazine in which she publishes her articles, and Sir Roger Percival, the "catch" of two continents. She refuses them because she cannot extirpate her deep attraction for St. Elmo, even though his "perverted nature . . . shocks" and "repels" her (279).

While Edna is in New York, St. Elmo remains in Georgia, slowly coming to realize that only he can atone for his sins. His first step is to effect a reconciliation with the Reverend Mr. Hammond, his (and Edna's) old tutor and father of the friend who had betrayed him. While Edna is delighted at the news, she still refuses to see St. Elmo or to listen to anyone else's plea for him, despite the social pressure that is brought to bear on her for her fastidiousness [during one visit home the text preached in the church is "Judge not, that ye be not judged" (429)]. Nonetheless, Edna is steadfast. Edna is sent to Europe with her pupils; meanwhile, unbeknownst to her, St. Elmo enters the ministry. When she returns from Europe, he appears in New York, once more declaring his love. Her prayers answered, now that St. Elmo is "saved – purified – consecrated to God's holy work" (470), Edna accepts him. Declaring himself "humble . . . grateful . . . proud," and "resolved to prove himself worthy of his treasure" (479), St. Elmo glories in his conquest. They are married, and Edna, listening to the "tremor" in his voice, "knew . . . that his dedication was complete," and that "now to be his companion . . . to be allowed to help him and love him, to walk heavenward with her hand in his; this – this was the crowning glory and richest blessing of her life" (481).

This, then, constitutes the Byronic overplot of St. Elmo, providing the thrill that compels readers for whom this schema of sexual attraction and repulsion provides vicarious pleasure. It is interesting to see how recent critics have interpreted this schema – a plot so prevalent in nineteenth-century women's novels that one contemporary reviewer criticized St. Elmo for using the "well-known" story of a "charlatan of literature" as its "central figure."[10] In Woman's Fiction, Nina Baym argues that the real attraction of the Byronic hero in women's novels is his function as an index to the heroine's power: "in a world where women are traditionally assumed to be the playthings of men nothing can be more satisfying than to see the tables turned."[11] For Baym, the significance of Byronic overplots lies in the power they assign women.

Extending her insight, we can note that the heroes' reformation also demonstrates one strategy nineteenth-century Christianity provided for resolving the struggle between male and female quests for domination, that is, that both parties submit first to God. In this schema, female power is both sexual and ethical: St. Elmo is rounded by the idea of woman as the saving influence on man, the one to bring him to God. The novel's epigram, a quotation from Ruskin, paves the way for this reading, proclaiming that

> Ah! the true rule is – a true wife in her husband's house is his servant; it is in his heart that she is queen. Whatever of the best he can conceive, it is her part to be; whatever of the highest he can hope, it is hers to promise; all that is dark in him she must purge into purity; all that is failing in him she must strengthen into truth; from her through all the world's clamor, he must win his praise; in her, through all the world's warfare, he must find his peace.

As almost any quotation from Ruskin in a nineteenth-century novel signals (*Sesame and Lilies* seems to have been universally read by women writers), the guidelines for *St. Elmo's* cover story are profoundly conservative, resting on a cultural code that inscribes women as morally superior but functionally subordinate to men. The Byronic overplot simply lends sexual interest to the doctrine that women's ultimate function is to guide men into the arms of God. Here, sexual and ethical opposites are fused, creating a set of binary oppositions that legitimize sexual tensions under the rubric of ethical imperatives.

Another recent reading of the Byronic lover emphasizes sexuality. Alfred Habegger sees the tension of the Byronic overplot within the context of nineteenth-century literature's oblique references to sex:

> The most important thing to remember about the social context of popular fiction in the nineteenth century is that sex outside marriage was taboo for women. One strange consequence of this was that weddings and even proposals became shorthand for sex: no reader could have been unaware that following the wedding ceremony would come something . . . that could not be spoken of. The reason why the scene on which everything depended in the novel had to do with love and its dread ceremonies is that the heart of the novel was an anticipated act of copulation. In an age when a man's declaration, "I love you" was tantamount to a proposal, these three words formed, quite simply, the most interesting speech-act there was.[12]

In this Big Bang theory of women's fiction, sexual energy is at the heart of women's novels; rather than sex simply lending interest to religious iconography, it was the texts' real creed.

I suggest that the basic tension in these novels is yet more complicated. In an age when marriage meant effacing the woman's individuality – when she was legally, socially, financially, and intellectually "covered" by her spouse – legal copulation was tantamount to obliteration. Novels like *St. Elmo* present a tension between sex-as-glorious-obliteration and self-as-gratification. (And also religion-as-glorious-obliteration, essentially the same, as illustrated by *St. Elmo's* plot, where the lover becomes a minister and the heroine, in submitting to him, also submits to a representative of Christ.) In carefully developing the heroine's independence, a novel like *St. Elmo* creates a countertheme fully as attractive – and as frightening – as its romantic one: the theme of individuality, of power in and of the self, of energy fueled not by sexual love but by self-love. In *St. Elmo*, this is presented through the heroine's seizure of written discourse, a source of cultural hegemony generally forbidden women. Here, the Ruskinean and the sexual thematics function to cover, or disguise, the counterlure of female self-definition and verbal power.

Throughout *St. Elmo*, subthemes, ambiguous wording, and strategic sentence placement create reading environments open to multiple interpretations. First, although Ruskin's definition of the true woman is placed so as to frame – and therefore influence our reading of – Edna's relationship to St. Elmo, in fact she is not so much a present agent in St. Elmo's conversion as an absent one. Although early in the novel she occasionally says or does something that pricks his conscience, they are actually separated through most of the novel. Of the five years she spends with Mrs. Murray, St. Elmo is gone on his wanderings for four; while he is home, she shuns him. During the two years she is in New York and Europe, she sees him only once, at a distance. Consequently his repentance and conversion, while initiated by his desire for her, is in fact effected without her.

In part, this phenomenon stems from the status of conversion ideology in nineteenth-century American Congregationalism; while sanctification was no longer a function of God's will alone, it still could not be effected by a third party. Rather, it was a matter entirely between a sinner and his or her God. But in this literature (and absences of the Byronic male are common, one function of his generic propensity to go wandering up and down upon the earth) the male's absence – or the heroine's absence from him – also signals a period of female self-development, of self-consciousness, and of self-preservation. Had St. Elmo won Edna's sympathies on her entry into the Murray home, he would have dominated her mentally and emotionally (as the major male protagonist succeeds in doing to the heroine in Susan Warner's *The Wide, Wide World*). In his absence, the young Edna develops along lines dictated by her own predilections, while her sojourn in New York strengthens her sense of self and establishes her independent (and triumphant) existence in the world. By the time they do unite, she is a force to be reckoned with, a woman who has won the hearts of the public and of three powerful and influential men – a phenomenon that, even to her, makes "her triumph seem . . . complete" (363).

With this, Edna's refusal to be an active factor in St. Elmo's conversion signals a covert rejection – despite authorial avowals to the contrary – of the heroine's major function to be her lover's "servant" and "queen." Baym points out that although Edna provides an example of moral steadfastness for St. Elmo, she actually refuses to help him; her declaration that she is "no viceregent of an outraged and insulted God" (279), and her unwaveringly and arrogantly judgmental stance, while it does ultimately bring him to his knees, also proves her deep reluctance to lose her own soul in trying to save his.[13]

The disparity between Edna's words about women's duties and her own conduct is evident not only in her behavior in the public sphere but also in the private. No matter how she defines female roles, Edna herself is not a self-abnegating heroine. Rather, she is a character adamantly determined to realize her own ambitions and preserve her psychological, as well as spiritual, integrity, going so far as to insist on her own prerogatives even with those for whom she bears genuine love and respect. For instance, when the Reverend Mr. Hammond, her old tutor and a thoroughly good man, begs her to come live with him and help him during what he believes is his last illness (380), she refuses, preferring to remain in New York, where her first book has just been published and where she can be on the scene as the reviews come out. Similarly, Mrs. Murray's motherly pleas that she come home to comfort her in her old age receive heart-torn, but steadfast, refusals. In the struggle between heart (the feminine) and will (the masculine), Edna's will consistently triumphs.

Second, and more significantly, Edna's ambition to know – even antedating her desire to publish – sets up a strong countertheme to the text's overt thematic. Although late in the novel Wilson implies that Edna's books are domestic tracts, for a large part of the novel Edna's mission is far from catholic. Edna herself admits that she is ambitious: Told that she has a heart disease, and must cut back on her labors, she cries out that "I love my work! Ah, I want to live long enough to finish something grand and noble . . . something that will follow me across and beyond the dark, silent valley . . . something that will echo in eternity!" (371). Authorial disclaimers notwithstanding, the work being described here is not the kind that "true women" were expected to produce. What Edna is saying is that she wants to be immortalized in her work, an ambition rigorously allocated to the male sphere. Similarly, her academic preparation and her plan for her first book exceed the requirements even for educated womanhood. Under pressure from the men who control the publishing industry, who continually tell her that "women never write histories or epics; never compose oratorios that go sounding down the centuries" (198), Edna shifts the form of her first book from scholarly exposition to didactic fiction, the latter a genre nineteenth-century publishers and reviewers considered appropriate for the feminine sensibility. But Edna does not shift her subject or her focus. The fictional framework simply disguises her critical intentions: Her novel features a woman who becomes disillusioned with the received truths of her own culture, searches for truth among other cultures, and inscribes her discoveries in a book that is essentially a critical history of pre-Christian thought. Edna's first book, then, is a massive analysis of world mythologies, a work that contemporary readers would recognize as part of the nineteenth century's new fascination with Biblical criticism and comparative cultural and linguistic studies.

Under Mr. Hammond's tutelage, Edna learns Latin, Greek, Hebrew, and Chaldee. Fascinated by ancient mythologies, she then conceives the ambition of performing "a rigid analysis and comparison of all the mythologies of the world [which] would throw some light on the problem of ethnology, and in conjunction with philology settle the vexed question" (109).

> Pushing the Polymetis aside, she sprang up and paced the long room, and gradually her eyes kindled, her cheeks burned, as ambition pointed to a possible future, of which, till this hour, she had not dared dream; and hope, o'erleaping all barriers, grasped a victory that would make her name imperishable (109).

The significant thematic subversions of this novel occur in the descriptions of Edna's scholarly goals and achievements, which take place within the context of continual verbal battling between male and female characters, and which detail Edna's struggle to grasp verbal power and to create a feminine mythology. As Gerald Graff points out in *Professing Literature*,[14] mid–nineteenth-century forms of classical education, with their stress on grammar and etymology, reflected the view that language study was prelude to intellectual self-development (29). Hegel had articulated this pedagogical philosophy in 1809, informing students that

> This centrifugal force of the Soul is above all the reason for the necessary separation by which it seeks to move away from its natural essence and condition, and why a remote and foreign world must be put before the youthful spirit. The barrier best suited to perform this task of self-division for the sake of education is the world and language of the ancients. This world separates us from ourselves, but grants us at the same time the starting point and leading string for a return to ourselves; for a reconciliation with it and a rediscovery of ourselves, but now a selfhood seen in the truly universal essense of spirit.
>   . . . Grammar has for its content the categories, special products and definitions of the understanding; therefore in learning it the understanding itself becomes *learned*.[15]

This educational philosophy excluded women a priori; they were associated with the imagination and the affections, not the understanding. It was barely conceivable that a woman could undertake the arduous task of educating her understanding – as Margaret Fuller's anomalous position demonstrates. Women's souls were soft, diffuse; the mental discipline classical languages required would destroy their femininity, develop the tough Selfhood that was antithetical to the nature of True Women. Given this gendered view of the study of classical languages, it is extremely significant that Edna learns not only Greek and Latin, but also Hebrew and Chaldee. Moreover, unlike most educated men of her day, Edna synthesizes and interprets[16]; her first book is a hermeneutic, not merely a taxonomic, investigation into the evolution of world myth, written from a female point of view. Finally, in acquiring her classical background, Edna has fulfilled the requirements for the Christian ministry.[17] It would be difficult to imagine a more radical appropriation of elite male intellectual culture than Edna achieves – a culture that, for all its dissociation from the realities of American life, clearly appealed to Wilson's patrician sensibilities.

Unlike George Eliot's male character Causabon, who embarks on a similarly difficult project, Wilson's female character succeeds, and the passages detailing her progress present an intellectual passion fully equal to the sexual passion inherent in the Byronic overplot. Although Wilson has various other characters censure Edna for her "ambition," and though, as Mary Kelley notes, in the nineteenth century's view Edna's heart disease is one of the consequences of her having stepped beyond her sphere,[18] there is an intensity – and a thoroughness – in the portrayals of Edna's studies that betray a true authorial fascination. This is also one root, of course, of Wilson's pretentious prose – in her zeal to display her character's erudition she is "forced" to display her own. Yet this prose also cushions the radical impact of Edna's project.

> The vastness of the cosmic field [Edna] was now compelled to traverse, the innumerable ramifications of polytheistic and monotheistic creeds, necessitated unwearied research, as she rent asunder the superstitious veils which various nations and successive epochs had woven before the shining features of truth. To-day peering into the golden Gardens of the Sun at Cuzco; to-morrow clambering over Thibet glaciers, to find the mystic lake of Yamuna; now delighted to recognize in Teoyamiqui (the wife of the Aztec God of War) the unmistakable features of Scandinavian Valkyrias; and now surprised to discover the Greek Fates sitting under the Norse tree Ygdrasil, deciding the destinies of mortals, and calling themselves Nornas; she spent her days in pilgrimages to mouldering shrines, and midnight often found her groping in the classic dust of extinct systems. Having once grappled with her theme, she wrestled as obstinately as Jacob for the blessing of a successful solution, and in order to popularize a subject bristling with recondite archaisms and philogic problems, she cast it in the mould of fiction. The information and pleasure which she had derived from the perusal of Vaughan's delightful Hours with the Mystics, suggested the idea of adopting a

similar plan for her own book, and investing it with the additional interest of a complicated plot and more numerous characters. To avoid anachronisms, she endeavored to treat the religions of the world in their chronologic sequence, and resorted to the expedient of introducing pagan personages. A fair young priestess of the temple of Neith, in the sacred city of Sais – where people of all climes collected to witness the festival of lamps – becoming skeptical of the miraculous attributes of the statues she had been trained to serve and worship, and impelled by an earnest love of truth to seek a faith that would satisfy her reason and purify her heart, is induced to question minutely the religious tenets of travellers who visited the temple, and thus familiarized herself with all existing creeds and hierarchies. The lore so carefully garnered is finally analyzed, classified, and inscribed on papyrus. The delineation of scenes and sanctuaries in different latitudes, from Lhasa to Copan, gave full exercise to Edna's descriptive power, but imposed much labor in the departments of physical geography and architecture (140–1).

This passage seems impenetrable, so packed is it with ornate descriptives. Yet it describes a scholarly investigation conducted by a woman. Embedding her story line in a remarkably overdetermined paragraph, Wilson creates a female protagonist who creates a female protagonist who has reinscribed the evolution of world religious history.

This strategy is typical of *St. Elmo;* the lavish, overwritten prose hides the novel's thematic and rhetorical heresies. The text contains an internal paradox: Its narrative design censures the protagonist's professional ambitions, while the details of the plot, the actual descriptions of Edna's hopes, fears, and acts, sanction them. The history of Edna's education demonstrates how the paradox evolves. Edna has pursued her preparatory studies with Mr. Hammond for four years; it takes her about two more to write this book. Soon after, she writes another, this one an advisory tract for women. Her tutor testifies to her intelligence when he tells one rejected suitor, Gordon Leigh, that "intellectually she is your superior" (161); her ability to focus on her work testifies to her zeal. In fact during the period of her education Edna's attraction to her work rivals – often, overrides – the intensity of her attraction to St. Elmo. The Angel with whom Edna wrestles most actively is the history of the Word and her own ability to appropriate it. In this context her tensions with St. Elmo spring as much from intellectual rivalry as from sexual attraction or ethical repulsion. Until she has succeeded in mastering the word, in seizing verbal power, St. Elmo exists only as a taunt to her powerlessness.

Though Wilson's narrator denies it, the story of Edna's writing career presents a viable alternative to the "normal" life of the married woman, a career that offers pleasures fully as deep. On the one hand, Wilson has her narrative design; on the other hand, she has a remarkable character whose successes are genuinely fulfilling. Even Edna recognizes that "my work is to me what I suppose dear relatives must be to other women" (370). In fact, during her time in New York Edna manages to have it all: her work, which gives her deep satisfaction and eventually enough money to free her from the need to teach; her charges, who feed her maternal needs; her literary friends, who introduce her to the cultural life of the city; her suitors, who provide sexual interest without sexual threat (only St. Elmo provides that, and he is hundreds of miles away); and her employers, who treat her as a member of the family rather than as a governess. To Mr. Hammond she admits that, although "I cannot say that I am perfectly content, . . . yet I would not exchange places with any woman I know" (412). Clearly the thrill of *doing* – of creating, debating (Edna does not "harangue from the hustings," but she defends her conservative stance warmly enough at dinner parties with prominent men), and influencing – generates enough satisfaction to make her, at times, "so happy that I believe the wealth of California could not buy this sheet of paper" (this is in response to a letter informing her that through her influence, a man has been brought back to his family from "haunts of vice") (411). Clearly Edna's quest for knowledge has evolved into a consciousness of power. And this power works on two levels, the personal and the public: It garners respect from and influence over intellectual New York, and it receives adoration from and influence over the troubled readers of her advisory tracts. She has become a Catharine or even a Henry Ward Beecher – famous, respected, pursued. For a female reader already committed to higher education for women, and willing to entertain the possibility that women might be able to live well without being married – in other words, for many of the proponents of Catharine Beecher's system – Edna's life presents an attractive alternative to marriage.

Yet, of course, Wilson does not sanction Edna's continued independence, instead truncating her career and subordinating her life – and mind – to St. Elmo's. But women bringing to their reading of *St. Elmo* a schema that privileges female accomplishment might well remember Edna's achievements rather than her renunciations. In her discussion of *St. Elmo,* Nina Baym points out that women read it and similar novels because they were intensely involved with the heroines, not the heroes.[19] To this I would add that the thematic intensity of Wilson's treatment of Edna's professional life, as well as some of the narrative idiosyncrasies of the text's style, are actually much more important and memorable to readers predisposed to entertain the validity of Edna's goals than is the novel's conventional dénouement. For women like Julia Dyson or Mary Parker (who, feeling that she was "frittering" her life away, in 1849 began to learn Latin),[20] the memory of Edna's intellectual life would be foregrounded, whereas her renunciation, predetermined by the text's Byronic theme and overt structure, would either recede into the background (the most likely event) or else frustrate their raised expectations.

Edna's silencing signals the major contradiction in this novel's plot, evidence of an authorial design in conflict with the way the story actually developed.[21] Elements in the rhetorical structure, however, have undermined the effects of this authorial design throughout the novels' course. As Edna's struggle to grasp verbal power undermines the authorial insistence on female subordination thematically, so the narrator's relationship with her reader subverts the effects of the author's narrative design. One way to examine this process is to look at the contract established between the narrator and her narratee as it develops through the course of the plot and as it reflects both Wilson's and her protagonist's authorial strategies. Throughout the story, the narrator stresses the didactic function of Edna's fiction. Examined in relationship in the novel's theme, stress on the didactic signals readers that Edna's publications lie within the realm of the acceptably feminine because they attempt moral uplift. Examined in relationship to the novel's authorial intentions, stress on the didactic function of Edna's fiction is the key to Wilson's own agenda. But Wilson's identification with this aspect of her character also shifts the balance of her authorial transaction with her readers. Examined in relationship to narrator–narratee contracts, the narrative stress on the didactic function of Edna's writing shows us how and why Wilson's agenda ultimately fails.

Embedding the didactic in the fictional describes Wilson's strategy in this novel as well as Edna's in her own. Edna's goals are mirrored in the narrative design of *St. Elmo,* where Wilson proleptically counters criticism of her own novel's packed prose by pointing to its didactic function. As Edna embarks on her second book, the narrator informs us,

> Edna unintentionally and continually judged her readers according to her own standard, and so eager, so unquenchable was her thirst for knowledge, that she could not understand how the utterance of some new fact, or the redressing and presentation of some forgotten idea, could possibly be regarded as an insult by the person thus benefited. Her first book taught her what was termed her "surplus paraded erudition," had wounded the *amour propre* of the public; but she was conscientiously experimenting on public taste, and though some of her indolent, luxurious readers, who wished even their thinking done by proxy, shuddered at the "springwater pumped upon their nerves," she goodnaturedly overlooked their grimaces and groans, and continued the hydropathic treatment even in her second book, hoping some good effects from the shock (439).

In other words, Edna is actively trying to teach as she writes, and is fearful lest her readers shy from her strategy: "If there should accidentally be an allusion to classical or scientific literature, which they do not understand at the first hasty, careless, novel-reading glance, will they inform themselves, and then appreciate my reason for employing it, and thank me for the hint; or will they attempt to ridicule my pedantry?" (439). But clearly, these are Wilson's problems, too; problems inherent in *St. Elmo's* narrative design. For that "hasty, careless, novel-reading glance" belongs to precisely the reader who follows overplots – like the story of Edna and St. Elmo – and has trouble processing less readily accessible material. Like Edna, Wilson is trying to capture those willing to think, to learn. In fact, in this passage the narrator, the author, and Edna come perilously close, while Edna's fictional readership and the "actual" narratee of *St. Elmo* are similarly conflated.

We have already seen how the narratee functions in early didactic texts; tracking her functional shifts is one way to understand the radical possibilities inherent in exploratory novels. As Robyn Warhol points out, engaging narrators and dramatized narratees (that is, a narrative "I" that addresses a listening "you") are common in nineteenth-century women's texts.[22] *St. Elmo,* however, differs from this norm in the extreme distance, even diffidence, of its narrative stance. There is little, if any, reaching out to the narratee. In comparison to most narrator–reader relationships in nineteenth-century women's novels, *St. Elmo's* narrative stance is distanced, even diffident; as if the narrator were afraid to make contact with her narratee. Instead she focuses almost exclusively – as if she had donned blinders to prevent her from seeing anyone else – on her characters, especially Edna. In the passage just quoted, Edna's "standards" are not generalized beyond Edna, and there is no hint that the accusation of "surplus paraded erudition" might apply to anyone else's book. Yet, of course, it also applies to *St. Elmo,* and Edna's standards are also Wilson's. By this internal logic, Edna's readers are also Wilson's readers, and the narratee is she or he whose "*amour propre*" is wounded by being presented with new or difficult ideas.

The address to Wilson's reader exists, then, but in a backhanded fashion that only serves to push Wilson's narratee onto the cognitive path the author wishes her to follow. Not wanting to be identified with the philistines, Wilson's narratee will be persuaded to read her novel with care, actually to process all those words and literary references and imaginatively to become Edna as she struggles with mythologies, the Word, and the culture that does not want her to speak. In 1881, for instance, Maude Rittenhouse read another of Wilson's novels, *Vashti; or Until Death Do Us Part.* Like many reviewers, Rittenhouse found Wilson's plot and vocabulary pretentious, even outrageous: "The main object of the writer seems to be to compose a book as entirely different from anything else ever written as possible," she told her diary. "Her girls of 16 talk philosophy, quote poems and the 'maxims of cynical Rochefoucauld.' Everybody in the book save one old maid is in love, not a person finds that love reciprocated, everybody dies but two. . . . nobody gets married, and the book stops without really ending." Severe criticism. And yet, Rittenhouse adds, "I suppose it did me good for it kept me running to the Dictionary or to an encyclopedia to see who Joubert is, or where the 'cheerless temple of Hestia' stands or stood, or to find what 'a wan Alcestis' and 'a desperate Cassandra he had seen at Rome' indicated."[23] Rittenhouse, who later became a writer and a defender of women's rights, reads both critically and defensively; for all its outrageousness, *Vashti* presents her with a model of education that she strives to emulate; she is captured not by the book's love plot or its plausibility, but by its erudition. Educationally aspiring herself, she does not want to be exposed by a novel more learned than she.

If *Vashti* sent Maud Rittenhouse to her dictionary, *St. Elmo* would have sent her to the library. The reviewer who noted Wilson's "deep love of scholarship"[24] identified a scholarly zeal that, for all its absurdity, does capture readers desirous of a classical education. In doing so, however, and involving that reader in Edna's intellectual pursuits, Wilson's narrator also subverts the author's ultimate design. As we see in Rittenhouse's response to *Vashti,* to engage in the ambitions of one of Wilson's heroines requires becoming intellectually if not emotionally involved in her activities, activities Wilson individually sanctions. But these pursuits also thrust beyond the sphere Wilson defines as legitimately female[25]; to partake of them sympathetically means putting oneself imaginatively beyond the pale. As a warning, in *St. Elmo* various characters caution Edna about her "ambition" even as they applaud her accomplishments; Edna's heart condition is not the only warning implicit in the text. Yet nothing fatal results from Edna's career. Not only is she extremely successful in her writing career, she is universally loved for her writing. Her success even makes Edna more sexually desirable to male characters who are themselves projected positively.

But Wilson truncates Edna's career with her marriage. After their wedding St. Elmo decrees that

> To-day I snap the fetters of your literary bondage. There shall be no more books written! No more study, no more toil, no more anxiety, no more heartaches! And that dear public you love so well, must even help itself, and whistle for a new pet. You belong solely to me now, and I shall take care of the life you have nearly destroyed in your inordinate ambition (480).

Ostensibly because of her heart ailment, possibly from his fear of an intellectual rival, St. Elmo's decree certainly stems from his wish to monopolize Edna. On the level not of plot but of narrative structure, however, St. Elmo's decree originates in Wilson's conservative reaction to the story she has *almost* told. For in fact, as with most exploratory novels, the ending of *St. Elmo* does not come as a logical sequence to the events preceding it; Edna's apparent acquiescence in St. Elmo's interdict alone flatly contradicts every explicit or implicit statement she has made prior to the last chapter. Edna's entire life – from her preadolescent reading of Plutarch and Dante to her lionization by the public – has been dedicated to her work. Despite the framework established by Ruskin's formula for true women, and despite Wilson's relentless conservatism, to have Edna's hard-won career thus abruptly terminated, and for her to offer no resistance, constitutes an ending that amounts to a lie, a divine decree by an arbitrary author; an ending that women readers who have gone through the cognitive processes necessary to understand what Edna does, and who as a result now identify with Edna's quest for intellectual independence and power, might well find a violation of their new self-image. The reader who has been encouraged to engage in Edna's pursuit, to enter, in Wolfgang Iser's terms, the virtual dimension where her own imagination fuses with the text, suddenly finds herself trapped in a narrative framework that denies her validity, that exposes the phallogocentrism of the culture that produced it.[26]

Other elements of *St. Elmo's* rhetorical design also protest such authorial predeterminism. The following paragraph, occuring early in the text, initiates a pattern that permits questioning of divine decrees. The penultimate paragraph of Chapter 3, this passage illustrates yet another way Wilson's novel hides radical (in this passage, atheistic) possibilities within the welter of prose surrounding them. Prior to the events it describes, Edna, currently just under thirteen years old, has left her birthplace in the Tennessee mountains. Rejecting kind neighbors' offers of protection, and also rejecting the male neighbor's recommendation that she get her "hankering after books" "out of your head" (a recommendation vehemently countermanded by his wife), Edna, with her grandfather's dog, embarks on the train to Columbus. Just after describing how the lonely girl falls asleep on the train, comforted by the touch of a baby's hand drooping near her, the narrator interjects the following passage:

> Diamond-powdered "lilies of the field" folded their perfumed petals under the Syrian dew, wherewith God nightly baptized them in token of his ceaseless guardianship, and the sinless world of birds, the "fowls of the air," those secure and blithe, yet improvident, little gleaners in God's granary, nestled serenely under the shadow of the Almighty wing; but was the all-seeing, all-directing Eye likewise upon that desolate and destitute mourner who sank to rest with "Our Father which art in heaven" upon her trembling lips? Was it a decree in the will and wisdom of our God, or a fiat from the blind fumbling of Atheistic Chance, or was it in accordance with the rigid edict of Pantheistic

Necessity, that at that instant the cherubim death swooped down on the sleeping passengers, and silver cords and golden bowls were rudely snapped and crushed, amid the crash of timbers, the screams of women and children, and the groans of tortured men, that made night hideous? Over the holy hills of Judea, out of crumbling Jerusalem, the message of Messiah has floated on the wings of eighteen centuries: "What I do thou knowest not now, but thou shalt know hereafter" (29).

This paragraph takes several apparently contradictory turns before it accomplishes its end. The first clause of the first sentence falls under the general rubric of pietistic writing: Its idea is that God holds even the sparrow in the palm of his hand. An ideal example of readerly prose, constructed entirely from other texts, the message of this passage is so conventional, its successive phrases come so easily (both rhythmically and imagistically), that a reader risks being lulled into inattention, thus missing the first turn, occurring in the second clause. There, the platitudes suddenly cease, and one of the century's great questions comes up: God may protect the birds, but what about people, especially this particular orphan? The question – the intimation of doubt – is continued in the next sentence: Is tragedy God's will – is it *divinely* teleological? – or is it naturalistically teleological? Is the universe, as Stephen Crane would claim thirty years later, "indifferent, flatly indifferent"? And does the imagery of Christian mythology – of silver cords and golden bowls – satisfy the "Why?" attendant on real chaos, "the screams of women and children, and the groans of tortured men"?

Rather like Melville, in *Pierre,* who also piously evoked the image of God holding a sparrow in the hollow of his hand, only to attack it as "a hollow, truly," Wilson here creates a tension between Biblical references that, like secular references to religious faith, have a tendency to lull, to point in expected directions – that is, to encourage the reader to fill in a well-known story – and skeptical questioning of the cosmic scheme. In this typically paratactic sentence, Wilson uses her freedom to expand the simple propositions of the sentence in order to pose unexpected, and potentially subversive, questions, to juxtapose a minor (and heretical) cultural code to a dominant one. Having done so, however, she apparently shifts back to the more conservative path: Evoking the landscape of the Holy Land, her narrator indicates that in fact the world is teleologically ordered, that God does have a plan. The choice, in other words, is made, and made for faith, and the question apparently closed. But the possibility of choice has been raised, the possibility of doubt proposed. The pietistic schema evoked at the opening and closing of the passage accounts for Edna's spiritual redemption; it does not, however, account for the deaths of other passengers, including the baby whose "innocent" hand had comforted Edna as she fell asleep but whose "sweet coral lips" are now "pinched and purple, the waxen lids . . . rigid . . . and the dimpled hand . . . stiff and icy" (31), and the dog who had been Edna's only living link with her past. While the authority of the dominant cultural code has been reinstated, elements of doubt remain. The narrator's brief recourse to alternative theories of causation has opened up new, and subversive, hermeneutic possibilities in the text.

The questioning of pious platitudes – or received wisdom – expressed in the passage quoted above also leads into the next level of both plot and theme: questioning of the apparently arbitrary decrees of a compelling but unjust God and, perhaps, of an equally compelling and unjust plot. As we have noted, Edna's anger originates in her belief that her Edenic childhood has been abruptly terminated by an apparently arbitrary act of God. Prior to her grandfather's death she is iconographically associated with nature and with nature's God. This was a standard association in nineteenth-century novels, part of a cultural complex signifying a virtuous woman. Like Sylvie, the child protagonist of Sarah Orne Jewett's later "The White Heron," this child has a deep affinity for nature. "Thoroughly happy," the young Edna loves "trees and flowers, stars and clouds, with a warm, clinging affection as she loved those of her own race. . . . To her woods and fields were indeed vocal, and every flitting bird and gurgling brook, every passing cloud and whispering breeze, brought messages of God's eternal love and wisdom, and drew her tender, yearning heart more closely to Jehovah, the Lord God Omnipotent" (17).

After her grandfather's sudden death, however, Edna rejects the God she regards as having cheated her: "bitter, rebellious feelings hardened her heart when she remembered that even while she was kneeling, thanking God for [her grandfather's] preservation from illness, he had already passed away . . ." (19). Her experience in the train accident – trapped under a beam with the dead baby across her chest – only serves to intensify her skepticism. "The chilling belief was fast gaining ground that God had cursed and forsaken her; that misfortune and bereavement would dog her steps through life; and a hard, bitter expression settled about her mouth; and looked out gloomily from the sad eyes" (19). Though Edna publicly repents her bitterness against God when she realizes that her trials are going to result in her becoming the ward of a wealthy woman, the doubts she has earlier expressed continue in the bitter character of St. Elmo Murray, who enters the novel just as Edna yields her own bitter stance. Questioning of divine decree, then, forms an intrinsic aspect of the plot.

But a doubting hero won over by a pious heroine is, of course, also integral to the master plot set by the theme of the Byronic male and the definition of woman's role. However, in *St. Elmo,* Edna's reassumption of faith – which indicates her willingness to subordinate her ego to a dominant force – is countered by her continuing obsession with knowledge and publication, an obsession that is at the center of the novel and that stands, ultimately, for Edna's power to define herself through writing. The ego willing to submit itself to God reasserts itself in the battle for verbal mastery. Moreover, the muted, but continuing, controversy *in* the novel over how much knowledge a woman should have continues the challenge to a priori definitions, especially those that deal with women's nature and place. Thematically, this is resolved by the authorial contention that women have the right to as much education as they wish, provided they use it to show other women their divinely appointed mission to tend hearth and home. Structurally, however, the conservative thematic is countered by the text's continuous focus on the phenomenon of a woman empowered through her writing.

Edna's successful career signals her triumphant appropriation of the Word, her seizure of a share of the marketplace, and her assumption of moral and intellectual hegemony in the public sphere. Once launched, Edna's power increases until the middle of the last chapter, when the Reverend Mr. St. Elmo Murray, now God's representative, walks into the house and abruptly terminates her public career, much as Basil Ransom would later terminate Verena Tarrant's in *The Bostonians*. If we consider all the readings there have been of the end of James's carefully plotted novel, we see all the more forcefully the arbitrary nature of Wilson's. For all her ideological protestations to the contrary, in Edna, Wilson has created a character who holds considerable authority in the public sphere – among men as well as women. St. Elmo's re-appropriation of that power satisfies the narrative design but denies Edna's entire experience. As Baym points out, in a genre determined by an a priori overplot, it is the narrative development, rather than the narrative design, that matters[27]; *St. Elmo* contains enough discontinuities of plot, theme, and rhetoric to alert readers to the possibility that women's quest for intellectual parity is not only viable but desirable. Readers already sympathetic to such quests would have engaged most intensely with Edna's struggle to appropriate myth history and to share the fruits of public discourse. For these readers, the most memorable portions of the novel would consist of Edna's intellectual triumphs, not her final submission.

Similar questions of power exist at the center of most exploratory novels, and similar thematic and rhetorical discontinuities undermine the texts' apparent ideologies. Despite their apparently conservative stances – stances, we must bear in mind, that seem far more reactionary today than they seemed 120 years ago – and despite their adamantly conservative closures, the middle portions of these novels explore profoundly radical possibilities for women, radical not in terms of male boundaries, but in terms of female ones. The Edna Earl of 1866 is the Ph.D. in Classical

Literature of today who (unthinkable in 1866) holds a chair at Harvard or Yale and is exploring myths of the Feminine. As we shall see, later novels like Louisa May Alcott's *Work* and Elizabeth Stuart Phelps's *The Silent Partner* thematize the covert radicalism of exploratory texts. In doing so, however, their authors shift the novels' formal structures into a didactic mode that makes little or no allowance for the free play of conflicting ideas. Didactic novels are, in Susan Rubin Suleiman's terminology, authoritarian fictions; in contrast to exploratory novels, they do not tolerate the propinquity of antithetical views.

St. Elmo is an appropriate text to begin studying the rhetorical adventurousness of exploratory novels because the density of its prose gives so much scope for the play of antithetical ideas. In Susan Warner's *Queechy* the prose is not dense but the textual codes are various. *Queechy* resembles *St. Elmo* in the multiple, antithetical, and unintended interpretations its multivalenced coding permits.

3

DECODING THE EXPLORATORY TEXT: SUBVERSIONS OF THE NARRATIVE DESIGN IN QUEECHY

In Susan Warner's *Queechy* (1852) the narrator is so distanced that it is often difficult to find her. Where the narrators in *Charlotte Temple* and *A New-England Tale* openly engage their narratees, lecturing them in full paragraphs and even chapters, *Queechy*'s narrator hides, concealing what few, full, value statements she makes within the body of seemingly objective narrative paragraphs, and preferring to guide her auditors through the more subtle means of modifying words and phrases. This narrative presence is what Wayne Booth calls a third-person reflector,[1] projecting her story from within the protagonist's own point of view. In comparison to *St. Elmo, Charlotte Temple,* or *A New-England Tale, Queechy* contains few passages of straight narrative commentary. By far the largest proportion of this nearly 800-page text is given to dialogue, and what long narrative passages exist tend to be either scenic: setting out landscape descriptions, for instance; or else psychological: reporting the heroine's inner thoughts. The remaining narrative passages are brief, often simply bridging devices ("After Fleda had got home"). None directly engage the narratee. This narrator seems to think that she can tell her story without leaving many markers to guide her readers' interpretation.

But *Queechy* is built on a multitude of codes that obviate the need for overt narrative comment. Susan Warner's second book (*The Wide, Wide World* was published in 1851), it rests on a long line of precursive texts that had already determined the ground rules – or written the codes – for American women's novels. By the 1850s, when the exploratory novel emerged in full, the codes were firmly established, present in the schemata readers brought to any given work, and therefore material to be evoked by writers. Thus, for instance, novelists could assume that readers would accept that the moral values of any given exploratory novel would operate within a Christian – generally a Protestant – frame of reference. Similarly, writers could assume that readers would share – or at least understand – their privileging of sentiment, or feeling. These were the two most prevalent culturally based codes in midcentury women's novels, and until very recently they were the only ones most twentieth-century critics perceived. Because these professional readers of the twentieth century were trained by the modernists to reject religious pieties as well as emotional expression, they have tended to lambast nineteenth-century women's novels as "pious" in addition to being "sentimental."

But, as Nina Baym pointed out in *Woman's Fiction,* other codes beyond the religious and the sentimental enter exploratory novels, most prominently the privileging of female experience – a code that, until recently, few of us were able to comprehend. Our ability to perceive its existence corresponds to what Jonathan Culler has labeled the "first moment" of feminist literary criticism: the premise that "women's experience . . . will lead them to value works differently from their male counterparts, who may regard the problems women characteristically encounter as of limited interest."[2] Devaluation of nineteenth-century women's novels is in part attributable to the predominantly male point of view among twentieth-century literary critics. As noted above, however, it is also attributable to the devaluation of piety and sentiment, values that twentieth-century critics assigned exclusively to women but that nineteenth-century writers and readers did not.[3]

Additionally, and inevitably, much has been lost through the passing of generations. To recreate readers' responses to literature of a past century, we should ideally be able to retrieve their complete experience. Since that is impossible, we can only strive to retrieve some of the symbolic and cultural codes – and those only very generally – predominant in the presumed readers' experiences and see how writers used them to create hermeneutic codes – codes that introduce, explore, or answer the enigmas posed by the text. I have found no private reader's responses to *Queechy;* in lieu of those, I am using a lengthy public response by a critic for *The North American Review.* This writer has an agenda for processing texts that rests on several dominant cultural codes. In addition, evidence from diaries continues to illustrate that many women in the reading community had aspirations and values running counter to those endorsed by *Queechy's* narrator. My reading of *Queechy,* then, like my reading of *St. Elmo,* is predicated on possibility rather than certainty; the possibility that women readers, given a common set of experiences, would as readily remember this heroine's achievements as her final obliteration under the aegis of a dominating husband.

One cultural code predominant in *Queechy* is the language of flowers. We have seen how this intertextual code is used to indicate, to "mark," heroines' natural piety, but Warner uses it to point to her text's thematic center. By the nineteenth century, the association of specific flowers with specific meanings had become a symbolic code, in large part reflecting liberal Protestantism's assumption that nature reflects God's intentions (in other words, it is a symbolic system compounded of other codes characteristic of a specific subculture). In *Queechy*, flower symbolism is also metaphorically linked to the valuation of Christian piety. The linkage creates a decoding device, a series of associations, that help readers locate and interpret the central problem of the text — how to preserve Christian purity despite living and acting in the world. *Queechy*'s ideal reader does not need interpretive guidance from the narrator because she already understands the relevant cultural and symbolic codes and can deduce the hermeneutic code from the narrator's manipulation of the cultural and symbolic.

The first indication of what the text's central problem will be is the phrase "unspotted from the world," which appears during the last conversation between the heroine, Fleda (Elfleda) Ringgan and her dying grandfather. They are discussing Fleda's mother, who died in Fleda's infancy.

> "Do you know what her last prayer for you was, Fleda?"
> "No, grandpa."
> "It was that you might be kept 'unspotted from the world.' I heard her make that prayer myself." And stretching out his hand the old gentleman laid it tenderly upon Fleda's bowed head, saying with strong earnestness and affection, *his* voice somewhat shaken, "God grant that prayer! – whatever else he do with her, keep my child from the evil! – and bring her to join her father and mother in heaven! – and me![4]

The phrase is a reference to James (1:27): "Pure in religion and undefiled before God and the Father is this. To visit the fatherless and widows in their affliction, *and* to keep himself unspotted from the world." Linked to Fleda's dead mother, and articulated by her dying grandfather, it is distinctly sacred in origin and intention.

The other reference is distinctly secular. In the novel, Fleda is also associated with flowers, from the wildflowers with which she decorates her grandfather's house in Queechy (a hamlet located in upstate New York), through the hothouse flowers sent her during her visits to a wealthy family in New York City and the flowers she cultivates for sale during her years of trial back in Queechy, to the enormous rose garden her lover creates for her on his estate in England. Almost any female reader in nineteenth-century America (and many male readers as well) would have had at least a passing familiarity with the language (the symbolic use) of flowers: They were a universal symbol, appearing pictorally in magazines, annuals, advertisements, and engravings; woven into fabrics, painted on china, embroidered onto dresses, knotted into lace. Guides to them

abounded. One was edited by Sarah Josepha Hale, editor for over thirty
years of the enormously popular *Godey's Lady's Book*.

According to its introduction, the fourteenth edition of *Flora's Interpreter*[5] had as its purpose the combining of interests in botany with a
better acquaintance with the beauties of American literature – a fusion,
not coincidentally, of nationalistic purposes with educational ones. As is
common with flower books, each flower is paired with an association,
usually reflective of an emotion or a state of being (ivy, for instance,
represents wedded love) as well as being defined and shown represented
in judicious quotations. Under the entry for pansies, for example, first
comes its latin name ("Viola, tricolor"); then its classification ("Class, 5.
Order 1. A European species of the violet, but cultivated here. It is called
tricolor from the union of purple, yellow and blue in its blossoms."); then
what it represents and a quotation ("Tender and Pleasant Thoughts."
"Pray you, love, remember / There's *Pansies* – that's for thought." –
Shakespeare); and then a long "Sentiment," in this case a poem by Mrs.
L. P. Smith.

> I've pleasant thoughts that memory brings,
>   In moments free from care,
> Of a fairy-like and laughing girl,
>   With roses in her hair:
> Her smile was like the star-light
>   Of a summer's softest skies,
> And worlds of joyousness there shone
>   From out her witching eyes.
>
> Her looks were looks of melody,
>   Her voice was like the swell
> Of sudden music, notes of mirth,
>   That of wild gladness tell.
> She came like spring, with pleasant sounds
>   Of sweetness and of mirth,
> And her thoughts were those wild flowery ones
>   That linger not on earth.
>
> I know not of her destiny,
>   Or where her smile now strays;
> But the thought of her comes over me
>   With my own lost sunny days, –
> With moonlight hours, and far off friends,
>   And many pleasant things,
> That have gone the way of all the earth
>   On Time's restless wings.[6]

Readers of flower books, then, were trained to see flowers as symbols as
well as plants. Even readers who did not turn to the actual flower books
would find floral symbolism explained in *Godey's* and numerous other

magazines; those exclusively for women, those for families, and (especially in the poetry selections) even those for general interest readers included references to flowers, pictures of flowers, explanations of flowers. In nineteenth-century culture, the language of flowers was ubiquitous.

Consequently it is not surprising that Warner (whose sister Anna loved flowers[7]) interleaved references to flowers with her narrative, drawing first on her readers' prior knowledge of the religious and symbolic codes and then assuming their ability to grasp the hermeneutic code (fading flowers develop spots; Fleda is a flower; therefore, the enigma is, how to keep Fleda from fading, from being torn from her roots, or, speaking nonmetaphorically, from being defiled by contact with corrupting forces). This complex of references forms the background for Warner's theme, but because the theme itself is never articulated by the narrator, it is a background only accessible to readers who already grasp its preconditional units. The rest of the novel operates similarly, drawing on symbolic, cultural, and hermeneutic codes assumed to be already extant in the reader's consciousness.[8] But in the complexity of this multivalenced coding, the author also leaves her text open to alternative readings, "closures" of ideas evoked by the codes and brought into conjunction in the text's thematic and rhetorical layers but inadequately addressed in the ending she mandates. *Queechy,* then, is like *St. Elmo;* in the tension between its rhetorical complexity and its author's intentions, it undermines some of its own ideological goals.

Briefly, *Queechy*'s plot is as follows. Fleda, an orphan, lives happily with her grandfather on a farm upstate (*Queechy* and *St. Elmo* share a common opening situation). Since the grandfather's physical decline, the farm has become heavily in debt, largely owing to a dishonest overseer, Dindenhover. On the same day that Grandfather receives notice that he is to be evicted, Fleda receives a letter from her mother's sister, Lucy Rossitur, inviting her to join the Rossitur family in Paris. That day, too, Fleda's adult cousin, Charlton Rossitur, and his English friend, Guy Carleton, stop by the farm. With Guy's mother, they are touring the area, and come to reaffirm Aunt Lucy's information that Guy's mother has volunteered to escort Fleda to Paris if she wishes to go. While Charlton Rossitur is a brash young man, Guy Carleton is an honest, sensitive gentleman. He and little Fleda are instantly attracted to one another.

The grandfather dies and Fleda goes to Paris. On the way she begins to convert Guy, whose major fault is his lack of faith and, hence, lack of purpose. Once in Paris, he leaves Fleda, ostensibly to meditate on his life; eventually he returns to his estates in England, where (having found that "power to its very last particle [is] duty," II, 388), he will devote himself to bettering the lives of his people. When he leaves her, Fleda gives him her grandfather's Bible. She is taken in by the Rossiturs, whom she soon loves, especially her cousin Hugh, a boy her equal in gentleness and piety (but not in intelligence), a character who becomes a strange alter ego to Fleda herself. After a year in Paris, they return to New York City, where, three years later, Uncle Rossitur fails. Since he is a gentleman, that is, a man without skills, he is not equipped to do anything, but he rashly accepts another relative's (Uncle Gregory) offer to run a farm upstate. The area is Queechy, and the farm, of course, is Grandfather's.

It is instantly apparent that Fleda is the only character capable of dealing with the family's reversals. Uncle Rossitur tries to hire men to run the farm for him and fails again; Aunt Lucy, for all her willingness, is able to do little beyond the family sewing. Hugh runs the sawmill on the property, a job well beyond his strength which eventually kills him. Fleda alone knows how to cope.

But it takes her a while to realize that she must do it. Although she takes "the brunt of the business [of settling in] on her shoulders" (I, 247), after the house is arranged she and Hugh essentially play for the rest of the summer. Only when the Irish servants quit and Fleda realizes, first, that there is no cash in the house to pay them and, second, that her aunt can herself neither cook nor clean and does not know how to find new "help" in this neighborhood, does Fleda's "ministry" begin (I, 241). As she takes charge, a cast of American rural characters begins to assume prominence in the action, characters who are outspoken, independent, and skeptical (or ignorant) of social conventions.

Fleda hires Barbara (Barby) Elster, a local young woman who, though she is an excellent woman and becomes a staunch friend of the family, regards herself as an American democrat who is "hiring out" (which can also be read as "doing the family a favor"), rather than as a professional servant. She has little respect for the social barriers between servant and employer, a factor that makes for constant friction between her and Fleda's Europeanized uncle. Hugh takes over the mill and effectively disappears from the novel until his deathbed scene. Fleda takes over the family's living, economic and emotional, at first managing domestic affairs – such as learning to bake bread, supervising Barby, finding materials for dinner and cooking it, arranging the table, and providing the cheerful face and patient attitude that keep Hugh and his mother afloat emotionally – then taking over the masculine business of farming.

In the middle of their second year at Queechy, Uncle Rossitur decamps, ostensibly to look after some lands in Michigan, actually because he can no longer bear his own failure. And fail he has, morally as well as financially. Warner's novels tend to have father figures patterned after Warner's own father, men who spend their time being physically and morally inert.[9] Rolf Rossitur is that figure in *Queechy*. Having hired Dindenhover – the same overseer who ruined Grandfather – Uncle Rossitur has destroyed whatever chance he had had of making a success of the farm. But his removal – like the absence of Mr. Carleton – also serves to clear the field for Fleda's full development. By the time Fleda has successfully organized a sugar-tapping experiment, her leadership is evident: She watches "her" men, then "went forward on the same principle that a sovereign princess shews herself to her army, to grace and reward the labours of her servants" (I, 405). She then proceeds to take over the farm. In this, too, she succeeds, largely because of her ability to handle the men she hires. "The farming plan succeeded beyond Fleda's hopes; thanks not more to her wisdom than to the nice tact with which the wisdom was brought into play" (II, 5). Like Alexandra Bergson, Willa Cather's protagonist in *O, Pioneers!*, written more than fifty years later, Fleda's ability to run the farm is tested by her tact in handling men who do not want to try new ways and in her willingness to learn all the intricacies of the art.

But the farm is not Fleda's only business endeavor. Though gardening is said to be a "masculine employment" (II, 68), she keeps two gardens, one for vegetables and one for flowers, selling her produce to nearby hotels catering to the summer trade. Here Fleda and her hired boy Philetus do all the labor themselves. She also keeps up "her own housewifery concerns, her share in Barby's cares or difficulties, her sweet countenancing and cheering of her aunt, her dinner, her work" (II, 6). In other words, Fleda does not just shift, she controls, learning as she does the difficulties, the skills, and the triumphs that successful labor, in both spheres, can bring. Her business enterprises (her work in the male sphere) serve her domestic labors (the female sphere), putting food on the table, clothing on the family's backs, and some degree of pride in their strides. In her work life, then, she is hermaphroditic, playing the nineteenth-century's definition of both male and female roles in the business of maintaining the family. The matrix of the family's nourishment, she is the center of all activities. Rather like modern professional women, Fleda learns to excel in both male and female spheres of endeavor.

This onerous labor is leavened by periodic visits to New York, where, dividing her time between Uncle Gregory's quiet house in Bleeker Street and a (largely female) family of friends, the Evelyns, in a more fashionable neighborhood, Fleda also learns about the joys and sorrows of life in high society. Liking the ease and advantages that wealth brings (she has a "strong natural taste for society" [I, 216]), Fleda dislikes the casual flippancy, the carelessness of others' feelings, that her friends exhibit. Nevertheless, she holds her own with them, responding to their railleries with her own wit and winning hearts, male and female, by her gentleness. In New York she is courted by Lewis Thorn (the "thorn" for this "lily" [*Queechy* I,

127, and Song of Sol. 2:2]), the villain of the story. He is a rich, nasty young man whom Fleda has disliked since meeting him in her childhood. This suitor is in addition to Mr. Olmney, a gentle young minister in Queechy whom she rejects because "there isn't enough of him" (II, 39), and Dr. Quakenbusch, a comic vernacular character. Guy Carleton also reappears while Fleda is in New York, but Fleda's "friends," who insist on teasing her about Thorn in Carleton's presence, keep them from serious conversation (a device to delay the plot), a fact that pains her deeply.

The crisis – and melodrama – of the story come when Thorn threatens to expose Uncle Rossitur (who finally returns from Michigan) for having falsely signed Thorn's father's name to a $4000.00 note some years previously. Rossitur flees; Fleda, on her own initiative, goes to New York, places ads in all the newspapers, and finds her uncle to tell him that she has "persuaded" Thorn not to prosecute. Thorn, however, reneges, threatening once more to expose Uncle Rossitur unless Fleda will marry him. Mr. Carleton intervenes, "persuading" Thorn to withdraw in his own turn. Carleton then returns to Queechy with Fleda, giving her her old Bible and refusing to take it back "unless the giver go with the gift" (II, 290). Surprised, tearful, but deeply pleased, Fleda agrees, and they proceed back to Queechy.

Fleda has to be extricated from her family commitments and American environment before they can marry, however, and it is six months before Fleda leaves Queechy forever. By then Hugh has died a lingering death, in Christ; Aunt Miriam is about to die similarly, and Uncle Rossitur has accepted a consulship to Jamaica. Leaving Queechy, Fleda and Mrs. Carleton sail to England, whence Guy Carleton has preceded them (to quell riots in his own and neighboring counties). Fleda and Guy are married within hours of her arrival, and she promises to share everything – all her emotional states – with him. He thus becomes "the one friend that was to take the place of all" (II, 369), and "the little asparagus-cutter of Queechy [is] transformed into the mistress of all this domain" (II, 389), with a husband who will "watch over . . . and tell [her]" how to "do . . . and be . . . just what [she] ought" (II, 387). Finis.

But of course that is not all of it. Because Warner has set up this story within a series of codes, she has also created the risk of subverting her overt idea. Much of the confusion stems from her own autobiographical concerns. Her ambivalence about women's working and her yen to be rescued by a rich Englishman – prominent in many of her novels – reflect her own situation as the (reluctantly) hardworking daughter of a failed father, and lead to her novels' fairy-tale endings. In *Queechy,* however, the imagery of nationalism complicates the schema of the fairy tale, introducing ideas of independence and moral autonomy that counter the ideas of dependence and moral subordination mandated by the fairy-tale structure. From the reader's perspective this thematic ambivalence pulls *Queechy* in opposing directions. On an abstract level, there is the confusion evident in the debate – present thematically in the novel – between the American system of self-government (which, though not projected without criticism, on the whole is seen favorably) and the English system of government by the aristocracy. On the concrete level, this translates into the tension between Fleda's development into an independent creator of her environment, an especially American theme, and her willingness to yield her autonomy to her husband. Finally, there is the problem of how to keep Fleda unspotted once she has quit her native soil. Each of these tensions is compounded by Warner's multivalenced rhetoric and the complex imagery on which the novel is built.

The debate between America and England frames this novel. Like Jane Elton, of *A New-England Tale,* Fleda Ringgan is portrayed as different from the ordinary run of human beings: "her spirit . . . like a clear still-running stream which quietly and surely deposits every defiling and obscuring admixture it may receive from its contact with the grosser elements around" (11), "in truth . . . made of different stuff from the rest of the world" (37). Also like Jane, Fleda is said to have inherited her exemplary nature, but Fleda's progenitors are cast in a culturally more significant framework than Jane's; as actors on the stage of the American experiment, a set of references that places this novel within one cultural code that we might label "the growth of a national literature." As we saw in Richard Henry Dana, Senior's letter to Verplanck about *The Spy* and *The New-England Tale* – and even more in *The North American Review* article to which he refers – this was an active endeavor, part of the early nineteenth century's movement toward cultural nationalism and, in the literary sphere, one of the motivations for those writers who later came to be known as local colorists.[10] Reviewers received *Queechy* within this framework: *Peterson's Magazine* found it "thoroughly American" in its depiction of country life[11]; *The North American Review,* in a lengthy essay saluting *The Wide, Wide World, Queechy,* and Amy Lothrop's *Dollars and Cents* as "truly indigenous novels,"[12] places "their pictures of American country life and character above all their other merits."[13] No matter what else readers thought about the book's style, plot, or sentiments, contemporary response was united in favoring *Queechy*'s faithful reflection of American life, especially its rural life. Even Elizabeth Barrett Browning identified it as "another American novel by a woman, very clever and characteristic."[14]

In *Queechy* the fairy-tale structure of the story is framed by – and in this case very much skewed by – the text's participation in the debate over the national character. In the introductory chapters, readers learn that Fleda comes from a line of American heroes. Her grandfather, a fifer during the Revolutionary War, served as an able state legislator later; her father was a military hero. Her grandfather's sister, Aunt Miriam Plumfield, is what Linda Kerber has denominated a Republican Woman: strong, pious, knowledgeable, capable, and mother of a fine American man.[15] Inheriting the best qualities of the revolutionary generation, Fleda is an exemplary heroine from the start, one whose education must come not in moral courage or character, but in keeping her moral character (keeping herself "unspotted from the world") even while recognizing her ability to create and control situations. This problem is analogous to the situation America faced after the Revolution, when its special status as a redeemer nation was threatened by the possibilities for corruption inherent in establishing a new order.[16] Fleda is not a rebel – on the contrary, she undertakes her cross-gender duties with great reluctance – but having shouldered the burdens of masculinity, she finds that she has established a new order, one where she, rather than the men around her, is at the center of the entrepreneurial as well as the domestic spheres.

Associated with the Revolution, with a family history of special purity, with a cast of American yeomen, and with a peculiarly American problem, Fleda's situation is carefully located within a context as much national as pious and sentimental. With the derivation of her moral nature, then, comes one set of cultural references: the valuation of the American experiment, of American independence and American religion, and the classification of distinctly American character types. Reviewers recognized this nationalistic impulse. *The North American Review,* for instance, classed *Queechy* among "these American novels of ours" that have

> a character of their own – humane, religious, *piquant,* natural, national. . . . They paint human nature in its American type; they appeal to universal human sympathy, but with special reference to the fellow-feeling of those whose peculiar social circumstances and trials fit them to be judges of the life-picture in whose background may be discerned so many familiar objects. They recognize the heart as the strong-hold of character, and religion as the ruling element of life. . . . [17]

For this reviewer, Fleda is an American flower, introduced within a uniquely American set of references.

Warner's portrayal of Queechy and its environs essentially buttresses this nationalistic code and places Fleda within it as a potential Republican Woman. This is accomplished by bringing into conjunction depictions of material objects, especially domestic objects; rural characters; and landscapes. Each depiction transcends its individuality either by being narratively linked to a particular association or by drawing on extant codes. Together, they create an environment that (despite exhibiting Warner's own class biases) argues for the American experiment. This positive portrayal of rural America also contributes, however, to the thematic ambivalence of this text.

Material objects, especially regarding food, its production, preparation, and social functions, are highlighted in *Queechy* and brought in to support its positive depiction of rural life. Interestingly, food is rarely mentioned during Fleda's flush periods in Paris and New York, probably because the social structure depicted prevented Warner from showing Fleda in the kitchen. The difficulty of associating a wealthy heroine with domestic details is revealed in the one scene in which Fleda learns how to make pastry – an event apparently so unusual that Warner has another character comment on it in surprise. In Queechy, however, food products are constantly imaged, in part because feeding the family becomes one of Fleda's chief worries, but also because they are vehicles for many of the positive associations the narrator wants her narratee to make. Simple food is often viewed as comfort, serving to ease communication and to reassure the mind through fortifying the body. Domestic comfort is one of the ground units in Warner's value system; for all her heroine's forays into the world of mansions and servants, the author actually rivals Harriet Beecher Stowe in the degree to which she privileges kitchens.

This tone is set in the second chapter, when Fleda and her grandfather return from their discouraging trip to Queechy Run.

> [Fleda] hurried up stairs to take off her wrappings and then came down to the kitchen, where standing on the broad hearth and warming herself at the blaze, with all the old associations of comfort settling upon her heart, it occurred to her that foundations so established *could not* be shaken. The blazing fire seemed to welcome her home and bid her dismiss fear; the kettle singing on its accustomed hook looked as if quietly ridiculing the idea that they could be parted company; her grandfather was in his cushioned chair at the corner of the hearth, reading the newspaper, as she had seen him a thousand times; just in the same position, with that collected air of grave enjoyment, one leg crossed over the other, settled back in his chair but upright, and scanning the columns with an intent but most un-careful face. A face it was that always had a rare union of fineness and placid-ness. The table stood spread in the usual place, warmth and comfort filled every corner of the room, and Fleda began to feel as if she had been in an uncomfortable dream, which was very absurd, but from which she was very glad she had awoke (I, 23).

This passage is built from small units of concrete images: the "broad hearth," the kettle on its hook, the grandfather in his cushioned chair at the corner of the hearth, one leg crossed over the other. By specifying exactly *what kind* of hearth, *how* the kettle hung, *where* the chair was placed, the narrator creates a specific locale, then links it to "comfort" by reiterating that and related words. The narrator here fuses her point of

view with Fleda's: The sensations are the child protagonist's; their artic-
ulation into values, the adult narrator's.

Warner names cooking implements because she knows her readers will
recognize them and associate them with the small chores of domestic life.
In the chapter referred to above, Fleda insists on cooking the muffins
herself "on top of the stove" (I, 24) rather than letting the hired woman
"clap 'em in the reflector" (a reflector oven was a tin box that stood with
its open end facing an open fire; heat reflected from the back wall and
cooked the food placed within[18]); later she appears holding "the little
iron spatula" (I, 27). That evening, roast apples and bowls of creamy milk
again comfort Fleda and her grandfather after they have had an anxious
discussion of their futures, and – in one of the narrator's rare direct
statements, the kind of statement that makes the reader conscious of the
narrator's existence – the narrator once more links the intake of food to
the comforting of the spirit:

> There is . . . deny it who can, an exhilarating effect in good wholesome
> food taken when one is in some need of it; and Fleda at least found the
> supper relish exceeding well. . . . She was just ready for anything reviv-
> ing. After the third mouthful she began to talk, and before the bottom
> of the bowls was reached she had smiled more than once. So her grand-
> father thought no harm was done, and went to bed quite comforted . . .
> (I, 39).

With flowers, food and its object-associations provide the bright spots –
the visual images of spiritual and physical health – in this novel. They
also point us to *Queechy*'s narratee: a woman who has participated in the
cooking process herself. Warner's domestic images draw on familiarity
with domestic implements and their uses (only a cook would understand
the difference between cooking muffins on top of the stove and using a
reflector). These are images that refer to cultural and symbolic codes
peculiar to a female audience that is not the privileged upper class, wom-
en who would understand Fleda's experiences and who, presumably,
may be susceptible to the lure of the fantasy conclusion.

The focus on detail associating domesticity with comfort is so firmly
established, however, that it may also function to reaffirm American
women's sense of their privileged status. The fusion of spiritual health
with gustatory comfort is especially evident in conjunction with Aunt
Miriam Plumfield, who provides the moral and material standard for the
novel's system of values. Grandfather's sister, Aunt Miriam

> was not at all like her brother, in feature, though the moral charac-
> teristics suited the relationship sufficiently well. There was the ex-
> pression of strong sense and great benevolence; the unbending up-
> rightness, of mind and body at once, and the dignity of an essentially
> noble character . . . (I, 69).

Always associated with good food and spiritual comfort, she is often seen in her kitchen, where she is invariably associated with pies, crullers, fat baked chickens, and newly baked bread. For instance, she provides the food when Carleton first comes to dinner at the farm:

> Aunt Miriam had sent down a basket of her own bread, made out of the new flour, brown and white, both as sweet and fine as it is possible for bread to be; . . . The superb butter had come from aunt Miriam's dairy, too. . . . Every spare place on the table was filled with dishes of potatoes and pickles and sweetmeats, that left nothing to be desired in their respective kinds; the cake was a delicious presentment of the finest of materal; and the pies, pumpkin pies, such as only aunt Miriam could make, rich compounds of everything *but* pumpkin with enough of that to give them a name . . . (I, 94).

In addition to food, Aunt Miriam provides spiritual nourishment. The most unflaggingly religious character in the text, she is Fleda's spiritual comfort and guide, the relative most concerned that Fleda remember her mission to remain unspotted from the world. Aunt Miriam's function as a provider of sustenance achieves the status of the spiritual.

In addition to concrete domestic imagery, concrete knowledge of crafts is also a positive value in *Queechy* and one that is associated with rural Americans. Rolf Rossitur, Fleda's Europeanized uncle, is most censured for his refusal to learn the minute particulars of farming, a criticism that can be seen as reflective of his way of life – and of the way of life of ladies and gentlemen in general. Certainly the local Queechy women fault Lucy Rossitur for her ignorance of hens, cows, and housewifery, and even the narrator somewhat acerbically remarks that "Mrs. Rossitur wearied herself excessively with doing very little" (I, 280). Even in his wealthy days, Rossitur *does* nothing, produces nothing; a gentleman living on his income, he likes to read books. In contrast, Uncle Gregory produces something: He is in the process of "collecting rare books for a fine public library the charge of which was now entrusted to him" (I, 219). (Presumably this is the Astor library, a historical event readers would have known about from the newspapers and that Warner slips in neatly here.[19]) Warner values people who really know the intricacies of their crafts; her characters are implicitly ranked through the amount of detailed information they reveal in their discourse. When Rolf Rossitur – always looking for the easiest way to do things – asks Seth Plumfield "what is the principal thing to be attended to in ploughing," he gets an answer that evokes all the hostilities farmers feel for city folk, hostilities that are part of the background for the tradition of comic dialogue between the Yankee farmer and the city slicker,[20] and that here are used to highlight Seth's competence and Rolf's incompetence.

"Well" [said Seth], looking up, – "the breadth of the stitches and the width and depth of the furrow must be regulated according to the nature of the soil and the lay of the ground, and what you're ploughing for; – there's stubble ploughing, and breaking up old lays, and ploughing for fallow crops, and ribbing, where the land has been some years in grass– and so on; and the plough must be geared accordingly, and so as not to take too much land nor go out of the land; and after that the best part of the work is to guide the plough right and run the furrows straight and even" (I, 259).

Fleda knows that though the information is right the tone is teasing; Rolf Rossitur does not. Constitutionally incapable of even contemplating mastering such intricacies, he quits before he begins.

In contrast, Fleda is willing to learn her arts and to take pride in exactly knowing what they will yield her. Telling her aunt that the local hotel keeper will give her "four shillings a bushel" for her peas, she continues: "and, aunt Lucy, I sent three dozen heads of lettuce this morning besides. Isn't that doing well? and I sent two dozen day before yesterday. It is time they were gone for they are running up to seed, this set; I have got another fine set almost ready" (I, 316). In knowing the specifics of what she is doing, Fleda, more than any of her Rossitur relatives, knows exactly where she stands.

Warner's rural Americans are also her most vivid characters. On the whole, these are portrayed with humor and admiration, although Warner's class bias is also most evident in these depictions. One of her most negative sketches of rural American women occurs in a chapter that, as contemporary readers would have certainly known, was Warner's variation on a stock comic scene in domestic fiction, the ladies' sewing and/or tea party. Modern readers know this scene best through writers like Mark Twain and George Washington Harris (*Sut Lovingood*), but in fact it was female writers who excelled in this parodic form. In *Queechy*, Fleda, in the course of her search for a new hired woman, is invited to a quilting party at the home of one of her candidates. Warner establishes this setting for her attack on American pretentiousness and its converse, the snobbery of the ignorant; the scene is not unlike the picnic of the parvenus in Cooper's *Home as Found,* and Warner's evaluation of it can be read in the battle metaphors she employs.

Some of the people present at the quilting party are Fleda's relatives; a fact she seems willing to forget – "Her aunt Syra Fleda recognized without particular pleasure and managed to seat herself at the quilt with the sewing-women and Miss Hannah between them" (I, 282) – but that they use as the justification for a concerted attack on the Rossiturs, "taking revenge" on the Rossiturs' patrician aloofness by asking Fleda questions she responds to as "home-thrusts" (I, 283). Some of the younger women are evidently trying to improve their education; toward these the narrator shows a double prejudice, her own and the company's – she parodies the speaker herself: ("'I should admire to travel in many countries,' said Miss Lucy. . . . 'I think nothing makes people more genteel. I have observed it frequently' "); but she also parodies the women who attack Lucy for her ambition.

> ". . . I was speaking abstractly, " [said Lucy].
> "What's abstractly?" said Miss Anastasia scornfully.
> "Where do you get hold of such hard words, Lucy?" said Mrs. Douglass.
> "I don't know, Mis' Douglass; – they come to me; – it's practice, I suppose. I had no intention of being obscure."
> "One kind o' word's as easy as another I suppose, when you're used to it, ain't it?" said the sewing-woman.
> "What's abstractly?" said the mistress of the house again.
> "Look in the dictionary, if you want to know," said her sister.
> "I don't want to know – I only want you to tell."
> "When do you get time for it, Lucy? ha'n't you nothing else to practise?" pursued Mrs. Douglass.
> "Yes, Mis' Douglass; but then there are times for exertion, and other times less disposable; and when I feel thoughtful, or low, I commonly retire to my room and contemplate the stars or write a composition."
>   The sewing-woman greeted this speech with an unqualified ha! ha! and Fleda involuntarily raised her head to look at the last speaker . . . (I, 283).

This Lucy is the possible candidate for the housekeeping job Fleda wants filled and, after seeing and hearing her, Fleda is relieved to find she is not interested. But Lucy also stands out in this situation because – bracketing Warner's prejudices – she reflects other American women, from Mary Guion at the turn of the nineteenth century to Maud Rittenhouse during the Gilded Age, who tried to improve their educations and to express their thoughts in writing. Lucy sounds absurd to those looking down at her from a position of superior education (Fleda and the narrator) or up from a position of inferior education and imagination (her interlocutors). But since Fleda, too, contemplates the stars, writes poetry expressive of her inner states, and has independently undertaken a course of reading designed to improve her education, Warner's snobbery here contradicts one of the aspects she most values about her protagonist. Yet, in this scene, the author's bias is supported by Fleda's. This is continued at the tea table, where Fleda realizes with horror "that the guests were expected to help themselves at will from these several stores [i.e., saucers of condiments] with their own spoons, transferring what they took either to their own plates or at once to its final destination, which last mode several of the company preferred" (I, 286). Food received as comfort in other situations is repugnant in this one, part of a ceremony Fleda reads as a tribe of alien beings cannibalistically trying to make her ingest them.

But this scene is Warner's most critical. While no other rural American characters are as exemplary as the Plumfields, the rest are portrayed as helpful, loyal, kind in their rough way, staunchly independent, self-possessed, and capable. Unlike the Rossiturs, rural Americans are sufficiently familiar with hard work to know how much of it Fleda does and to read her character correctly. Barby, the hired woman, loyal to the end, represents the best among them; Philetus, the stubborn, lazy, but good-natured hired boy, the worst. Most are comic characters, but the comedy rests on a rich appreciation of their merit.

In contrast to these folk, urban Americans (the Evelyns) and Europeans (with the exception of Guy Carleton) are portrayed in a far less favorable light, being on the whole superficial, narrow in their kindnesses, and ignorant of the kind of work that goes into making their lives comfortable. Though Fleda loves the material comforts and sophisticated conversations of the Evelyn home, it is also through the Evelyns that she encounters real evil, in the person of Lewis Thorn, and genuinely corrupt values, in the devaluation of piety and sincerity that characterize high society. Contemporary reception, both positive and negative, reflected the novel's dual values. *The North American Review* applauded its portrayal of the corruption of high life, seeing it as Warner's courageous criticism of American manners: "our authoress is on impregnable ground when she takes the golden rule as her standard of manners. . . . As good republicans, we ought to thank her for indicating the basis whereon we may build, even in this land of equality and fluctuation, a politeness more gentle . . . than ever prevailed in the court of the Grand Monarque. . . ."[21] *Peterson's Magazine,* on the other hand, found Warner's (whose pseudonym was Elizabeth Weatherell), depiction of high society inauthentic: "In delineating fashionable life . . . Miss Weatherell utterly fails: it is evidently a subject of which she knows nothing."[22] What is clear from both reviews is that *Queechy* sets up an implicit opposition between rural and urban Americans and, through Fleda, illustrates its bias in favor of rural virtues. Though her choice, finally, turns against Queechy and all it represents, in fact the people Fleda has known there have been the soil from which her fine flowering has sprung.

Finally, the description of the Queechy landscape also betrays an authorial predilection for the rural American scene. A large proportion of what straight narrative passages exist is given to the landscape, and the meticulousness with which it is described is, like the attention to material detail, the valuation of detailed knowledge of domestic and agricultural arts, and the portrayal of rural character, a sign of allegiances that undermine the declared preferences of the text.

> The valley was very narrow, only divided into fields by fences running from side to side. The table-land might be a hundred feet or more above the level of the bottom, with a steep face towards it. A little way back from the edge the woods began; between them and the brow of the hill the ground was smooth and green, planted as if by art with flourishing young silver pines and once in a while a hemlock, some standing in all their luxuriance alone, and some in groups. With now and then a smooth grey rock, or large boulder-stone which had somehow inexplicably stopped on the brow of the hill instead of rolling down into what at some former time no doubt was a bed of water, – all this open strip of the table-land might have stood with very little coaxing for a piece of a gentleman's pleasure-ground. On the opposite side of the little valley was a low rocky height, covered with wood, now in the splendour of varied red and green and purple and brown and gold; between, at their feet, lay the soft quiet green meadow; and off to the left, beyond the far end of the valley, was the glory of the autumn woods again, softened in the distance. A true October sky seemed to pervade all, mildly blue, transparently pure, with that clearness of atmosphere that no other month gives us; a sky that would have conferred a patent of nobility on any landscape. The scene was certainly contracted and nowise remarkable in any of its features, but Nature had shaken out all her colours over the land, and drawn a veil from the sky, and breathed through the woods and over the hill-side the very breath of health, enjoyment, and vigour (I, 44).

This is landscape that has been observed and measured, described with the eye of a painter obsessed by detail, much as, a dozen years later, the American Pre-Raphaelite painters would seek to embody Ruskin's principle of "truth to nature" in paintings that explored the minute particulars of small natural objects.[23] At the same time, this passage also reflects the concern for landscape and the sublime evident in the Hudson River Valley School of painting, a concern that overlaps with the text's religious commitments. Paradoxically, this description also posits an American landscape fully as aristocratic as anything in the Old World, made for nature's nobility. A countryside promoting "health, enjoyment, and vigour," this is the right place to keep a heroine "unspotted from the world."

In *Queechy* then, the most extensive, detailed, and original writing concerns the most uniquely American aspects of the novel. This is the setting into which Fleda is born; it is the land and people in which she is rooted. Most importantly, it is the setting in which she develops into a woman who can excel in both male and female spheres of endeavor. Yet Fleda's accomplishments are consistently devalued by the narrator. From the scene introducing her, when the child spots a poorly buckled strap fastening the horse to the cart, to her mastery of the mysteries of farming, Fleda is established as an extraordinarily competent woman. The narrator, however, chooses to stress Fleda's delicacy and gentleness rather than her strength and determination, a stress satisfying the cultural mandate that heroines be gentle, submissive, and physically frail. The portraits of Fleda and Ellen Montgomery (heroine of *The Wide, Wide World*) according the *The North American Review,* show them to be "true women," characterized by "modesty," "due humility," "sweetness," and "goodness," qualities this reviewer favors, in contrast to the "strong minded women" Fleda and Ellen's "truly feminine" natures preclude.[24] These elements also provide the rationale for the novel's dénouement, in which Fleda essentially gives up on the American experiment, marrying Carleton, moving to England, and placing herself under the protection of a man who likes to control other people.

Queechy is constantly alternating between these two codes, the narrator evoking Fleda's submissivess and frailty, the action evoking her determination and mental strength. Even while the narrator insists on Fleda's essential gentleness, for instance, Warner's rhetorical texturing also demonstrates her heroine's unusual aggressiveness. In passages such as the following, Lawrence's old warning that we should "trust the tale, not the teller," seems appropriate. For though the narrator claims that Fleda is meek, the action shows that in fact her tongue is quick and her acts definitive. In this scene, the narrator shows how Fleda handles the relationship between Barby and Mr. Rossitur. Barby, let us remember, does not regard herself as the Rossiturs's inferior (one cultural code this character signals is the "servant problem," a subject of perennial controversy[25]). When Barby intrudes upon the family in a leisure hour to ask a domestic question, Mr. Rossitur is furious, "springing up and advancing towards the kitchen door." Fleda throws herself in front of him.

> Mr. Rossitur's wrath was high, and he would have run over or knocked down anything less gentle that had stood in his way; but even the harshness of strength shuns to set itself in array against the meekness that does not *oppose;* if the touch of those hands had been a whit less light, or the glance of her eye less submissively appealing, it would have availed nothing. As it was, he stopped and looked at her, first scowling, but then with a smile.
> "*You* manage her!" said he.
> "Yes," said Fleda laughing, and now exerting her force she gently pushed him back towards the seat he had quitted, – "yes, uncle Rolf – you've enough else to manage – don't undertake our 'help.' Deliver over all your displeasure upon me when anything goes wrong – I will be the conductor to carry it off safely . . ." (246).

It is in the tension between the narrator's assertion of Fleda's gentleness and her depiction of Fleda's pushing her uncle back into his chair that this novel exhibits its own internal oppositions. Laughing and crying are Fleda's two primary emotional responses to other people; whereas crying serves a variety of functions, laughter is in great measure a physiological gesture of appeasement. Here, while communicating this message through facial gesture and sound, and supplementing it through eye gestures also culturally calculated to appease, she is also said to use her hands "gently." These are all acceptable feminine actions, expressing Fleda's awareness of her subordinate gender and generational status to her uncle. But the upshot of her actions is that she pushes Rossitur back into his chair. To "exert force," gently or not, is to oppose, whether or not the narrator claims that is what is happening. Fleda "exerts force" against the angry man. "Gently" is the narrator's adverb; the narrator's information, however, is that Fleda stopped Rolf, thus achieving her goal. Moreover, at the end of her act she has gained control over one more area of the family's life, their relationship with their one remaining domestic.

Here the tension between what the narrator *says* Fleda is communicating and the acts readers *see* Fleda *perform* creates areas of ambiguity into which, or out of which, readers are free to "read" what they think are Warner's real intentions. The textual and linguistic layering permits more than one interpretation; in the rhetorical tension between activity and passivity, such "areas of indeterminacy" permit readers to cognitively isolate such ambiguous scenes and to draw from them interpretations that undermine the *apparent* meaning of the text.[26] Here, Fleda's apparently contradictory stances enable her to succeed where a less complex heroine would fail; her sweet gentleness gives her first moral, then act/ual power over her companions.

Another area of narrative denial about Fleda's accomplishments occurs in reference to her education. Here, the narrator first establishes Fleda's superior capacities through associations drawing on readers' familiarity with other heroines attempting to educate themselves. Like the other protagonists we have seen (and like Lucy Flint, whom we have also seen parodied for her pretensions), Fleda craves an education. As a child at her grandfather's house, she reads what few books and pamphlets are there: the Encyclopaedia, *Quentin Durward, Rob Roy, Guy Mannering,* the *Knickerbocker, The Christian Magazine,* "an odd volume of *Redgauntlet,* and the *Beauties of Scotland*" (I, 57). During the flush years in Paris and New York she and Hugh have tutors in music, French, Italian, and art, and undertake an unsystematic program of reading. Because both children are considered delicate, neither is sent to school, and the narrator, in one of her rare evaluative statements, suggests that their "somewhat irregular and desultory education" (I, 217) might have been better. Nevertheless

For Fleda this doubtful course of mental training wrought singularly well. An uncommonly quick eye and strong memory and clear head, which she had even in childhood, passed over no field of truth or fancy without making their quiet gleanings; and the stores thus gathered, though somewhat miscellaneous and unarranged, were both rich and uncommon, and more than any one or she herself knew. Perhaps such a mind thus left to itself knew a more free and luxuriant growth than could ever have flourished within the confinement of rules. Perhaps a plant at once so strong and so delicate was safest without the hand of the dresser. At all events it was permitted to spring and to put forth all its native gracefulness alike unhindered and unknown (I, 218).

Even here, the narrator is juggling two antithetical assumptions: one, related to the ongoing debate about the quality of women's education, essentially attacking girls' schools; the other, deploring parental care-lessness about their children's education. With these, her underlying theme is that Fleda is exceptional. Projecting Fleda as a plant once more, here the narrator suggests that the kind of education Fleda might have encountered had she been formally educated would have stunted rather than encouraged her intellectual growth. Certainly her cousin Marion, educated at a convent school in France, develops neither mental nor moral resources. But the harvest Fleda "gleans" from the opportunities afforded her are one more testimony to her exceptional nature, not a program the narrator sees appropriate for all children. Certainly it does not work for Hugh: "Hugh's mind wanted the strengthening that early skillful training might have given it. His intellectual tastes were not so strong as Fleda's; his reading was more superficial; his gleanings not so sound and in far fewer fields, and they went rather to nourish sentiment and fancy than to stimulate thought or lay up food for it" (I, 219). What works for Fleda, then, does not work for all children. The point is, however, that it *has* worked for Fleda; the narrator has taken some pains to tell us that Fleda's rare intelligence has flourished under this plan.

The nature of Fleda's reading program is spelled out in a scene that borrows from the reading habits of many American women, and is, then, a reference to yet another female code – the quest for educational opportunity. In the novel, Uncle Gregory asks to see Fleda's reading diary, "a neat little book covered with pink blotting paper" (I, 221), and humorously reads it aloud.

> "Now for it," said the doctor; – "let us see what this English amounts to. Can you stand fire, Elfleda?"
> "Jan. 1. Robinson Crusoe."
> . . . .
> "Jan. 2. Histoire de France."
> "What history of France is this?"

> Fleda hesitated and then said it was by Lacretelle.
> "Lacretelle? – what, of the Revolution?"
> "No sir, it is before that; it is in five or six large volumes."
> "What, Louis XV's time!" said the doctor muttering to himself.
> "Jan. 27. 2. ditto, ditto."
> "'Two' means the second volume I suppose?"
> "Yes sir."
> "Hum – if you were a mouse you would gnaw through the wall in time
> at that rate. This is in the original?"
> "Yes sir."
> "Feb. 3. Paris. L. E. K."
> "What do these hieroglyphics mean?"
> "That stands for the 'Library of Entertaining Knowledge'" said Fleda.
> "But how is this? – do you go hop skip and jump through these books,
> or read a little and then throw them away? Here it is only seven days
> since you began the second volume of Lacretelle – not time enough to
> get through it."
> "Oh no, sir," said Fleda smiling, – "I like to have several books that I
> am reading in at once, – I mean – at the same time, you know; and then
> if I am not in the mood of one I take up another" (I, 221–2).

Dr. Gregory's examination continues for several pages of the text, revealing a list that includes Johnson's *Tour to the Hebrides*, Goldsmith's *Ani-
mated Nature*, Paley's *Natural Theology*, Marshall's *Life of Washington*,
Spenser's *Faerie Queene*, and Milner's *Church History*, as well as, for leav-
ening, Marryat's *Peter Simple*. "History, fun, facts, nature, theology, poetry and divinity!" as the doctor declares.

This is the reading list of an exceptional fifteen-year-old. But Warner
takes care to inform her reader in a footnote that it is also "A true list
made by a child of that age" (I, 221n). And, certainly, extant reading
diaries from the period support her claim. Like Fleda's, often these are
small books carefully decorated by their owners. Others were originally
printed to be used as miniature almanacs, and have preprinted page for-
mats that leave little room for personal commentary. In 1833 Louisa Jane
Trumbull, then aged eleven, recorded reading that ranged from the *Juve-
nile Miscellany*, through William Weston's *Attributes of God*, to Scott's
Peveril of the Peak (which she notes "is the first novel I have ever read").[27]
One year later her list includes Burke's *On the Sublime and Beautiful* and
John Knox's *Memoires*.[28] When Julie Newberry tried to give up novels in
1870 she substituted Ruskin, Bacon, and a book on chemistry.[29] And
Katherine Johnson, a young woman whose diary entries – actually
lengthy reviews of the books she read – show that she approached books
as much for their information as for the imaginative pleasure they
yielded, lists forty-eight books written in English, thirty-three in French,
and five in Italian in her formal list at the back of the reading diary she

kept between 1868 and 1871. These range from novels, through history and travel books, to works on art and aesthetics.[30]

Fleda Ringgan's range of reading, then, was not so remarkable as it might seem to modern readers, and her systematic record of the books she read reflected the literary habits of many other women. Moreover, her plan of self-education in the absence of formal schooling is an example of the efforts women made to lift themselves from the slough of ignorance in which they felt mired. Wealthy Julia Newberry recorded that her lack of schooling came from "being abroad so much, and traveling all the time,"[31] while Ann Parker, a middle-class New York matron, lamented, "Very little leisure for reading. When will it come?" some weeks after commencing to study Latin and "sundry" other "improving things."[32] Fleda's whole plan and execution of a reading program mirrors the ambitions of many of the women who read Queechy; in this reading context, her success first, at completing the books she started and, second, sufficiently understanding what she read to be able to use it profitably in conversations and arguments with men amounts to a fictional ideal, a model for aspiring readers.

But Fleda's educational accomplishments – later she begins to publish her poetry – constitute one aspect of Warner's simultaneous use and abuse, or extension and inversion, of established cultural codes. On the one hand, this aspect of the novel echoes familiar themes and mirrors readers' own aspirations. On the other hand, late in the novel Warner proceeds as if this education had not happened, projecting Fleda as so uneducated and inexperienced that she must beg her future husband to instruct her. By the time she arrives at the Carleton estate in England, the witty girl who had held her own in New York society, learned French and Italian in Paris, read widely if eclectically, published her poems in popular journals, and run a household and a farm by herself has been so transformed that the epigram to the chapter introducing her to England is a passage from The Merchant of Venice portraying "an unlesson'd girl . . . / happy / . . . that her gentle spirit / Commits itself to your's to be directed, / As from her lord, her governor, her king" (II, 374). From active to passive female, American entrepreneur to English aristocrat, in her passage between these spheres Fleda has lost her hard-earned education as well as her independence. As in St. Elmo, here the narrator takes back a competence assigned an unmarried protagonist in order to make her character material fit to be molded by a male hand.

Of course it is in the development of her capability as a farmer that Fleda is most exhaustively and ambivalently portrayed. Fleda's learning process is described with the same attention to detail as Edna Earl's, but in Queechy each apparent triumph is succeeded by a narrative disclaimer. Unlike her Uncle Rolf, Fleda is willing to learn the intricacies of farming from her Uncle Seth, and to personally oversee Earl Douglass, the man she has asked to be her overseer. Conservative and crotchety, Earl resists all innovations, but Fleda handles him with the same diplomacy and perseverance that she used with everyone else.

> Earl Douglass was sometimes unmanageable, and held out in favor of an old custom or a prevailing opinion in spite of all the weight of testimony and light of discovery that could be brought to bear upon him. Fleda would let the thing go. But seizing her opportunity another time she would ask him to try the experiment, on a piece of ground; so pleasantly and skilfully that Earl could do nothing but shut his mouth and obey . . . And as Fleda always forgot to remind him that she had been right and he wrong, he forgot it too, and presently took to the new way kindly (II, 5).

Similarly, she learns to give orders, even in front of genteel visitors; she sends a city friend into gales of laughter as she asks Douglass to try curing clover hay in cocks, rather than in the sun, knowing that the "heft" should be "about a hundred pounds," and that Douglass should not cut more than he can put up in one day (II, 23–4). She becomes so skillful that Douglass regards her as the head of the family; when he comes to her – rather than to her uncle – for permission to settle on a price for the corn, he reports (concurring) that Seth Plumfield has declared her to be "the best farmer in the state" (II, 160).

Warner's ambivalence about this triumphant foray into the masculine is evident in her narrator's frequent reports of Fleda's exhaustion, recourse to tears, and migraine headaches. Fleda's paralyzing migraine headaches tend to develop either in situations where she does not have effective control over events or, paradoxically, in situations where she has taken full command in a masculine endeavor. The first occurs when she hears Guy Carleton curse. Professing deep disappointment in him (I,173), Fleda develops a headache so severe that her appearance shocks Carleton into backing out of a duel to which he had committed himself, thus obeying Fleda's wishes rather than those of his "honorable" male companions. Another occurs the day after Fleda has organized – and led – the expedition to tap the sugar maples on her family's property (I, 404). Though they are laid to "extraordinary nervous agitation or too great mental or bodily trial" – in other words, like Edna Earl's heart condition, to activities that strain her "feminine" mental and physical composition – in fact, they are signs of Fleda's ambivalence about her own status. In this Fleda shows the insecurity Mary Kelley notes in *Private Woman, Public Stage;* she likes to run things, but she also feels she should not have to do so.

But Warner's continual harping on this theme runs counter to the experience of many nineteenth-century women, who not only worked hard – often at jobs defined as male – but who also valued themselves within that context. Moreover, other publications urged women to expand their spheres of activity. A review of Elizabeth Starling's *Noble Deeds of Woman; or, Examples of Female Courage and Virtue* (1850) reminded readers that

> woman's sphere of action is not, at all times, to be so circumscribed [i.e., to the domestic sphere]: her integrity, fortitude, courage, and presence of mind, may frequently be called forth by adventitious circumstances. In extraordinary times, as are those in which we live, she may be placed in situations of difficulty, if not danger: let her then prepare herself to encounter them, by studying the examples now presented for her contemplation.[33]

Extraordinary circumstances call on women's hidden strengths (and this text defines the entire period as extraordinary; implying that the condition is chronic); works like *Noble Deeds* sanction forays into the male sphere.

Farm work was one of those long-term "exceptional" circumstances; then as now, farm women shared agricultural labor with men. Some managed to combine intellectual interests with domestic and agricultural duties. Late in the century Annie A. Mackey, a Nebraska farm woman, kept a commonplace book in which she used quotations from her reading as springboards for her own ideas, meditating on the American character much as Warner does in *Queechy*. [34] Her essays on "Taste," "Blank Faces," and "Humor" show her to be a reader for whom hard work did not devalue a sense of self, place, and intellect. Some women even cheerfully performed tasks extraordinary by any standards (and read women's novels while they did them): In 1881 seventeen-year-old Virginia Benton, journeying west with her family, reported that "Pa and John went to Goose Creek. I read Marian Grey (consider it slush). – kept the mules from straying and killed a rattlesnake."[35] Neither of these diarists display Fleda's pathological ambivalence about work; they may grow tired, frustrated, and impatient, but they accept hard labor as part of their own definition. *Marian Grey* is a novel by Mary Jane Holmes about a passive, timid woman who transforms herself into one educated, independent, beautiful and irresistible; it is a fair bet that the girl who found it "slush" would have had little empathy with Fleda's tears.

In *Queechy*, Fleda's development into full-fledged independence is cut short by the exigencies of the author's narrative design, which mandates that she be rescued from her peril (actually, Carleton recues Rolf Rossitur, not Fleda) and transported to England.[36] As in *St. Elmo*, this reverses the heroine's development, denying the validity – even the reality – of everything she has learned. As we have seen, even her educational accomplishments are declared null. Most importantly, she sees herself as a blank slate on which Carleton can now write his version of her character.

> "I am afraid you will find me wanting," [Fleda says to Carleton] "and
> when you do, will you put me in the way of being all you wish me to
> be? . . ."
> "My dear Elfie," he said, "what do you consider yourself deficient in?"
> Fleda spoke with a little difficulty.
> "I am afraid in a good many things – in general reading, – and in what
> are called accomplishments – "
> "You shall read as much as you please by and by," said he, "provided
> you will let me read with you; and as for the other want, Elfie, it is
> rather a source of gratification to me." Elfie very naturally asked why?
> "Because as soon as I have the power I shall immediately constitute
> myself your master in the arts of riding and drawing, and in any other
> art or acquisition you may take a fancy to, and give you lessons
> diligently."
> "And will there be gratification in that?" said Fleda.
> His answer was by a smile. But he somewhat mischievously asked her,
> "Will there not?" – and Fleda was quiet (II, 324).

Stripped of her accomplishments, shifted from independence to dependence, it is no wonder Fleda is silent – in her choice to marry Carleton
she has in effect silenced herself forever. Carleton likes her "want" because it gives him a chance to fill it, to provide her with "*con*-tent." But
this "wanting" Fleda, so deficient in all "accomplishments," is not the
same heroine who ran the farm or partied in New York. As in *St. Elmo*,
she has been reduced by authorial fiat.

But just as Warner's regressive desire for "protection" undermines the
forward movement of Fleda's independence, so counterthemes, many
related to the idea of American independence, undermine that regression.
To understand these we need to look first at the character of Hugh and
how he functions in the novel, then at what his and Fleda's roles mean
within the American context of this tale. Fleda's Cousin Hugh is a textual
remnant of the book Warner thought she was writing but did not quite
succeed in doing. The most anomalous figure in this novel, Hugh is in
part a figure like little Eva, of Stowe's *Uncle Tom's Cabin*. In his piety (for
instance in his deathbed scene, during which he implores his parents to
come to Christ so that they can all meet in heaven) he functions as a sign
of religious truth, or warning – a child sent not to live for himself, but to
bring his erring parents to Christ. He does not, however, serve that
exemplary function prior to his deathbed scene. Eva is an exemplary
figure throughout *Uncle Tom's Cabin,* but, until he starts to die, Hugh is
an almost evanescent one in *Queechy,* difficult to bring into focus.

A peculiarly nineteenth-century configuration of passive piety and intellectual sweetness – the kind of character that, in other novels, usually
dies in childhood[37] – in *Queechy* Hugh may best be viewed as Fleda's alter
ego, a shadow possibility for the heroine that actually evolved – rather

like the outlines of trial figures one sees on old paintings. As such, he is one aspect of the authorial ambivalence imbuing this novel. Always projected in tandem, Fleda and Hugh seem almost interchangeable: Both are beautiful, both love books, both love God, and each loves the other: "They were everything to each other" (I, 214); in each other they find "everything – love, confidence, sympathy, society, help; their tastes, opinions, pursuits, went hand in hand" (I, 195). When Fleda begins to publish her poetry, she uses "Hugh" as her pseudonym. But Hugh has also been consistently portrayed as Fleda's inferior. Though both are regarded as delicate, Hugh is clearly more so, with a tendency to melancholy, with less intellectual acumen than Fleda (I, 219), and with no aggressive energy at all.

Within the nineteenth century's iconography of male and female qualities, Hugh is far more feminine than Fleda. Though he does not complain about the family's misfortunes, and though he takes on the heavy burden of the mill, he never takes charge as Fleda does; rather, he leans on her strength. Moreover, he is sexless – despite their time in each other's arms, and that they are in their late teens well before he dies, he and Fleda maintain an entirely presexual relationship. And it is Hugh who gives up the world, renouncing his dreams of college, turning to his Bible for instruction, and deciding that "I have good time and opportunity to furnish myself with a better kind of knowledge, that I shall want where college learning wouldn't be of much use to me," a speech which "Fleda . . . did not like" (II, 10). Meanwhile Fleda, equally burdened, lives and flourishes, growing in competence and self-confidence as her farm begins to pay. In these aspects, *Queechy* anticipates James's *Portrait of a Lady,* featuring a heroine whose activity takes center stage and a male protagonist whose delicacy keeps him from acting males roles but enables him to participate in the cultural valuations of sympathy, piety, and submission generally only associated with women. Seen as two parts of a whole, Fleda and Hugh exhibit Warner's confusion over the limits of female nature, capacities, endurance, and desire.

The crossed roles played by Fleda and Hugh are also indicated by the fact that Fleda is free to leave Queechy only after Hugh's death, not just because he begs "that you will not let anybody take you away while I want you" (II, 315) but also because in some way he *is* Fleda, in her capacity for passive renunciation. While she has participated in Queechy's life, exhausted but very much involved, Hugh has withdrawn so steadily that he finally has no option but to die. When he does he bequeaths "all my part of [Fleda]" to Mr. Carleton (II, 346). Since Fleda gives up her independence on her marriage, an independence clung to as long as Hugh was alive, one might see Hugh's legacy as the feminine passivity that Fleda held at bay during her years in Queechy but that she exchanges for her masculine aggressiveness when she leaves to become Carleton's wife.

Together, Fleda and Hugh reverse roles, and she is unable to yield her masculine competence until he bequeaths his femininity to her on his death.

Fleda's move from the masculine back into the feminine also marks her movement from American independence to English class stasis. Much of Fleda's move into the feminine takes place during a hiatus in New York, after Fleda has left Queechy and her friends (or their graves) but not yet sailed for England and Mr. Carleton. Exhausted, she lies for weeks watching the ships off the Battery, feeling that she is "alone, broken off from her old friends and her former life, on a little piece of time that was like an isthmus joining two continents. Fleda felt it all exceedingly; felt that she was changing from one sphere of life to another" (II, 372–3). One cultural code that explains this imagery is the nineteenth-century notion of "separate spheres" for male and female endeavor. Having acted in the male sphere for so long, it takes Fleda weeks of listless depression to move back into the feminine. The other cultural code involved nationality; Fleda is preparing to move from the American scene, characterized by nonconformity and social mobility, into the English, characterized by tradition and social stasis. To make these transitions she must empty herself, renounce – as Hugh had renounced; and, as we have seen, she does so successfully. When she reaches Carleton, she is ready to welcome him as her "lord . . . governor . . .king." At least one contemporary reviewer objected to this ending on patriotic grounds. "There seems a slight lurking of prejudice, hardly consistent with the general patriotism of Miss Warner's books, in this setting up of English people as models of virtue and good-breeding, and almost a solecism in sending across the water for an immensely wealthy English husband for the sturdy little American Fleda, whose breeding of hap and hazard certainly have fitted her so admirably for making some indigenous swain happy."[38] Fleda's English husband, then – or rather, the happy ending in which Fleda rejects her national identity – violated the cultural code mandating loyal American heroines.

Yet Warner does not quite end Queechy on this note. After the wedding ceremony Fleda endures the scrutiny of her new English relatives at the wedding breakfast, where Fleda's American speech becomes a subject of discussion. Asserting that "I will not assure you . . . that I will not always keep a rag of the stars and stripes flying somewhere" (391), Fleda raises an issue that, within this staunchly Tory context, echoes the book's original emphasis on Fleda's Revolutionary ancestors. In addition, she responds to a nobleman's query as to whether she has "anything of a rebellious disposition," by replying (as had her revolutionary forebears), "Not against any lawful authority" (II, 391). His Lordship quickly leads the subject to the status of women in the nineteenth century; the association between two kinds of revolt is made here by the most conservative speaker in the novel. When Lord Peterborough asks if Fleda thinks that women "ought to stand more on that independent footing from which lordly monopoly has excluded them," and if she thinks that "the rights of the weak ought to be on a perfect equality with those of the strong," Fleda responds: "The rights of the weak *as such* – yes, my Lord" (II, 392). This answer is as reactionary as any Edna Earl might make, and endears Fleda to the men around her. The women, however, "looked rather puzzled" (II, 392). The subject is then closed, and the novel ends.

Still, its brief introduction, especially within the context of the tension between England and its erstwhile colony, serves as a reminder that this novel embodies two contradictory themes: the theme of independence, evoked in all of the references to the American Revolution and displayed in Fleda's victory over her circumstances; and the theme of dependence, evoked in the narrator's insistence on Fleda's feminine weakness and displayed in the regressive movement of the novel's dénouement. Moreover, the story itself often raises these issues, casting them as an argument between American independence, which often displays itself in brashness, and English class distinctions, which create a smooth exterior but which also – as Carleton's hasty trip home illustrates – foster unrest, even riots, among the people. In addition, the English women's implied opposition to their countryman's conservatism suggests that yet another kind of revolt may be brewing in English society. Certainly among the Americans with whom Fleda has come in contact, those identifying themselves with Europeans have been proved morally inferior and practically incompetent. Of the English themselves, only Guy Carleton has any favored status in the author/narrator's eye.

Finally, Fleda herself has been quick to defend her country and her compatriots in the past: In the section dealing with her sojourns with the Evelyns in New York, an entire chapter is given to her debate with an Englishman over the relative merits of English and American governments. Fleda, victoriously, has insisted that the democratic system encourages its people to develop morally, whereas the English system gives them no opportunity to learn through experience of self-government. Certainly Fleda's own period of independence – of making her own decisions – has proved the validity of her position. In a novel whose central theme is to find a way to keep its protagonist "unspotted by the world," Fleda's American experience, which has preserved her purity by forcing her to exercise her mental and moral judgment, has given her what Milton would have seen as an experienced virtue, not a blank one. Moreover, both Fleda and her Plumfield relatives have grave doubts about her ability to maintain this kind of purity among Carleton's sort of people. The specter of "independence" raised by Lord Peterborough then, can be seen as a reminder that the ability to create and control may not be something that can – or should – be relinquished.

The dubiousness of this regressive movement is also underscored by the reversal of Fleda's and Carleton's roles of moral authority and by the increasingly ominous hints about the force of Carleton's will. Like the heroes in many women's novels of the period, Carleton is absent for much of the novel. Not quite a Byronic hero, he is nevertheless initially alienated, purposeless, and prone to go wandering to and fro on the earth. Since Fleda succeeds in making him face his godlessness early in the novel, his absence is laid not to prolonged alienation but to the time it takes to convert him from a haughty member of the landed gentry into a benevolent one. Still a dominating character, for all his courtesy – even his mother claims he always gets his own way – Carleton is cast, and casts himself, as Fleda's protector. Fleda likes this; she would be glad to have him in charge of her all the time. But though she is always happy to have him "managing things about her, and even . . . managing herself" (II, 317), his ten years' absence is a necessary part of the plot if the heroine is to have any room for development, just as Rolf Rossitur's departure for Michigan is necessary for her emergence into full-fledged entrepreneurship.

But by the end, all this is reversed. Not only does Fleda give up her independence, she also seems to have yielded her moral authority; by the time Carleton begins paying regular visits to the farm – during the period when Hugh is dying – he has assumed the position of moral leadership: Fleda increasingly defers to him in all questions pertaining to the spirit. Yet for all his Christian benevolence, Carleton is also an aristocrat, bent on getting his own way and controlling everyone around him; *The North American Review* claimed that Carleton "carries his pretentiousness into the region of melodrama."[39] His hasty trip back to England occurs when a local uprising threatens his power; his authority over his people is evinced when Fleda is told that "he can introduce and carry through any measure; neither ignorance nor prejudice nor obstinacy seem to make head against him" (II, 380). And its import for Fleda is clear when Carleton tells her that now he has her "under safe control" (II, 388).

Queechy, then, does not satisfactorily "close" both strains of its narrative concerns. Laboring under contradictory imperatives – to cast a women's novel in the American mode *and* to tell a story that will meet psycho-cultural imperatives to see women, by nature empty, filled with both "*content*" and "*content*" through a dominating male agency, *Queechy* continually undermines its own propositions. On the one hand, there is clear analysis of the American scene, especially its rural aspects, and of the rural American character. Though not without criticism, on the whole this is projected favorably. In addition, the praise and the tangible rewards Fleda receives – the sense of having created an independence – weigh heavily in texts produced in antebellum America. Finally, the "escape" to England, with all its fairy-tale motifs (mansion, servants, park, rose garden), is projected as an escape into childhood – Fleda is repeatedly comforted by her sense of "being a child again."

But his reverse *Bildung* fuses sexual and national politics to suggest that regression may be, after all, just a fairy tale – that just as the country is not going to revert to its colonial status, "protected" by a mother country, so women who have learned to create and control should not necessarily want to regress to the status of children. Fleda's marriage remains as it looks: a fairy tale (as the marriage of Mrs. Wallis Warfield Simpson to Edward VIII would be eighty years later), a titillation. As attractive as this ending is for the romantically inclined – Fred Pattee's foolish schoolgirls – Fleda's success at mastering her circumstances is equally compelling for the democratically inclined "mothers . . . papas . . . and sober bachelors" *The North American Review* identified as the extended readership for this book. When Fleda creates, controls, and nourishes in Queechy, she becomes an autonomous figure, consolidator of male and female roles who can thrive in the open Yankee atmosphere.

The thrust of the *Bildung* action in this text then, is toward increasing power and independence. And while Fleda's migraines, exhaustion, and tears undermine the emotional authority of that movement, her emotional endorsement of the landscape (in which she feels truly comfortable) and, most importantly, her ultimate goal to remain uncorrupted (possible in Queechy, as evinced by her Aunt Plumfield and cousin Seth; unlikely in England, where she requires "protection" by her reformed spouse) bear enough weight to enable readers to create an alternate configuration to the closure indicated by the overt text. The memorable sections of *Queechy* concern Fleda's education in independence, just as those of *St. Elmo* concern Edna's passionate intensity over her work. Perhaps because these passages reflect the writers' own life histories – their struggles to master some aspect of the male sphere – or perhaps because in writing about women who choose to involve themselves in activities generally reserved for men the writers pay more attention and detail to their writing, it is these episodes the overt texts do not want to sanction, rather than the conventional closures, that convey the energy and power of these works and that lay the foundations for texts that will begin actively to question – and finally challenge – their need to deny their protagonists the fruits of hard-won experience.

PART III

NARRATIVE REBELLIONS AND TEXTUAL DESIGNS

4

INSCRIBING AND DEFINING: THE MANY VOICES OF FANNY FERN'S RUTH HALL

Fanny Fern's (Sara Payson Willis) 1855 novel *Ruth Hall*[1] is the story of a woman who, losing her economic security on her husband's death, and finding herself sole support of two small children, becomes a highly successful popular writer. The book has autobiographical elements: Willis did lose her first child and first husband and was thrown out on the world to fend for herself. Like her heroine, she too went through a period of trial before she found her vocation as a writer.[2] *Ruth Hall* records some of her actual experiences; more importantly, it records how she felt about them. There's a wicked mood in the portrayal of some of her fictional characters that suggests she was reaping revenge on those who had wronged her. Certainly her contemporaries understood that: The novel was soundly condemned in some quarters because it furiously satirized Willis's brother. *Peterson's Magazine* commented that "Much as we see to praise in the work, we cannot, however, keep down a suspicion that it is intended to pay off certain old scores of fancied neglect or insult; and this, we confess, we are sorry to see. We do not mean to say that the author has not been badly treated; but only that the public does not and cannot know the merits of private controversies. . . ."[3] With this one reservation, *Peterson's* liked *Ruth Hall; Godey's,* on the other hand, took such offense at the family scandal that it essentially refused to review the book: "As a writer, the author of this volume has been very successful and very popular," the reviewer begins. And concludes: "Her success and popularity may be increased by this 'domestic tale;' but, as we never interfere in family affairs, we must leave readers to judge for them-selves."[4]

Twentieth-century readers have not been offended by Willis's personal attacks, but many have been offended by her language. The text's mix-ture of the sentimental with the cynical confused early critics like Fred Pattee and Helen Papashvily, to whom flowery rhetoric was simply a sign of debased or manipulative emotion. Recent critics, however, have focused on that mixture, seeing it as a sign of the novel's bifurcated sensibility. Both Baym's *Woman's Fiction* and Kelley's *Private Woman, Public Stage* tackle the thematic implications of *Ruth Hall*'s dualities, Baym discussing them as deviations from the generic norm of nineteenth-century women's novels, and Kelley seeing them as an expression of the contradictions inherent in the life of any nineteenth-century woman who accepted the prevailing definition of women's nature at the same time that she sought power in the public sphere.

Additionally, Ann Douglas Wood's "The 'Scribbling Women' and Fanny Fern: Why Women Wrote" (1971) and Joyce W. Warren's introduction to the Rutgers University Press reprint of the novel (1986) explore the novel's linguistic radicalism as well as its thematic divisions. Anticipating Kelley, Wood studies *Ruth Hall* within the framework of women writing, suggesting that the excessively "feminine" language used in women's novels was a facade that helped the authors to write, to produce, without facing the social and psychological consequences of doing so. Fern's work she sees as exceptionally forthright but also "confused"; according to Wood, Fern "waged a curious and confused battle in which she often utilized the techniques of the subculture to fight against it" (17), manifesting this confusion through her "two selves . . . two voices, one strident and aggressive, the other conventional and sentimental" (18). Though she views Fern's dual voices as unintentional, Wood recognizes Fern's deliberate manipulations of her culture's gender conventions, especially their conventions about women's writing. Warren, on the other hand, sees the sentimental rhetoric as a reflection both of the period's rhetorical tastes and of the protagonist's initially innocent state of mind (*xxvii*). Whereas Wood sees Fern's florid writing as only partly premeditated, then, Warren sees it as a deliberate strategy.

With Warren, I take Fern's sentimental voice as a conscious creation. Rather than seeing it as a reflection of Ruth's innocence, however, I suggest, with Wood, that Fern used the sentimental mode against the subculture that mandated it as proof that the writer was a "true" woman.[5] But the problem lies not, as Wood claims, in Fern's "confused battle." Rather, it lies in our confused reading. Our interpretive conventions have been inadequate for assessing just how deliberately nineteenth-century women writers were capable of manipulating the writing conventions of their day. *Ruth Hall* is an excellent text to begin reexamining this question because in it Fern used sentimental imagery and language patterning as means, first, of disguising her goal to project a woman who grows into self-definition and verbal power and, second, of bringing the worldview implicit in the sentimental mode into doubt. In exploiting and subverting a rhetorical mode not only closely associated with women's writing but also commonly held to be reflective of women's nature itself,

Fern was actively challenging the prevailing nineteenth-century view of ideal women.

Fern's manipulation of these conventions occurs both in the associations she evokes for her protagonists and the specific words and syntactical patterns she employs. Iconographically, Ruth is framed by a variety of the culture's cherished associations with good women, with flowers, for instance, and, fused with them, God.

> Ruth had a strong, earnest nature; she could not look upon this wealth of sea, sky, leaf, bud, and blossom; she could not listen to the little birds, nor inhale the perfumed breath of morning, without a filling eye and brimming heart, to the bounteous Giver (29).

Passages such as this draw on readers' prior acquaintance with other texts, especially flower books and the language of flowers, which, as popularizations of mid–nineteenth-century American Protestantism's conviction that nature reflected its creator, also projected blossoms in tandem with God. "I am the spirit that dwells in the flower," begins one poem in Hale's *Flora's Interpreter*.[6] Another ends on a typically pious note: "I would that thus, when I shall see / The hour of death draw near to me, / Hope, blossoming within my heart, / May look to heaven as I depart."[7]

Twentieth-century readers have trouble with such language; our only response to it seems to be to dismiss it as "sentimental" and "stereotyped." But as we have seen in *Queechy*, it is more useful to see works employing it as intertextual constructs. Within any given text, sentimental language functions as a system of codes, or shorthand symbols designed to help readers know where a character stands in the value hierarchy of a (presumably) shared world. By associating Ruth with flowers and piety Fern creates a protagonist her readers will recognize as deeply feminine, a woman who feels as a woman should feel, and who therefore qualifies as a heroine the general culture can accept. Similarly, Ruth's maternal solicitude "marks" her as a woman who knows that her most important function lies in her nurturing duties, while her lovingly subordinate relationship with her husband valorizes her as a woman who, as a contributor to one gift-book phrased it, knows that "she is made to be cherished and loved, and to be so, must confine herself to that refined and delicate sphere, the charms of which, form her principal claims to the affection of man."[8] These were the images that defined a good woman in the middle of the nineteenth century, that created her image – realities notwithstanding – in the public eye. They are facets in the complex of associations we call sentimental.

In *Sacred Tears: Sentimentality in Victorian Literature*, Fred Kaplan points out that British Victorian sentimentality was a rearguard action struggling to defend eighteenth-century concepts of the moral affections against the encroachment of a realist worldview that denied human nature the possibility of transcending its own limitations.[9] Similar concepts undergirded American sentimentality. Since one function of the female icon in nineteenth-century literature was to represent a retreat from – or alternative to – the realist worldview, the sentimental language that engendered her served as a sign of her difference from male characters, who tended to be associated with harsh "realities" and described in the language of commerce. Women were especially associated with feeling. Certainly this kind of inscription appealed to reviewers of *Ruth Hall;* *The Knickerbocker* singles out the scenes when Harry dies and when Ruth is forced to give up his clothes as "touching" enough to merit extensive quotation,[10] while *Peterson's* found "an earnestness, breathing through the whole, which is often terrible."[11]

The problem for us – as twentieth-century readers for whom the concepts no longer have validity – lies in learning how to interpret sentimental language and its associations and, if possible, in determining its effects on contemporary readers. One interpretive strategy is to examine the patterns into which sentimental passages fall – to see just how consciously writers are employing them. The dual narrative voices of *Ruth Hall* indicate a writer trying to transcend the language and references that had already created her heroine. For Fanny Fern, the answer to the dilemma of a priori characterization lay in its unveiling, in a work that is as intent on demonstrating how the society defines and circumscribes women as it is in developing its plot. Fern's own strategy is to orchestrate a variety of voices, all focused on the central character but all exhibiting their own will to power as they inscribe (and therefore define) the protagonist. The question of voice is at the heart of this novel, then; the work is structured to show, first, how Ruth is defined by the voices of her culture; then, to suggest what kind of voice she might have when she finally begins speaking and writing for herself.

As with other nineteenth-century novels, it is difficult to determine how private readers perceived these opposing discourses. Reviewers generally reflect the novel's dualism in the way they alternate between criticizing its exposure of family squabbles and praising its sentimental episodes. But reviewers, as Baym points out, tend to uphold cultural stereotypes, and often it is necessary to read between their lines to determine exactly which values they are supporting and which they are opposing. What they dislike, we should examine closely. In *Ruth Hall,* they dislike Fern's anger, her furious, and linguistically barbed, attack on real people. But the novel makes it clear that the brother, in-laws, publishers, and employers Fern attacks stand for the establishment that deprives women, first, of ways to achieve economic independence; and, second, of the voice to protest their helplessness. The cultural values reviewers were upholding, then, mandated women's silence and dependency. But as we have seen, nineteenth-century women readers admired members of their sex who conquered their misfortunes, who became famous for their achievements, and who spoke out in the world.

Some readers – not many – also recorded sensitivity to the artificiality of language chosen to project sentimental idealism. Julia Newberry objected to Lydia Sigourney's "Lucy Howard's Journal" because Howard's "language seems to me too studied, and her words are the longest she can find,"[12] and another reader mocked the studied repetitions sentimental literature employed – singling out one of Fern's especially florid novels as well as Fern's brother Nathan's *Home Journal*. "Wonder if you ever read 'Rose Clark' by Fanny Fern?" Lucy Sherwin wrote to her sister Nancy in 1862. "Wonder if you have ever read 'Ernest Linwood' by Caroline somebody? Wonder if you read the Home Journal? . . . Wonder if this repetition of the word wonder will divest it of any of its old charm, or invest it with anything new?"[13] Finally, we know that most women were actively reading literature by and about women in search of models for conduct and ambition. *Ruth Hall* offers two models, each presented through a particular linguistic mode; the one the reviewers disliked embodies Fern's anger against sentimental language and the model of female behavior it inscribes.

In *Ruth Hall* the concern for defining (inscribing) proceeds through a continuous alternation of sentimental (or iconizing) and cynical (or iconoclastic) modes. As I have already noted, by the mid-nineteenth century the function of sentimental prose, especially clichéd prose, had evolved from a verbal representation of ideal qualities – the exaltation of sentiment for the specific didactic purpose of demonstrating moral excellence – to the evocation of chords of associations already constructed by prior texts. In other words, sentimentality itself had become an intertextual construct, functioning to evoke reflexive responses – usually emotional responses – rather than to stimulate readers to measure their own behavior in terms of moral ideals.

Another way of seeing this is as a convention, a shortcut to making popular literature readily accessible – of making what Roland Barthes calls the readerly text,[14] or Hans Robert Jauss, the culinary text[15]: the text that draws so heavily on standard plot lines and conventional values that it can be "consumed" without requiring much effort on the reader's part. Readers who indulged in the "fast read" that Augusta Evans Wilson castigated as "the hasty, careless novel-reading glance"[16] could find in sentimental clichés assurance of their emotional responsiveness rather than challenge to their moral behavior. Consequently, when the narrator of *Ruth Hall* interprets Ruth sentimentally – when, for instance, she says that in marriage Ruth's "craving heart" had "at length found its ark of refuge" – she is sounding a note that will stimulate readers to assume that empathy with Ruth's loneliness will be rewarded by Ruth's (and, by extension, their own) rescue by a life-long companion; in other words, that little girls deprived of love will find it and live happily ever after.

In Wolfgang Iser's terms, such language stimulates the creation of a gestalt, or illusion, on the reader's part; in *Ruth Hall* the illusion is clearly that we are reading an updated version of *Cinderella*. But Iser's model for the reading process also suggests that in all reading such illusions are continually altered and even destroyed by the continual input of new information.[17] In *Ruth Hall* this process is intensified by the interruptions of the narrator's voice speaking in its iconoclastic mode, which in the first part of the novel alternates with the sentimental mode to create an almost continuous pendulum of raised and lowered expectations about exactly what constitutes the nature of this woman. To conflate Iser and Peter Rabinowitz[18] (that is, to conflate phenomenological and rhetorical paradigms of narrator–reader relationships) for a moment, perhaps we can see this process of creating and destroying expectations as a method of forcing readers to shift rapidly back and forth between audience levels. Here, the most naive – or the most intertextually dependent – audience accepts the narrator's interpretations in the sentimental mode, thus creating the gestalt for the Cinderella paradigm in the novel. But while all readers "receive" the sentimental interpretation, other interpretive modes exist as well. The narrator's cynical commentary challenges attentive readers to doubt the fixed truths of the iconizing clichés. The result is that those readers are continually challenged, forced to question the gender values implicit in the voice that iconizes the silent, loving, and ultimately victimized woman.

This alternation of voices, each revealing a worldview that contradicts the worldview of its opposing voice, is continued in the voices of other characters (including some who are only present in their letters to Ruth), each of whom reveals her- or himself as she or he defines Ruth. This is *skaz*, written speech fashioned to represent oral patterns revealing socially distinct points of view[19]; in this novel the narrative voices initiate the central dialectic and the other voices continue the process of dual (and contradictory) inscription. The play of many voices, then, is Fern's primary tool for first rendering the verbal–political power structure of gender relationships in mid–nineteenth-century American culture and then casting the values associated with it into doubt.

The narrative voice introducing Ruth calls on the intertextual context of her readers by presenting the protagonist as a deprived child who, like Cinderella, is emotionally abused by her family despite her own exemplary qualities. This paradigmatic child has spent her childhood craving love, especially from men, and has been denied it, especially by her father, Mr. Ellet, a tight-fisted religious hypocrite, and her brother, Hyacinth, a sensuous fop. Love here is a synonym for recognition: The narrator's brief review of Ruth's childhood suggests that her companions have defined Ruth less in terms of her own emotional needs and personal talents than in terms of her usefulness for their selfish purposes. Her father, for instance, uses her as a vehicle for tyrannizing her mother; her classmates tease her for being studious and then borrow her compositions to cover up their own deficiencies; her brother makes it clear that her existence is of no consequence to him, ignoring her presence and assuming she is the maid when she performs small services for him. Ruth's response to this refusal to value or even admit her existence has been to retreat into silence, to voluntarily isolate herself: Because none of her acquaintances is willing to take the child on her own premises, "Ruth was fonder of being alone by herself" (14). Although this move evokes accusations that Ruth is "odd" and "queer" (14) because she refuses to play the public roles her society dictates, it does not signal Ruth's rejection of her culture's gender definitions. Rather, in isolating herself Ruth tacitly agrees that her female voice should not be heard. The alternative to being a silly woman is to be a silent one.

Predictably, Ruth's first sense of public identity comes through her first experience of sexual notice, when she acquires a beau: "She had arrived at the first epoch in a young girl's life, – she had found out her power!" With this discovery, the narrator continues, had come a change in bearing: "Her manners became assured and self-possessed. *She*, Ruth, could inspire love! Life became dear to her. There was something worth living for. . . . She had a motive, an aim; she should *some* day make somebody's heart glad. . . . her twin-soul existed somewhere" (15–16). This is traditional women's power, defined as power to attract in order to serve. Harry Hall, her husband, becomes that soul mate, and in her marriage Ruth lives "in a sort of blissful dream" (18), delighted by "this new freedom, this being one's own mistress."

Both the sentimental voice and the cynical voice interpret Ruth's progress to this pinnacle of womanly happiness. The first approves it: Ruth's search for a love object and her discovery of self-worth in the reflection of a loved one is consistent with prevailing definitions of female nature: "it is not admiration which that young beating heart craves; it is love," the voice solemnly informs us (17). Moreover, Ruth's power is limited to the evocation of sexual love. Thus happiness, freedom, and self come about through the agency of a male, the gestalt called for by the Cinderella paradigm in the novel. Intertwined with this interpretation, however, is the other voice, which disillusions the reader as quickly as the first panders to her. This is the voice that characterizes Ruth's first admirer as a "smitten swain" who accompanies his floral tribute with "a copy of amatory verses" (15). "Swain" and "amatory" were still in use in the midfifties, but self-consciously; the 1854 edition of Webster's suggests that "swain" is only appropriate for pastoral poetry, and the reviewer who employed "swain" in reference to *Queechy* clearly meant it to refer to a sturdy country lad. Used as Fern uses these words, in a paragraph otherwise composed of very simple language, "amatory" and "swain" become metalinguistic markers, signaling the narrator's dubiousness about the ultimate importance of the phenomenon she is recording. As she describes this Cinderella's discovery of sexual love, she begins to bring the values implicit in the cultural paradigm into doubt.

In fact, in this passage the iconoclastic voice alternates so continuously with the sentimental voice that even in this first chapter the notion of love as the *summa* of woman's power is undermined. The play of voices is so continual that the passage is worth quoting in full.

> In the all-absorbing love affairs which were constantly going on between the young ladies of Madame Moreau's school and their respective admirers, Ruth took no interest; and on the occasion of the unexpected reception of a bouquet, from a smitten swain, accompanied by a copy of amatory verses, Ruth crimsoned to her temples and burst into tears, that any one could be found so heartless as to burlesque the "awkward" Ruth. Simple child! She was unconscious that, in the freedom of that atmosphere where a "prophet out of his own country is honored," her lithe form had rounded into symmetry and grace, her slow step had become light and elastic, her eye bright, her smile winning, and her voice soft and melodious. Other bouquets, other notes, and glances of involuntary admiration from passers-by, at length opened her eyes to the fact, that she was "plain, awkward Ruth" no longer. Eureka! She had arrived at the first epoch in a young girl's life, – she had found out her power! Her manners became assured and self-possessed. *She,* Ruth, could inspire love! Life became dear to her. There was something worth living for – something to look forward to. She had a motive – an aim; she should *some* day make somebody's heart glad, – somebody's hearthstone bright; somebody should be proud of her; and oh, how she *could* love that somebody! History, astronomy, mathematics, the languages, were all pastime now. Life wore a new aspect; the skies were bluer, the earth greener, the flowers more fragrant; – her twin-soul existed somewhere (15–16).

Here we have what Mikhail Bakhtin would call "double-directed discourse," two voices, expressing two worldviews, occupying the same linguistic space.[20] Lines such as "her lithe form had rounded into symmetry and grace" belong to the sentimental mode of projecting a heroine as she matures physically (i.e., into sexual maturity); "Eureka!" to a worldview that questions Ruth's adolescent discovery that sexual maturity means power. "Eureka" is not even listed in the 1854 *Webster's;* though it may have become famous by the discovery of gold in California in 1848, it was not the kind of word generally associated with a tender young woman's sexual awakening. One way to look at its occurrence in this passage is as a sign of the adult narrator's perception of adolescent sexuality. Within the context of *Ruth Hall*'s development, however, it is also the voice of a narrator commenting on one of the culture's favorite sexual myths. Her facetious equation of Ruth's discovery of sexual power with the discovery of gold suggests that readers should reevaluate the idea that sexual maturity is the crowning achievement of a woman's life.

To read this paragraph as without ambiguity is to see it only through the lenses called for by the sentimental mode. Recognizing it as double-directed discourse, however, mandates moving between narrative modes – that is, being forced to evaluate the worldview implicit in each. Once this movement has begun, most readers perceive that these worldviews are antithetical. The opposition can be resolved by seeing the book as confused – as the product of a writer who did not understand her own motives; or as ironic – as the product of a writer who is consciously manipulating writing conventions. The frequency of double-direction occurring in the midst of the sentimental mode in *Ruth Hall* suggests that the latter is the most appropriate response. But to discover irony in the novel means to believe that from its inception the text embodies radical doubt about "woman's power," its awakening, and its manner of defining and limiting a girl's life.

Thematically, grounds have already been laid for this rhetorically layered skepticism. As with flower imagery, this is intertextually determined. As we have seen, throughout the nineteenth century most writing directed to or about women valorized education, from diary entries by young women who, like Mary Guion, lamented her "neglected education"[21]; through educators like Catharine Beecher, who called for the establishment of women's universities even in the midst of disavowing the franchise[22]; to the many women's novelists who portrayed heroines like Edna Earl, who lust for education far more than they do for lovers. In *Ruth Hall* the classmates who wondered "why [Ruth] took so much pain to bother her head with those stupid books, when she was every day growing prettier, and all the world knew that it was quite unnecessary for a pretty woman to be clever" (16) are in turn denigrated by the narrator, who praises Ruth's academic seriousness and treats it as an integral part of Ruth's own nature – that is, emphasizes this aspect of the protagonist as none of her fictional companions do. If the specter of "love" makes this studious girl forsake her studies and dream only of making some male happy, the initial highlighting of her academic zeal and its subsequent dismissal once the possibilities of "love" are discovered should also bring "love" into question. And of course Ruth's education, especially her writing skills, will become vitally necessary to her livelihood later in the novel. Finally, the narrator notes that Ruth's recognition as a love object is only "the *first* episode in a young girl's life," implying that there will be others. And the others – as subsequent events show – do not lend credence to the durability of sexual power.

Poor little rich girls usually marry at the end of the novels that concern them. One who marries in the first chapter (itself an unusual event in nineteenth-century women's fiction) must be destined for a sea-change; the Cinderella paradigm does not take us beyond the wedding. For Ruth, this begins in yet more voices inscribing her, from yet other centers of personal desire. Having set the tone for multiple views of her protagonist, the narrator moves to a rear seat in this text, leaving the process of defining Ruth to other characters.

One of the first to "redefine" Ruth after her marriage is old Mrs. Hall, her mother-in-law, who sees her as simultaneously incompetent and cunning. Jealous because she perceives Ruth as having stolen her son's love, Mrs. Hall interrogates, castigates, and generally intimidates Ruth about her imperfect housewifery, her curls, and what the parsimonious Mrs. Hall perceives as her extravagance. Declaring, "that girl is no fool. . . . she knows very well what she is about: but diamond cut diamond, *I* say" (31), Mrs. Hall makes Ruth into an antagonist and conducts an almost open, one-sided warfare with her. To this Ruth offers almost no resistance. ". . . Ruth kept her wise little mouth shut; moving, amid these discordant elements, as if she were deaf, dumb, and blind" (23).

Her silence is interpreted by the narrator in the sentimental mode: "Oh, love! that thy silken reins could so curb the spirit and bridle the tongue, that thy uplifted finger of warning could calm that bounding pulse, still that throbbing heart, and send those rebellious tears, unnoticed, back to their source" (23). For all its floridness, this voice is a protesting one: In iconizing the good wife it also brings the injustice of her situation into question. "Ah! could we lay bare the secret history of many a wife's heart, what martyrs would be found, over whose uncomplaining lips the grave sets its unbroken seal of silence" (23). Silence, in other words, may be the sign of an ideal wife – forgiving, uncomplaining, accepting her inferior status in her intimate relationships – but it also makes her a martyr, a sacrifice to an unjust system – a system that runs counter to God's wishes. If uncomplaining wives are martyrs, those who oppress them are tyrants. Certainly Mrs. Hall is a tyrant, but in moving out from the specific case to the general situation, the narrative voice implicitly takes in the entire system of intimate relationships women experience in their marriages. Here, the "system," the total cultural valuation of female sacrifice, is implicitly cast as tyrannical. And those who accept women's silence as acquiescence in the system are themselves in complicity with the forces of oppression.

Most importantly, the wife who moves "deaf, dumb, and blind" among "discordant elements" is the woman who has removed herself from the play of voices that define her, accepted their inscription as definitive, opted out of the possibility of inscribing herself in opposition to their words. As she had done in her girlhood, then, during her marriage Ruth retreats from conflict rather than meeting its challenge, thus acting in complicity with her own oppression. Her complicity has its very real compensations; not least of which is to be defined by her lover as his beloved, his queen: "Did not [Harry's] soul bend the silent knee of homage to that youthful self-control that could repress its own warm emotions, and stifle its own sorrows, lest *he* should know a heart-pang? . . . Ruth read it in the magnetic glance of the loving eye . . . and in the low, thrilling tone of the whispered, 'God bless you, my wife' . . ." (23–4). As Ruth's story is told prior to her husband's death, her victimization by others is a minor irritant in a life that shows an accommodation to being defined from the outside.

Ruth's early years are marked by two sanctioned modes of female behavior: first silence, then entreaty. Ruth's first pleas are in behalf of her first child, Daisy – emblem of her mother's innocence – who dies of croup; they are not successful. Her first movement out of these patterns occurs as Harry is dying, when she refuses to leave his room. Resistance joins entreaty to become her dominant modes of response during the early period of her widowhood, when she alternately pleads for money to support her daughters and resists the family's efforts to take the children away. Again, neither mode is successful. Ruth's own voice – a voice that speaks for her own self-interest – does not sound until after the narrative has detailed her move to the city and her unsuccessful efforts to get work as a seamstress, laundress, and schoolteacher – about the limit of occupations open to unskilled women during the time. This period is recorded through the voices of Ruth's "friends," none of whom wish to acknowledge her needs; through the voices of prospective employers, who want to exploit her; and even through the voices of two male residents in her boarding house, who see her as sexual prey.

Two apparently irrelevant stories of other women are interpolated into this stretch of the novel. One concerns Mrs. Leon, a wealthy, intelligent, beautiful woman whose husband incarcerates her in an insane asylum, where she dies of grief and neglect. The second, a comic sketch about an Irish-American family that could easily have been one of Fern's light newspaper columns, concerns Mrs. Skiddy, Ruth's landlady. Like Mary Austin's "The Return of Mr. Wills" some fifty years later,[23] this sketch bears a feminist punch. Once Mrs. Skiddy discovers that her erring husband has finally deserted her, she takes nominal as well as practical control of her affairs and flourishes at it. When Mr. Skiddy writes a year later to ask for money to come home, she refuses. "Drawing from her pocket a purse well filled with her own honest earnings, she chinked its contents at some phantom shape discernible to her eyes alone; while through her set teeth hissed out, like ten thousand serpents, the word 'N–e–v–e–r!' " (109).

Ruth's own decision to try writing for a living comes directly after these interpolated stories. Clearly they delineate the two choices facing her: Either continue to be defined and controlled by others, and die from it, as had Mrs. Leon, the model of upper-class wifely forebearance; or begin to define herself and take control over her life, as had Mrs. Skiddy, a "comic," lower-class character. As with many other women's novels of the mid-nineteenth century, the unacknowledged model for the successful heroine's behavior is the lower-class woman, whose status frees her from the gender definitions and restrictions of the middle and upper-middle classes. For the heroines of these novels, such freedom and consequent self-definition come only in isolation, in the *lack* of protection by others. These heroines have to learn what it is like to be entirely freed from familial and class "protections."

In *Ruth Hall*, Ruth comes to understand this slowly. Her most important lesson comes on the eve of her rebirth as a writer, when she sends her initial sketches to her brother Hyacinth, editor of the *Irving Magazine,* assuming that he will help her launch her career. Not only does Hyacinth reject them, but he informs her that she has no talent and advises her to seek some *"unobtrusive"* employment (116). Whether or not Willis's own brother actually sent her a similar letter, the incident's occurrence in the novel demonstrates the uselessness of class and family ties. With this, it also reinforces the society's dictum that women must be neither seen nor heard. In other words, Ruth's unprovoked fall from grace has thrust her into a world where she must labor not only to create a speaking self but to be responsible for it, to protect herself. Finally understanding this, Ruth moves from entreaty and resistance to challenge, swearing that "I *can* do it, I *feel* it, I *will* do it" and embracing her children "with convulsive energy," the first energy she has shown.

Ruth's evolution into a writer is chronicled, as had been her evolution into a wife, largely through other voices, from those of editors who use her naïveté against her to those of fans whose letters assume that she is rich and powerful. Ruth's own voice develops as she learns how to pit these antithetical voices against one another for her own gain. Here, Mary Kelley's study helps illuminate the dilemma Ruth faces in learning to articulate her demands; she must learn to be aggressive in order not to be victimized, but she must counter the unfeminine aggressiveness by showing her deeply womanly exceptional circumstances: She is the sole support of two young children, one of whom, in fact, has been "captured" by her wicked grandmother on the premise that Ruth cannot support her; during much of the story, the child patiently awaits rescue. As Kelley demonstrates, her children's needs legitimize Ruth's aggressions in her own eyes as well as in her contemporaries'. Certainly it provides a "cover" that allows Ruth (and Fern) to write and also to maintain their status as "natural" women in their society's eyes. But though the sentimental narrative voice stresses Ruth's parental anxieties, the iconoclastic voice emphasizes Ruth's evolution into a professional writer whose own voice is at least as business oriented as it is parental.

Ruth's initial encounters with the two editors who first publish her work exhibit these tensions. Narrative time is collapsed here; though the two encounters with editors are shown occurring on the same day, they illustrate modes of business acumen and self-confidence that come developmentally far apart. Rather than exhibiting Fern's confusion or carelessness, this temporal fold successfully accomplishes Fern's purpose of showing the inadequacy of feminine passivity and the necessity of business aggressiveness in the pursuit of a livelihood. Ruth's first interview is with Lescom, the editor who has published her first sketches and whose dialogue reveals his insistence on putting all of Ruth's reactions into gender-defined patterns. Lescom begins this interview by congratulating Ruth on her popularity; her first articles have been copied by Lescom's wire-linked "exchanges" and are netting him new subscribers. When Ruth's "eyes sparkled, and her whole face glowed" at the news, he patronizingly responds that "Ladies *like* to be praised." But Ruth hastily disclaims a desire for admiration, admitting a desire for success only "because it will be bread for my children" (130). In this scene, when Ruth, pulling her gloves off and on and pleading family responsibility, finally "muster[s] courage" to ask that her success be translated into money, she fails. The voice of the womanly woman who pleads family responsibilities is clearly not the appropriate one to wrest pecuniary rewards from the business world.

Ruth's second interview of the "day" is more successful. Mentally reviewing Lescom's "business practices" as she goes to the next magazine office, she realizes that her best interests lie in her ability to play one editor off against another, and her voice has a very different ring in the next editor's office. The novice author who had twisted her gloves in front of Lescom speaks out firmly in front of Tibbetts: When the second editor realizes she is "Floy," the pseudonym under which her articles have been published, he pressures her either to write for him under a different pseudonym, or to write for his journal exclusively. This time Ruth does not mention her family. Rather, she casts her reply in terms of self-interest and trade, the appropriate "language" for communicating with a man who sees literature in terms of producers and consumers. Ruth meets Tibbetts's demands by asserting that "if I have gained any reputation by my first efforts, it appears to me that I should be foolish to throw it away by the adoption of another signature; and with regard to the last, I have no objection to writing exclusively for you, if you will make it worth my while" (132). Her speech gains her a second job but little profit; it does, however, mark an important step in her evolution from passive victim to active speaker. Not only does she speak, she demands; not only does she demand, she does so in the language of the business world. And she also gathers ammunition for further attacks. Overhearing Tibbetts's plan to exploit her services as long as he can, she thinks to herself, "Thank you gentlemen. . . . when the cards change hands, I'll take care to return the compliment" (132).

Ruth's success as a writer is evinced in the letters she receives in response to her articles. These range from simple appreciation of the mark she has made on the writers' lives, through demands that she provide pecuniary help through her literary skills, to proposals of marriage. All perceive Ruth as powerful. Their accumulated effect is to make her understand that she is wielding a very different kind of power than that which she had experienced as a girl. Through her writing she is creating a self, not just a persona; Ruth (like Sara Payson Willis) writes under a pseudonym, but as she masters her craft the distinction between Ruth and "Floy" becomes increasingly blurred.

Shortly after signing an exclusive contract with John Walters, an editor who has offered an honest remuneration, Ruth receives another business offer that is placed, narratively, to echo the major thematic question of the book: the relative merits of love, or sexual, power versus economic power. Again, the debate is presented through the agency of letters, disembodied voices that project Ruth. The first letter to Ruth is a request for her autograph, her sign of her own existence. The second is an offer of marriage from a rich Southerner who offers her "a box at the opera, a carriage, and servants in livery, and the whole heart and soul of Victor Le Pont" (153). Like the self-consciousness of "amatory" and "swain" used earlier by the narrator, the double-direction of the voice that reports this proposal highlights the artificiality of the culture's sexual mythology. Here we have the end of the Cinderella story, the retreat from worldly struggle; this narrative thread – if carried through – would fulfill readers' intertextually created expectations for a retreat into stasis, the triumph of sexual love, the reassumption of protection. *Ruth Hall* rejects this. Rather, "the next [letter] was more interesting. It was an offer to Floy from a publishing house, to collect her newspaper articles into a volume. They offered to give her so much on a copy, or $800 for the copyright" (153). Ruth gives the marriage proposal to her toddler for drawing paper and keeps the book proposal for herself. "'Well, well,' soliloquized Ruth, 'business is accumulating'" (153).

In addition to showing that Ruth has become far more interested in business power than in love power, Ruth's new voice also demonstrates how positively she has responded to the image of her projected in the letters. Trying to decide whether to accept the flat fee or risk the royalties, knowing that the flat fee would enable her to redeem her other daughter from her in-laws immediately but also might lose her thousands of dollars if the book is successful, Ruth refuses the "temptation."

> Ruth straightened up, and putting on a very resolute air, said, "No, gentlemen, I will not sell you my copyright; these autograph letters, and all the other letters of friendship, love, and business, I am constantly receiving from strangers, are so many proofs that I have won the public ear. No, I will not sell my copyright; I will rather deny myself a while longer, and accept the per-centage;" and so she sat down and wrote her publishers; but then caution whispered, what if her book should *not* sell? "Oh, pshaw," said Ruth, "it *shall!*" and she brought her little fist down on the table till the old stone inkstand seemed to rattle out "*it shall!*" (153).

This voice marks Ruth's rebirth; it shows her conviction that she can effect economic power through her writing and signals the beginning of an entirely different mode of discourse in her business relations.

When one of her former editors threatens to defame her in retaliation for her move to Walters's magazine, Ruth not only refuses to be intimidated, she even moves differently. The woman who had stood in editors' offices nervously pulling her gloves off and on now "smiled derisively," then answers in a tone soft enough to constitute an intimate threat in return:

> "Mr. Tibbetts, you have mistaken your auditor. I am not to be frightened, or threatened, or *insulted,*" said she, turning toward the door. "Even had I not myself the spirit to defy you, as I now do, for I will never touch pen to paper again for 'The Pilgrim,' you could not accomplish your threat; for think you my publishers will tamely fold their arms, and see *their* rights infringed? No, sir, you have mistaken both them and me." And Ruth moved toward the door (157).

Ruth is not entirely accurate here: Tibbetts has not mistaken her; he has continued to act upon the assumption that his is the hegemonic voice in their relationship. The difference lies in Ruth, who now projects herself through a sense of her own pecuniary power and who knows she has earned the right to claim a new group of "protectors," men who acknowledge her existence in the world of commodity values. An indication of the shift in gender perspective that her new stance implies is the suddenly archaic language her erstwhile employer speaks:

> "Stay!" exclaimed Mr. Tibbetts, placing his hand on the latch; "when you see a paragraph in print that will sting your proud soul to the quick,

know that John Tibbetts has more ways than one of humbling so imperious a dame" (157).

Once more, Fern's language calls attention to itself, a sign that her speaker can no longer be taken seriously within the novel's discursive world. Both the phrases ("sting your proud soul to the quick," "Humbling so imperious a dame") and the scenic placement (the man preventing the woman from leaving the room) evoke eighteenth-century seduction novels and their degraded descendents, nineteenth-century melodramas; in a work by Richardson or on a Bowery stage, this passage would introduce a rape. Here, it illustrates the sudden impotence of the male figure. Ruth has found her voice, through writing; her self-inscription and self-creation work in tandem. This voice, rather than the others, articulates the new kind of woman the novel finally projects.

The portrait of Ruth's daughter Nettie supports this latter image. Nettie is "courageous, impulsive, independent, irrepressible, but loving, generous, sensitive, and noble-hearted," the child who has weathered her mother's trials and found her own voice (198). "Independent" is the key word here; despite Ruth's earlier claim in response to Nettie's query whether *she* will become an author that "no happy woman ever writes. From Harry's grave sprang 'Floy'" (175), the fact is that Nettie will never experience her mother's cold plunge into the world and language. Rather, Nettie already reflects her mother's success in her verbal dexterity and confidence; she is a punster and an avenger who vows to cut her wicked grandmother's head off (192). Her linguistic maturity and her confrontational readiness show that Nettie – easily nettled – will become a woman for whom independence and self-reliance are axiomatic.

Notwithstanding, the novel appears to end on the sentimental note. The last chapter shows Ruth and the children visiting Harry's grave, where the sentimental narrator reports that "the moon had silvered the old chapel turrets, and the little nodding flowers glistened with dewdrops, but still Ruth lingered" (211). But the arousal of feeling here focuses largely on scene, rather than action. Action, in fact, works against the paradigm evoked by the association with Harry, the life that has passed. Although Ruth's implicit request that Walters promise to bury her next to Harry both evokes her marital happiness and reasserts her status as a true woman, loyal and deeply feeling, it also suggests that Ruth has no intention of remarrying, an unusual ending for a women's novel of the period. In addition, the family's pending removal to an unspecified part of the country evokes American male rather than female myths of success.[24] The narrator's voice, in other words, seeks to evoke associations that the plot does not support.

This is consonant with the many voices that have defined Ruth and her circumstances throughout the novel. In this last chapter, as in the first, the narrator speaks rather than Ruth herself. But it is a mistake to assume that the narrative voice projects confused authorial values. Rather, the dominance of the sentimental mode in this section works as a disguise, a deliberate strategy rather than evidence of a split consciousness, a continuation of the process of dual inscription that is one of the novel's themes. The tension between the image of the silent, devoted woman as the iconizing narrator presents her, and the characters' futures as the plot anticipates them, suggests that Fanny Fern understood how to manipulate her society's conventions at the same time that she was determined to change them. This scene comforts the reader hesitant to endorse a heroine who has learned to live, and speak, for herself – like *The Knickerbocker* reviewer, whose reading allowed him to "infer . . . although this last is not very explicitly stated" that the "poor widow finally succeeded . . . in winning . . . a husband."[25] This reader is processing *Ruth Hall* through the Cinderella paradigm, assuming that the ending the cultural plot – the plot suggested by the narrator's sentimental language – denotes as "happy" will in fact transpire. But the novel's actual plot implies that Ruth has chosen a future in which she will be both self-supporting and outspoken. For all her indulgence in a day of nostalgia in the graveyard, Ruth is no longer silent, and the plot suggests that her next performance in a wifely role will be when she is dead. Meanwhile Ruth clearly anticipates a new life for herself and her children. By the end of the story, *Ruth Hall* has inscribed a new woman, one who will write her own story rather than allowing it to be written for her.

5

EXTENDING AND SUBVERTING: THE ICONOGRAPHY OF HOUSES IN THE DESERTED WIFE

The Deserted Wife, by Emma Dorothy Eliza Nevitte (she called herself E.D.E.N.) Southworth, is a spiritual autobiography; Southworth's presentation, in her thirty-first year, of her own life to her readers. Like *Queechy,* it is a fictionalized record of its author's tribulations after losing the protection of the man she expected to support her. Unlike *Queechy,* it grants its heroine rewards compatible with her experience. Southworth employs the standard cover story of loss and retrieval, but she is far more skeptical of male strength, and far more confident in female talent, than any of the writers we have seen so far. Southworth was intensely, even obsessively, concerned with revising the image of women in the public imagination, and *The Deserted Wife* transcends fictional autobiography to become spiritual *bio*graphy, the story of the nineteenth-century American woman in her imaginative quest for self-determination.

Southworth herself *was* a deserted wife. Married in 1840, at the age of twenty-one, she followed her husband to Wisconsin only to return to Washington, D.C., four years later, with one small sickly child and another on the way. According to her later letters, Frederick Southworth "abandoned us and went to Brazil" after her grandmother's husband refused to help them.[1] Friendless and penniless, Southworth taught school, cared for her house, nursed her children, and wrote fiction, beginning by publishing short stories in *The National Era* in 1845 and working up to an exclusive contract for the serialization of her novels with Robert Bonner's *New York Ledger* in 1856.[2] The years between were often desperate. In a brief autobiographical sketch written for John Hart's *The Female Prose Writers of America* Southworth remembered that "My time was passed between my housekeeping, my school-keeping, my child's sick-bed, and my literary labours. . . . It was too much for me. . . . Still I persevered. I did my best. . . . Yet neither child, nor school, nor publisher received justice."[3] Nevertheless, the end was triumphant; when *Retribution,* her first book, was published (serially in 1849; in full in 1850),

> Friends crowded around me – offers for contributions poured in upon me. And I, who six months before had been poor, ill, forsaken, slandered, *killed* by sorrow, privation, toil, and friendliness [sic] found myself born as it were into a new life; found independence, sympathy, friendship, and honour, and an occupation in which I could delight. All this came very suddenly, as after a terrible storm, a sun burst.[4]

This journey – from desperation to delight, poverty to prosperity, dependence to independence – is recorded in Southworth's second book, *The Deserted Wife* (1850).

Briefly, *The Deserted Wife* is about four women, each of whom experiences a period during which she is left "unprotected," that is, without the active guidance of a parent or male protector. Hagar Churchill, the central protagonist and heroine of the tale, is Southworth's spiritual double; thin, dark, sallow – the antitype to beauty in nineteenth-century American culture – she is clearly patterned from Southworth's memories of her childhood self: "At the age of six, I was a little, thin, dark, wild-eyed elf, shy, awkward and unattractive," she recalled.[5] Hagar is also high-strung, passionate, jealous, and untrusting. After she marries – a step she takes with much trepidation – she commits herself to her husband; having let him become "every thing to her,"[6] she becomes passionately jealous of her cousin Rosalia, a lifelong rival. When her husband deserts her – leaving her alone with twin daughters and an as yet unborn son – she refuses to divorce him (Emma Southworth was granted a bill of divorce but apparently never acted on it).[7] Like Southworth, Hagar and her children pass a winter of despair, destitute and alone. Unlike Southworth, Hagar cannot teach. But she can sing. Revisioning her own relatively private career as a writer in terms of the very public career of a singer, Southworth makes her fictional heroine an international star. By the time Hagar has become rich and famous, her husband has repented his folly. By the time she has conquered her passions, he has conquered his pride. They are reconciled, and the novel – with Southworth's fantasy (she and her own husband were never reconciled) – ends.

But this sketchiest of summaries does not and cannot do justice either to the complications of the novel's plot or the complexity of its theme. Reaching well beyond Southworth's own fantasies, the iconography of Southworth's text lends it a wide-reaching cultural significance. A "domestic" novelist, that is, one whose subject is women and their lives (lives which the culture, not the writers, defined as essentially domestic), Southworth first deliberately thematizes the nineteenth century's association of women and houses, thus turning an icon endemic in her society into a problematic in her text. A writer committed to shifting popular images of women from the nineteenth century's valorization of the "Angel in the House" – passive, obedient, and happy to be defined by others – to a recognition of women's talents for active self-determination, Southworth then fuses domestic imagery to a narrative framework evoking ancient Western regeneration myths. Imbued with Romantic concepts of alienation and redemption, she finally casts the story of her heroine within the paradigm of the spiral return. Her use of a female protagonist as the "hero" of her own quest – the regenerator of her life, lands, and people – demonstrates Southworth's conscious effort to change readers' perceptions of women's capacities for realizing active power. To this end she simultaneously exploits, extends, inverts, and subverts popular images of women and the kinds of power they wield.

Like the other novels we have examined, *The Deserted Wife* has a "cover" story, the story of a woman who, moving out from the circle of male protection, ultimately and happily returns to it. Like Catharine Beecher's introduction to her *Woman Suffrage and Woman's Profession*, Southworth appears to set forth her themes in her preface to *The Deserted Wife*. Unlike *Retribution* (1849) or *The Mother-in-Law* (1851), her first and third novels, *The Deserted Wife* does not seem to have been serialized before publication. By the time it appeared, both *Retribution* and *The Mother-in-Law* had appeared in *The National Era*, and Southworth's reputation for excess was beginning to be established. The Preface to *The Deserted Wife* functions to deflect readers' initial attention from that excess, to set up an interpretive framework directing readers to perceive the novel as an argument against divorce, an exploration of its causes, and a call for better physical education for young women.

"In no other civilized country in the world is marriage contracted, or dissolved, with such culpable levity as in our own," she begins, and proceeds to analyze "the *causes* and the means of *prevention*, of unhappy marriages." After listing Americans' failure to "impress the duty of PRUDENCE . . . FIDELITY . . . [and] FORTITUDE," she claims that

> but it is PHYSICAL EDUCATION, in its relation to the happiness of married life, that I wish to discuss. . . . no moral education can be completely successful, unless assisted and supported by a good physical training. . . . A girl cannot be a useful or a happy wife, and she cannot make her husband and her children happy, or even comfortable, unless she be a healthy woman. . . . American children [grow up sickly and marry]. They cry out in their agony for separation, divorce, for reform in social laws, when the truth is, no reform would cure their evils without a reform in their personal habits; such a reform as would give health, consequently good humor, and lastly happiness.[8]

In her search for analogies, the author introduces the idea of the questing knight: "In the old times of chivalry, a knight must have proved his prowess before he could successfully aspire to the hand of his lady-love. The days of knight-errantry are long past, but in the age of man, or of the world, the days of moral warfare are never over . . ." (27). Throughout this introduction, Southworth argues from a conservative stance, implicitly drawing on her readers' prior acquaintance with arguments against divorce and social legislation in general, and substituting personal responsibility (here even more depoliticized by being projected as defects of the body) for social.

But physical health figures little, if at all, in the novel itself, and the issue of divorce occupies a very minor place. Although Hagar does refuse her deserting husband a divorce, does win him back in the end, and does appear to give up her career, these are actually minor aspects of the novel, structurally subordinate to their thematic antithesis: Hagar's growth into a thoroughly self-reliant woman who, were it not for the demands of the cover story, has little need for a husband (especially one like Raymond) at all. Raymond deserts Hagar because he thinks he wants to marry Rosalia who, it transpires, is his sister and therefore not marriageable anyway; and Hagar, who knows him better than he knows himself, does not refuse him a divorce; she only demands that he wait until a year has passed. In fact, in the novel itself, the question of divorce is overshadowed by Hagar's growth in the absence of a male protector, a theme clearly echoing Southworth's own discovery, after her desertion, that she could succeed without a husband. As she put it in her autobiographical sketch

> That night of storm and darkness came to an end, and morning broke upon me at last – a bright, glad morning, pioneering a new and happy day of life. First of all, . . . my 'life sorrow' [i.e., the fact of having been deserted] was, as it were, carried away, or *I* was carried away from brooding about it. Next, my child, contrary to my own opinion and the doctor's, got well. Then, my book, written in so much pain, published besides in a newspaper . . . accepted by the first publishing house in America . . . and subsequently noticed with high favor. . . .[9]

These lines record a woman's breakthrough into consciousness of her own capability – her ability not only to mother and to write but to succeed in the public arena and to make money, and influential friends, by doing so.

Despite having only a tenuous relationship to the novel's plot, Southworth's preface serves two interrelated functions. First, it deflects readers' attentions from her heroine's power; and second, it reshapes readers' perceptions of the stylistic flamboyance for which Southworth was roundly criticized in the press. As Baym notes, typical of early reviews of Southworth's work was the tart remark by *The Literary World* that *The*

Deserted Wife "sacrifices probabilities to the intense. . . . We cannot help thinking that our estimable authoress has lived more in the world of fancy than in the world of realities."[10] By suggesting that *The Deserted Wife*'s major theme explores the causes of divorce, Southworth attempts to gain a place for her novels within respectable – and didactic – literature, to redeem them from the onus of having first appeared in newspapers and from the charges of artificiality leveled against them.

Her success is evident in the shift in critical perspective documented by Nina Baym in her reception study of antebellum fiction, *Novels, Readers, and Reviewers.* As Baym notes, reviewers first criticized Southworth's flamboyant writing, then, perceiving it as the basis of her popularity, praised it.[11] But reviewers not only changed their perceptions of Southworth's style. In addition, they began perceiving a moral element in the work: In its review of the 1855 edition, *Godey's* held that *The Deserted Wife*'s exploration into the causes of divorce combined "the strongest incentives to purity and forbearance, with the most elevated sentiments of love and constancy."[12] "Morally," this review began, "this is a most beautiful and instructive novel. . . . We greatly approve of her views in the Introductory chapter on the subject of 'marriage and divorce.'" This review focuses so much on the Preface that it is open to speculation whether the reviewer had read the rest of the novel. In any case, the deflecting purpose of the Preface succeeded. Readers bringing with them schemata devaluing divorce eventually came to see the novel as contributing to public morality. Years later Southworth recorded that a "Professor Powers," who had been given *The Deserted Wife* by his father, a Baptist minister, had asked her "if it was not a source of great comfort . . . to reflect on . . . the many youths I had taught and hearts I had comforted."[13]

Interestingly, in the few places where Southworth does try to link her story to the declared intention of her introduction, her narrative takes on a didactic cast. Though there are scattered references to the "reader" throughout, in only one extended passage does the narrator actively confront her narratee, engaging her attention by addressing her directly, fashioning her prose in a distinctly oratorical pattern, and directing her auditor's attention to her interpretation of the text. At the crisis of the story, just before Raymond deserts with Rosalia, the narrator stops the narrative flow to summarize the action, freezing her scene as she evaluates where it – and she – stands.

The part of the chapter given to this narrative analysis is divided into three parts, each serving a specific function in the communication between narrator and narratee. The first sets out the narrator's intentions, establishing her relationship to the narratee and forestalling objections to her interpretive design.

> Three circumstances combined to bring on the catastrophe of this household wreck, three circumstances, reader, that I wish you to notice, as I desire particularly to call your attention here, and now, to the great importance of the formation of character in childhood and youth, and to the awful truth that the blackest treachery, the deepest guilt, the direst misery, the utmost perdition of men and women may sometimes be traced to the smallest, seemingly the most harmless mistakes in the education of boys and girls. Perhaps I have already been tedious upon this subject; perhaps I have dealt "in vain repetitions;" yet, in tracing the rise and progress of a guilty passion, can I be too emphatic in forcing the causes that produced this upon attention? These causes, then, I said there were three that conspired to bring down this impending thunderbolt (391–2).

This narrative confrontation with the reader is more typical of didactic novels than of exploratory. Here the narrator is so impassioned by her subject that she feels compelled to continue, to spell out the problems facing her characters, reminding her readers that the character histories given earlier had a point and that the narrator's purpose in recapitulating them is to help readers prevent themselves from arriving at a similar impasse.

The second part outlines each character's tragic flaws.

> Firstly. Hagar's jealousy. We have seen how inevitably that jealousy sprang from a want of faith that had been chilled to death in her heart by the coldness and neglect of her guardians in infancy. We have seen how that jealousy, by its violence, exasperated the anger of her husband; by its injustice, alienated his affections; by its pertinacity, suggested and kept before him the evil thought until it grew familiar. So much for its baleful effect on Raymond. Its influence on Rosalia may be summed up in a very few words – by manifesting itself in coldness and aversion, it threw the tender-hearted and guileless girl upon the ready sympathy and affection of Raymond for consolation. Do you now see the madness of this jealousy, and its powerful agency in bringing the desolation of heart and home it feared and dreaded?
>
> Secondly. Rosalia's tenderness – tenderness unsupported by strength of principle, heart unprotected by mind. We have seen that this softness was no more nor less than the feebleness of a character enervated by fond and foolish indulgence in her infancy. We have seen . . . We have seen. . . .
>
> Thirdly. The self-indulgence of Raymond. A delicacy cultivated and refined for years into an effeminacy that *seemed* harmless enough, yet that, as time passed, insidiously undermined his moral strength, rendering him daily more averse to self-denial, until he became incapable of self-resistance (392–3).

While the first part of this homily was structured on a repetitive framework expressing the narrator's desires, doubts, and desperation ("I wish," "I desire," "Perhaps I," "but can I be"); and the second essentially outlines the problems; the third part shifts to the characters' alternatives.

> Could either of several good principles now have been brought into exercise, it would have, even *now* arrested the impending catastrophe; could Hagar, by prayer, by effort, have thrown off her jealousy, have practised faith, candor, charity – could she have shown kindness to Rosalia, who was entirely innocent in thought, word, and deed – could she have pitied and forgiven Raymond, who, as yet, was guiltless in act or intention. Or, could Rosalia have sought aid from heaven, and balanced her gentleness upon its feet, by self-sustaining strength. Or, lastly, could Raymond have awakened and aroused his great latent moral force from the bathos of luxury in which it was half-drowned; could he have risen and shaken himself like a lion in his strength, throwing off the moral lethargy stealing upon him; could he have risen as Samson arose in his might, breaking the fetters that bound him, they might yet have been saved (393).

Relying, as she tends to do, on strong parallel structures to strengthen the force of her argument, here the narrator implies that there *are* alternatives – that the wise narratee, seeing herself or himself reflected in the narrator's description, may avoid such a catastrophe.

But the story itself does not show such alternatives. Having fulfilled her didactic duties, the narrator shifts back to her story mode at the conclusion of this third passage, claiming that though "they might yet have been saved," nonetheless "Alas! They seemed all under a spell, while the cloud of destiny came on, and on" (393). Since the whole idea of destiny has already been questioned earlier in the novel, reference to it here should make the reader suspicious of the narrator's intentions. Certainly the shift is a narrative ploy, a way to ease back into the story, but it is also significant because it signals a concomitant shift from the didactic mode – which has occupied some 4 pages of the 530-page novel – back into the exploratory. And the remainder of the story evinces little interest in the question of divorce, or physical education, or any of the other stated concerns of the introduction. It *is* interested in moral inadequacies, but as the basis for moral re-creation rather than as tragic flaws, especially in regard to the heroine of the text. Moreover, the narrator ceases addressing an identifiable narratee as soon as she shifts back to the exploratory mode.

For all its pretensions to moral conservatism, *The Deserted Wife* is actually about women's need to recognize themselves as integral individuals, able to control themselves, to think and act for themselves independently of spousal or social approval, and therefore to recognize their value in and for themselves. During the course of the story Hagar moves from a state of uncontrolled passion and social alienation to a state of controlled passion and social integration. While Hagar's name is clearly meant to signal the concubine Abraham cast out on his wife's bidding, rather than retelling the biblical story of a woman permanently rejected by the established powers, Southworth recasts her Hagar's tale into the story of a woman who returns to become the source of power. When Raymond returns to Hagar at the story's close he returns to a woman who has become the acknowledged leader of the neighborhood, and has earned the right to bear herself regally. Unlike the biblical Hagar, then, this character returns; moreover her return is not to the same place from whence she set forth; rather, it is to a higher status in her moral and marital relationships.

The conceptual difference between Augusta Evans Wilson's Edna, from *St. Elmo,* and Southworth's heroine is crucial here; Hagar Churchill's "journey" demonstrates the emergence of the American heroine into Romantic selfhood, reflecting Schiller's idea of progress through alienation and reintegration.[14] Southworth's sense of triumph about her own accomplishments is thus embodied in *The Deserted Wife,* but the novel transcends spiritual autobiography to become an exemplary narrative designed to teach female readers how to become the heroines of their own lives.

Despite her desire to analyze her characters' defects for her narratee, this narrator does not function like the narrator of a didactic novel. Where the narrator of a didactic novel would shape her entire narrative to illustrate the consequences of her characters' weaknesses, continually engaging the reader's attention in order to point out the relationship between moral inadequacy and divorce, this narrator allows herself to become involved in exploring the psychology the moral flaws reveal. She is, in effect, carried away by her investigation into her characters' psychological makeup, and, following these through her plot, ends up demonstrating not that all moral inadequacies are a priori irremediable, but that some kinds of flaws – especially flaws of will and passion – may result in remarkable virtues. In contrast to heroines of other nineteenth-century women's fiction, especially Gerty, of Maria Cummins's *The Lamplighter,* or Ellen, of Susan Warner's *The Wide, Wide World,* both of whom learn that they must extirpate their will before they can be loved, *The Deserted Wife* explores its protagonist's mastery of self-control, a process that leads to Hagar's judicious use of her will and consequent power over her environment.

In addition to readers searching for portraits of self-creating women, this novel would speak to readers struggling to conform to the social mandate that women not express anger or any other passion. Young Louisa Trumbull, for instance, struggled to control her temper: "I have I think in part at *least* overcome the petulant disposition which I think is my cheif [sic] and principal difficulty," she told her diary. "When I feel angry and ready to give some sharp answer I keep still and do not say a single word. I have found this a very effectual method to conquer my disposition and I shall try and persevere and at length I hope to become a pleasant girl."[15] Similarly, Julia Newbury told her diary in 1869 that "I've made one grand resolution and that is to *hold my tongue*!!!!! It certainly is a 'little member, and kindleth a great fire.' "[16] Novels like *The Deserted Wife* indicate that silence is not the only option for women with "difficult" dispositions, suggesting instead that learning to control passion is one aspect of genuine moral growth, a spiritual expansion seen not as a movement toward simple perfection but toward psychological complexity. To this end the story examines its protagonists' innate natures, the social forces that mold them, and their abilities to break out of those molds. In the process *The Deserted Wife* becomes a story that explores individual women's capacities for independent action and self-creation rather than emphasizing the moral flaws that lead to divorce.

As in *Queechy,* there are historical references that place this story within an American context. Unlike in *Queechy,* however, these are not heroic. *The Deserted Wife* is set in Maryland, and the narrative begins by carefully distinguishing Marylanders from their Northern brethren, an invidious comparison unusual for a Southern writer and an indication of Southworth's thoughtful criticism of the South and its institutions.

> The character of the first settlers of Maryland and Virginia is known to have been very different from that of the Pilgrim Fathers – as opposite as the idle, gay, and dissolute cavalier to the stern, laborious, and self-denying Puritan. Their purpose in seeking the shores of the Western World was also widely different from that of the first settlers of New England – the object of the latter being spiritual liberty; the end of the former, material wealth. And their history . . . has been as broadly diverse. The children of the Pilgrim Fathers have reached the highest seats in the temples of Fame and Fortune – the descendants of the first aristocratic settlers of Maryland and Virginia have seen themselves outstripped in the path of success and honor by the children of the very menials of their father's house.
>
> This is emphatically the case in Maryland. . . . unlike the Pilgrim Fathers they were deplorably destitute of these natural and necessary qualifications for success in a new and unsubdued world (31).

The ancestors of Southworth's protagonists, then, unlike Warner's, are not brave Revolutionary yeomen but improvident gentlemen farmers. From these come the "sterile heath and ruined Hall" that Hagar inherits when the male Churchill line dies out. But Southworth uses the physical elements of Hagar's inheritance in a particularly fruitful fashion. From the image of the decaying house, Southworth builds the dominant metaphorical structure of her text; from the image of the ruined land, she structures a quest for her heroine; against the image of failed male ancestors, she structures a story leading to the conclusion that women will succeed in rebuilding the promised land.[17]

In *The Deserted Wife* houses are metaphors for women's capacities for independence. Part of Southworth's narrative strategy is to project each female character through her association with a particular type of house, each reflecting its owner's abilities – or inabilities – to grow emotionally, to move out from the dependent status of domesticity into the independent status of economic self-support and public action. In this Southworth, like Warner, is drawing on cultural codes that were especially meaningful to her readers. Southworth's substitution of houses for lands in projecting her heroine both acknowledged the domestic ambiance of most nineteenth-century women's lives and reflected the new importance domesticity and domestic architecture had assumed in nineteenth-century culture. In using architectural associations as part of her narrative structure, Southworth was employing imagery that already spoke eloquently to a readership for whom domestic architecture had become an iconographically significant new art, and for whom ever-increasing mobility created a nostalgia for the imaginary virtues of their childhood homes.

Like Andrew Jackson Downing, the popular American architect whose *The Architecture of Country Houses* (also 1850) fused architectural and moral concerns, Southworth sees her characters' dwellings as reflections of their abilities. But where Downing's houses reflect their male owners' public (that is, financial) success, Southworth's also reflect her female owners' mental and moral worth. Both, for instance, see vine-clad cottages as signs of a female domain, as houses that exhibit the domestic intimacy of devoted mothers and daughters. But Southworth subverts the ideological assumptions of this popular image even while she exploits it, evoking images of rustic maternity only to then question the moral and intellectual capacities of women whose primary function is to make a nest. Similarly, while Downing praises villas for fostering ". . . the development of the intellectual and moral nature which characterizes the most cultivated families,"[18] in novels like *The Mother-in-Law: A Tale of Domestic Life* (1851)[19] Southworth portrays the ruthlessness which may also characterize the owner of a prosperous house. Knowing that power – visibly manifested in opulent homes – comes from mastery of the public, not the private, sphere, Southworth reserves mansions as the rewards for women for whom nesting is only one aspect of life; who view themselves as multifaceted beings and are courageous enough to exert themselves in their own behalf.

Heroines or villains, Southworth's female protagonists see themselves as movers and shakers. Perhaps their extremes are set by *Vivia or, The Secret of Power* (1857), in which the heroine functions as a living symbol of Christian triumph over adversity for all the other characters, and *The Mother-in-Law*, where the villain is a truly terrifying woman whose passion for self-aggrandizement leads her to crush deliberately her daughter's will and attempt to destroy all who thwart her. In both these novels women own houses that reflect their capacities for intellectual, emotional, and economic power regardless of its ethical value. *Vivia*'s heroine and its villain both live in mansions that face each other on hilltops. In *The Mother-in-Law* the horrific mother, Mrs. Armstrong, lives in a grand house, while the heroine who will eventually overpower Armstrong works her way up to become mistress of the mansion that represents Armstrong's nemesis. Both novels feature minor characters who (though they possess the virtues of passivity and self-abnegation that often mark heroines created by less flamboyant writers) in these texts are anti-heroines, occupying small, comfortable cottages which they tend not to leave, and possessing ambitions which they tend not to realize, in large part because they lack the courage to make their wishes come true. Perhaps significantly (and certainly most enjoyably) *The Mother-in-Law* also features one wonderful character, Gertrude Lion, an Amazon who lives in the forest in a large house appropriately named The Lair, and who gets what she wants – even her man –by picking it/him up and carrying it/him off.[20]

Southworth's association of women with houses not only demonstrates her grasp of the culture's obsession with domestic architecture, but also her grasp of its psychological origins and its implicit contradictions. For Gaston Bachelard, a twentieth-century phenomenologist whose analysis of domestic imagery grows out of his own roots in nineteenth-century Romantic philosophy, houses are female, nourishing, "the non-I that protects the I."[21] Southworth comprehends this deep-seated cultural code, correctly reading it as one aspect of the era's search for protection, for a center of stability in an unstable world. But where Bachelard's analysis is male centered, seeing both houses and women as protective enclosures for a subject who cannot, by definition, be female (i.e., the "non-I," one formulation of the classic definition of woman as Other), Southworth focuses on the potential of the "non-I," exploring her capacity to become an "I," a subject in her own right. To do this she must also contend with the contradictory idea that women, the protectors, in turn need protection by men.

In other words, Southworth extends the cultural association of women and houses, only, ultimately, to destroy it; the women on whom her novels focus are those who have learned that they can provide their own protection and, in doing so, also learn their value to themselves, for

themselves, rather than their value only in relation to others. In Southworth's novels "protected" women are women with little egos of their
own; each sees herself as the "non-I" who comforts others – as wife,
mother, and/or neighbor – but rarely as an "I," an integral individual.
Being "unprotected" tests a woman's capacity to develop self-reliance, to
integrate self and world. Those who succeed earn the status of heroines.
In Southworth's novels, then, houses fit the spirits who own them: Her
self-reliant women own mansions, her self-abnegating spirits own cottages. While she begins with the standard plot of the unprotected female,
Southworth's exploitation of the cultural association of women and
houses implicitly recognizes "protection" as the responsibility of women
toward themselves, rather than the function of a parental or male "other."

Historical investigations into the cultural association of women and
houses or Bachelard's topoanalysis (the term he uses to describe the
phenomenological evaluation of the sites of our intimate lives) are not the
only ways to approach Southworth's houses. As we have seen, the first
chapter of *The Deserted Wife* raises the issue of a failed American ancestry
and the problem of inheriting a wasted land, while the Introduction to
the novel evoked the image of knight errantry. In *The Deserted Wife*,
Southworth domesticates and feminizes these heroic references, substituting houses for lands and self-reliance for maidens' hands. Here, the
heroine's house also functions much as do male heroes' lands in regeneration myths. Like the knight whose task is to cleanse himself of sin and his
country of the evils that have laid it waste, in this novel the heroine's task
is first to master herself, then to redeem her house from destruction, and
finally, by example and precept, to revive the community that looks to
her estate for social and moral leadership. But, unlike the neoplatonic
form of these myths, Hagar's story demonstrates a spiral concept of the
return; though she reassumes her domestic role, she does so as wiser,
better, and far more powerful than before.[22] With the personal victory
attending her return goes the larger suggestion that the new redemptor of
the moral landscape may be a woman who has learned the lessons her
ancestors did not.

But Hagar's story comes late in the novel, after Southworth has established the capabilities of all four female protagonists. These are first
paired generationally and then compared and contrasted for tempera-
ment and potential. Three follow the path valued by the culture and
exhibited in most women's novels: They move from stasis (seen in its
gender connection as a state of protection); to discomfort (i.e., lack of
protection); back to stasis (protected once again). Only Hagar returns to a
different kind of stasis, one where she, having established her own capacity to protect herself, has achieved a higher moral, psychological, and
economic state.

In *The Deserted Wife,* Emily May – with Sophie Churchill one of the first, or "mother" generation – exhibits the most conservative attitude toward her own and other women's unprotected state. When her husband, a thoughtful minister many years her senior, dies Emily becomes owner of Grove Cottage, a single-storied house notable for its unimaginative simplicity during an era when even parsons' cottages had at least two stories and as many picturesque angles as their owners could afford.[23] In keeping with the image of the woman in the vine-clad cottage, Emily is the most self-consciously mothering of the women, even delaying a second marriage for ten years so that she can devote all her energies to her son. But Emily is as intellectually and emotionally simple as her house is architecturally. Emily represents women who see themselves as they are seen by their neighbors, and her energies are directed to rearing her son, keeping her house, and maintaining the status quo. Though she is not evil – and Southworth's novels abound in evil characters – her acts have evil effects because her loyalty to local standards prevents her from questioning her community's norms. As long as she is guided by her husband, her natural generosity flourishes (when we first meet her she is outfitting infant Hagar at her own time and expense), but as soon as he dies, her conformity overrides her generosity and makes her cruel to anyone who seems to deviate from local conventions.

Southworth's view of this character is nowhere better exhibited than in an argument between Emily and her son Gusty about Hagar's willingness to receive male visitors even though she lives alone and is therefore "unprotected." Discussing her, Emily remarks that "Hagar has given room for talk by getting into an anomalous position. Why *should* people find themselves in inconceivable situations? *I* never did, yet I was an unprotected girl." To which Gusty replies, "Dear Mother, Lewis Stephen . . . was drowned last summer, in a gale of wind! – Now, why *should* people be drowned in a gale of wind? *I* never was, and *I* have been in a gale of wind." And his mother responds, "Gusty, *hush!* You talk like – like a young man" (507).

Gusty does talk like a young man; he is secure enough to tolerate Hagar's improprieties and to question the rules that suffocate her. In contrast, Emily's inability to sympathize with Hagar stems from the threat Hagar's independence poses to her own security. Like the neatness and constancy of her cottage's decor, the neatness and constancy of her ideas about decorum are her insurance against community censure. Late in the novel, when curious neighbors query her about events at the old Churchill mansion, now Hagar's property, Emily – suddenly echoing the Apostle Peter – not only denies any knowledge of current events but also any connection with either Sophie Churchill or Hagar, formerly her good friends. Reflecting on her disclaimer, the narrator suggests that "In truth the character of Emily had sadly deteriorated since the death of the good and wise old parson, and since her marriage with a weaker, if not a worse man" (567).

Yet Hagar evaluates Emily and her second husband most accurately. "They acted as their nature made it necessary," she tells Gusty, ". . . and their conduct does not grieve . . . me . . . ; perhaps it inspires some contempt" (503). Coming from the person Emily has most wronged, Hagar's remark highlights the difference between the two women. Hagar, born defensive, develops generosity as she matures, while Emily's moral nature withers as she ages. In contrast to Hagar, who has always been her own judge, Emily's sense of self is socially determined. She is the minister's widow, Lieutenant Gusty's mother, the village women's friend; fresh rice cakes and pots of tea are her stock in trade. Consequently she can brook no irregularities in her conduct. As neat and uncomplicated as her cottage, she never even contemplates challenging the rules that circumscribe her life.

Sophie Churchill, the other protagonist of the mother generation, illustrates a more courageous, though no less traditional, response to being "unprotected." Sophie, Hagar's aunt, has been left guardian of Heath Hall as well as of her niece; when she assumes her duties, Hagar is three years old and the Hall a neglected mansion. While Emily, the ideal housewife, is always happy because always occupied, in her youth Sophie is often bored. As her future husband shrewdly notes, her capacities are larger than her employments – she has more talent than mere housewifery can satisfy, but has never learned how to use it. Not until she finds a vocation in service – first as a teacher, then as her husband's nurse – does she begin to utilize both her own and her mansion's capacities. Meanwhile, because the estate is potentially rich, she gains two suitors, both of whom see her as part of her inheritance and speak of (and to) her as if she were a piece of property. Wishing to marry one, but trapped into marrying the other, Sophie is presented with marriage as the end to her freedom, a forced mating with the Reverend John Huss Withers, a man who has charmed the neighborhood but in whom Sophie correctly detects cruelty.

Clearly, the intertextual context of this aspect of *The Deserted Wife* is the Gothic romance, with Sophie the victimized female. But again, as with Emily in her cottage, Southworth exploits a popular image only to question its validity. Here, she suggests that in fact women – even women in novels – need not marry ogres unless, at some level, they choose to do so. After Sophie realizes that she is in fact going to marry Withers, "she sat there with cold clasped hands and rigid features, letting fate encompass her, but feeling in her profoundest soul the painful consciousness that *she herself,* and not another, was making her own misery"

(107). Even though Withers had earlier told Sophie that he was her destiny, "a net of circumstances from whence there is no escape" (93), Southworth suggests that women can avoid such traps if they are brave enough to defy the men who set them and the communities that permit them to do so.

Lacking that courage, Sophie finds there are other ways to control her "destiny." Her "courtship" – disguised as pastoral visits by the Reverend Withers, who knows she cannot refuse to admit her minister – is conducted in one of the Hall's few habitable rooms, a parlor cheerfully papered with scenes from Fox's Christian Martyrs. Sophie studies the wall to avoid looking at Withers, often finding herself in deep contemplation of the sacrifice of St. Petronella, an early Roman martyr who died in Christ after resisting a Count Flaccus's efforts to make her marry him.[24] Sophie does not successfully resist her Count, but she does finally "escape" the fate marriage to Withers spells, by secularizing religious transcendence; she becomes a willing sacrifice, a mother/saint who turns her house into a hospice and herself into its mother superior. Informed that Withers is mad, and that she can have her marriage annulled, she embraces rather than rejects the marriage bond, claiming that "The Lord has given me something to do, for His sake, and endowed me with strength to do it . . . to dress the wounds of this poor warrior . . . to raise and nurse him back to health . . ." (128). Sophie thus gains control of Withers through a process Helen Papashvily, discussing the novels of Caroline Hentz, describes as the phenomenon of the "mutilated male."[25] In becoming Withers's loving and forgiving nurse, Sophie gains control of the relationship, making her hitherto useless house into a womb wherein she can nourish her child/man. In the process she changes from a victim – "a trembling, shrinking, suffering victim, offered in *useless, objectless* sacrifice," to a victor – "a cheerful self-possessed human soul, who had solved the problem of her destiny, and held the answer in her hands" (130).

Through the spiritual inversion of her relationship with the man who owns her, Sophie creates a viable selfhood; though the outward circumstances have not changed (Withers still abuses her during his manic spells) she moves from purposeless to purposeful self-sacrifice, a mother, who, having no children of her own, makes her husband into her child and her house into a structure to protect him. His rehabilitation becomes the object of her existence and compensates for her lost freedom. By transforming the outlines of her circumstances, then, she transcends her plight, much as the martyrs on her wallpaper transformed their earthly tortures through faith in an invisible God. She and Withers keep Heath Hall until his death eight years later, managing only nominal improvements, but at least halting its deterioration. Like the Hall, Sophie's voluntary martyrdom is a holding action against disaster; her control over

Withers illustrates one way a woman can buttress her sense of self against a "protector" whose goal is to destroy her.

Emily and Sophie, then, are the mother generation, women who see themselves in terms of their nurturing functions and who achieve limited success in the novel's fictional world. But they are the precursors of Hagar and Rosalia, the latter the positive and negative exemplary heroines of this text. In addition to rearing Gusty (Emily's biological son) and Raymond (Withers's son by his first wife), Emily and Sophie also rear Hagar, who is Sophie's niece, and Rosalia, who they think is Sophie's niece as well but who actually turns out to be Raymond's sister. The plot and theme thicken as the younger generation matures, and Southworth's inversion of some of the culture's most dominant gender-based stereotypes doubles its force.

One cultural code Southworth is at pains to destroy is the character distinction between dark and fair women. As Leslie Fiedler pointed out, in nineteenth-century American fiction dark women tend to lose out in the marital struggle, while their fair sisters marry the heroes.[26] In *The Deserted Wife* Southworth exploits and subverts these images much as she exploits and subverts the association of women with houses. Blond, blue-eyed Rosalia, for instance, is the protagonist who best fits the culture's image of the ideal female child, endearing herself to everyone but Hagar, who – rightly – regards her as a threat to her own tenuous security. Introduced to Heath Hall as Sophie's orphaned niece, Rosalia's appealing ways become part of the feminine "cure" for Withers's malady. Southworth, however, inverts the culture's values, showing that Rosalia's power is also her great weakness. Though she may fit the mold of true womanhood, she does not qualify for heroism; Rosalia is not made of valiant stuff. Because she craves love, responding to its slightest sign, she has no foundation for an independent ego and is incapable of discriminating between love objects.

Southworth turns these character defects into plot material: Rosalie is the only character in the novel not to have a home of her own. In addition, she is the female most needing protection. As Rosalia confesses to Hagar late in the novel, in her childhood she loved *everyone:* "the poor old negroes . . . the blind horses, and the crippled children, just as warmly as I loved you, . . . and Gusty, and Sophie . . ." (574–5). Rosalia's sense of self is so impoverished that she can only see her own image if it is reflected in the eyes of those who claim to love her. For instance, when Hagar and Raymond both neglect her after their marriage, she "grew . . . dejected, – pining for the love, the tenderness . . . which was the great necessity of her life; without which she could not exist" (387). When Raymond begins to pursue her, she naively receives his advances as if they were the attentions of a devoted relative to a deserving child, and when she realizes that his intentions are sexual, she submits, feeling herself "in the power of a will stronger than my own" (574–5). Because she does not have the power to say no – or even to imagine that she could do so – she is the most dangerous of the novel's four women, both to herself and the others.

Perhaps her insubstantial self-image is the reason why Rosalia is only seen in other people's houses. Since Southworth's women own houses proportioned to their capacities for growth in power and control, it is logical that a girl deficient in ego would also be without a home of her own. Certainly she is the only woman in the novel to be projected as psychologically stunted, a defect attributed as much to Sophie's neglect of her during Withers's illness and her years at a young ladies' boarding school as to having been universally indulged. Her education having left her "tender and defenseless as the conservatory exotic," she is unable to make moral decisions: "Had Rosalia's intellect and conscience, her moral accountability for the use of time and talent, been cultivated in the same proportion as her sensibilities and affections, she would not have been thrown thus helpless upon the tenderness and sympathy of others; she would have possessed a self-sustaining principle, would have found occupation in mental resources . . ." (390–1). In other words, a woman's moral education should teach her to rely on herself, so that she will not feel obliterated if affection is denied her. To be self-sustaining is to be a morally active agent.

Interestingly, since Rosalia does not possess this principle, Southworth does not hold her morally accountable, treating her as if she were an unfortunate child, always needing care. One reason she does not develop a moral system of her own may be the inconsistency in moral standards to which she is exposed. Because she lives first with her mother, then with Sophie and Withers, then with Emily May, then at a boarding school, and finally with Hagar and Raymond, consistency – whether of people, values, or location – is not a part of her experience. Lacking her own source, her own place to return to at her own volition, Rosalia is far from the centered, morally active woman Southworth values. She is not called to account for herself until after she runs away from Raymond – who has coerced her into going to Italy with him – and hides in the Court of a powerful Duchess who protects her.[27] By the time she finds out that Raymond is her brother, she has developed enough self-reflection to reevaluate her conduct in the past and to recognize her responsibility for her future.

Marrying Gusty (the one honest, if comic, male in the novel), and inheriting enough money to allow him to buy a small estate, she achieves a "happy" end to her state of unprotection, but not a heroic one. One sign of her low status in Southworth's system of values is the fact that she must marry to find a permanent home. Rosalia is a pawn to be won by others' wills; she has none of her own. As a woman who owns neither herself nor her house, she represents the antithesis to the heroine in *The Deserted Wife*.

Emily's, Sophie's, and Rosalia's responses to being "unprotected" are the backdrop to Hagar's, a woman who learns to depend on her own resources and who grows to fit her mansion. Unlike the others, Hagar is a born alien; ugly by conventional standards, she is also extremely sensitive to any apparent rejection. In addition, she is a far more complex character than her foils, a compound of conflicting loves and hates; proud, passionate, and wilful. Most of her battles are fought on two fronts: with people who try to circumscribe her activities, and with her own passions, which overwhelm her reason and complicate her difficulties. While neither Emily nor Sophie ever really questions her own assumptions, and Rosalia realizes her failings only at the end of her adventures, Hagar battles with herself throughout. Here, too, Southworth consciously works with established cultural codes. First, she extends the character of the "dark lady" of American fiction, making Hagar wilful and passionate. Whereas most dark ladies – Cooper's Cora Munro, for instance, or Southworth's own Juliette Summers, in her first novel, *Retribution* (1849) – who do not renounce their passions are not suffered to live, in *The Deserted Wife* Southworth's heroine not only lives but prospers, honing her passions and learning to use them for her own benefit. Southworth's heroine differs from her contemporaries in that, for her, self-mastery leads to self-knowledge and independence, rather than to submission and self-abnegation. While other novelists' heroines – Fleda Ringgan is perhaps the best example – are left blissfully yielding all responsibility for their lives to Jesus and a strong, authoritarian husband,[28] Southworth's heroine is left self-supporting, mistress of her house, and conquerer of her husband's will.

Because she transforms herself and returns to transform her environment, Hagar is also projected as a classically mythic heroine, perhaps best understood as one manifestation of the hero in Joseph Campbell's *The Hero with a Thousand Faces*. The mythic aspect of Hagar's adventures may also suggest a clue to Southworth's popularity. For myths appeal to our deepest consciousness, our sense of the relationship between self and world; and if we add, to our understanding of the function of myth, Bachelard's suggestion that images of houses appeal to our deepest sense of selfhood, we have a structure to explain the significance of Hagar's quest. When Hagar undergoes a transformation that leaves her firmly in possession of herself, her house, and her destiny, readers respond as though to a personal triumph, an imaginative retrieval of our own sources of identity and a projection of our own abilities to triumph over adversity.[29] And when Hagar returns to redeem her neighborhood, female readers, at least, can read in her act the possibility for matriarchal leadership.

When Hagar inherits Heath Hall it is badly deteriorated, having seen only a brief revival during Withers's few productive years. After his death and Sophie's remarriage, it is left to the wind and rain. Like the land of the Fisher King in the primal myth of regeneration,[30] the Hall's condition represents the condition both of Hagar's spirit and of her power (as owner of the neighborhood's dominant estate) to influence the moral level of her community. Her heroic task, then, is first to conquer the passions that alienate her, then to reconstruct the Hall, and finally to revive the degenerated neighborhood.

Perhaps the hardest task Hagar faces is to learn how much of her difficulties are caused by herself, and how much by the cruelties of others. Her own nature is as much her enemy as her salvation. While Rosalia yields to those she loves, Hagar possesses and demands; consequently Rosalia has often been granted the right to be cuddled and comforted by the kitchen fire, while Hagar has been banished to the chill of a cheerless attic. In these as in many instances, Hagar often inspires the harsh treatment she receives. Having always had Sophie to herself, for instance, Hagar "conceives" jealousy of Withers shortly after he and Sophie marry, while her foster mother is too busy to attend to her. Even though Sophie subsequently returns to her, Hagar never forgives both adults for their "neglect." In addition she and Withers have a tempestuous relationship, born as much from her fierceness as from his sporadic madness. Left to her own devices, especially during the periods when Sophie turns Heath Hall into a nursing home for Withers, "the wild child took to the wild scenes of nature" (148), where she lives out her "fiery blood" in communion with the equally fierce animal world. Similarly, although in later years her husband is by far the most blameworthy partner in the failure of their marriage, her jealousy triggers his interest in Rosalia, and her inability to control her passions helps drive him toward the mild, even-tempered girl.

On the other hand, Hagar's griefs are not altogether her own fault. When Raymond urges her to marry him, she responds that "my experience has so schooled me, that I am afraid to launch my happiness in the uncertain seas of other hearts" (226), a fear subsequently justified when she does. Shortly after the ceremony she observes that "it was strange, queer – a few words had been pattered over by a fat old gentleman in a gown; and lo! all their relations were changed. It was curious; her very name and title were gone, and the girl, two minutes since a wild, free maiden, was now little better than a bondwoman; and the gentle youth who two minutes since might have sued humbly to raise the tips of her little dark fingers to his lips, was now invested with a lifelong authority

over her" (247). Certainly the "gentle youth" sheds his disguise as soon as
the fatal words are pledged; he is his father's son, and his goal is to take
Hagar away from the Hall to his own smotheringly overrefined villa,
where he tries to strip her of everything that she values as her own. But
unlike Sophie, Hagar fights, insisting that "I will not let your cold,
damping, implacable will extinguish my life and soul. . . . *I* have a will!
and tastes, and habits, and propensities! and loves and hates! yes, and
conscience! that all go to make up the sum total of a separate individuality
– a distinct life! for which *I alone* am accountable, and *only* to God! . . ."
(299).

Hagar is the only female character in *The Deserted Wife* to respect her
own imperatives. When she is presented with the classic dilemma of
married heroines – to submit or to resist – she resists, rejecting Sophie's
lessons about the usefulness of submission. Despite her filial devotion to
Sophie, she refuses to take her maternal advice or to see her as a role
model, even when Sophie's way seems to offer the only solution. For
instance, when Raymond tries to send their twin babies out to nurse so
that he can monopolize Hagar, Sophie uses all her experience with Withers to coax, flatter, and cajole Raymond into bringing a nurse into the
house instead. Since Raymond was using Hagar's maternal love as a
weapon in his battle to crush her, Sophie's victory is an important one.
But Hagar is too proud to manipulate her man, refusing to compromise
and insisting that shifting houses – from her own to Raymond's – does
not also mean shifting responsibility for her life. Increasingly obstinate,
thin, and haggard from anxiety and a new pregnancy, she withdraws
from the fray when she perceives Raymond pursuing Rosalia. Thus she
leaves an open field for Raymond to fall in love with their innocent and
pliant guest.

Hagar's transformation begins when Raymond accepts a post in Italy,
leaving Hagar and her children behind but coercing Rosalia to join him.
Discovering that he has left her destitute, Hagar quits his house and
returns to Heath Hall, now a ruin surrounded by a fragmented and
intolerant neighborhood. There, faced with poverty; with three children,
all under three; with the Hall in ruins; unable to sew for a living and
without enough education to teach (because in her youth she had refused
to study), Hagar passes a bitter, lonely winter, a season made worse by
her neighbors' self-righteous hints that they know her husband has deserted her and that they do not approve of her receiving visits from men.

But Hagar's nadir precipitates her rebirth, and her choice of a career
recapitulates the development of her independence. During her brief
marriage she had cultivated her voice, at first because Raymond liked to
hear her sing. Failing "entirely," in the parlor *lieder* he preferred, however,
as her marriage deteriorated she had

abandoned the seemingly vain attempt to make her music agreeable in the drawing-room. She cultivated the art – *her* art by vocation and adoption – with all the passionate enthusiasm of her ardent nature; it became her solace. . . . at length her soul began to struggle for freer, fuller utterance – for the revelation of its *own* individual life and love – and Hagar became a poet and a musician – . . . at last she attained the power of revealing her *own* poetry – breathing her *own* music (374–5).

As she struggles to free herself from the confines of a restricting marital mode, so she struggles to free herself from the confines of a restricting musical one. Now she determines to make this, her sole talent, be her livelihood. Her decision is made from her sense of pride in herself, not because she feels forced to compromise her name for pecuniary concerns. "There was nothing in Hagar's pride to prevent her from embracing this career – her pride was strictly *personal*. She could not have been proud of her descent, of wealth, had she possessed it, of social position, or of any external circumstance whatever – but she was proud of herself, that self that came alone into the world, and would go alone out of it" (503).

Hagar's triumph over her circumstances is at once fantastic (a successful career as a singer is not an option open to most deserted women) and sternly realistic (her success depends on her at last conquering her own nature). Like Edna Earl or Ruth Hall, she buries herself in her work until she becomes mistress of her art. Unlike Wilson or Fern – or Cather, whose *Song of the Lark* would, much later, also chronicle the slow transformation of a country girl into an opera singer – Southworth does not take her reader through Hagar's learning process, presenting it instead as a *fait accompli*. Nevertheless, Hagar's success suggests how strongly Southworth felt about the importance of lone women discovering that they can build their lives by their own efforts.

Mary Kelley has carefully examined the economic motives for the careers of many nineteenth-century American women writers, and has noted their ambivalence about their exposure to the public eye.[31] Certainly poverty initiated Southworth's career, as well as her fictional heroine's, and her reluctance to establish a "tough" (i.e., male) business relationship with Robert Bonner kept Southworth herself in a state of relative dependency.[32] But it is interesting that in this novel Southworth chooses *such* a very public career for her heroine. Unlike Augusta Evans Wilson, who in *Beulah* as well as *St. Elmo* makes her heroines teach and write for their livings, or Susan Warner, who in *Queechy* has her heroine farm and write, Southworth's heroine is assigned a profession unparalleled in its public exposure. While the author shows her insecurity about Hagar's profession by her narrator's insistence on the rectitude of Hagar's private life, she also does not hesitate to portray her heroine as the focus of public attention: showing Hagar standing alone on a stage, wearing an elaborate headband and bracelets fashioned in the shape of serpents, and charming the multitude with her voice. This outcast Hagar then, is also Eve, a progenitrix who embraces, controls, and flaunts her temptations. As such, she is Southworth's model for a woman who can revel in her independence.

Significantly, the epigram heading the chapter that describes Hagar's decision to launch her own career, a chapter entitled "Hagar's Resurrection," quotes a poem by Frances S. Osgood[33] that is a feminized version of Emerson's call for solitude as the necessary environment for mastery of self and other.

> Once more alone – and desolate now for ever,
> In truth the heart whose home was once in thine;
> Once more alone on life's terrific river,
> All human help, exulting I resign.

> At last I task the joy of self-reliance;
> At last I reverence calmly my own soul;
> At last I glory in serene defiance
> Of all the wrong that could my fate control (499).

To prepare herself for her career Hagar leaves Heath Hall, taking her babies and going to New Orleans, where she "sinks . . . for at least a year or two, her old in her new existence" (505).

Literally, she breaks all her ties to absorb herself in her new environment; mythically, she embarks on the journey to find the Holy Grail of self-reliance, a journey that entails leaving the old self/house before returning to fully possess and renew it. Clearly, self-mastery is part of her trial, the discipline that completes her conversion. After a time she emerges, famous as Mrs. – ,

> a lady as remarkable for the stern asceticism of her private manners as for the brilliant success of her public career. Hagar's greatest motive . . . had been to achieve, by the only means in her power, an independence, and she had made a resolution of reserve, self-denial, and solitude, as the only way of reserving her from falling into her besetting sins of wildness and reckless gaiety, and towards which everything in her present life would conspire to draw her (505–6).

Seen mythologically, during this period Hagar conquers her own demons; seen pragmatically, she matures, learning circumspection and self-control, not in order to please Raymond but to further her own career; seen within the context of nineteenth-century ambivalence about women's public careers, she balances the flamboyance of her appearance on stage by the reticence of her domestic life. Most importantly, it is clear that the success of her quest rests on self-control, self-reliance, courage, and hard work.

The significance of Hagar's resurrection is not that she becomes famous but that she does not allow the demands of the world to destroy her
sense of self, any more than she allowed Raymond to do so. Rather,
struggle with the world refines her, and she emerges confident and triumphant. As a sign of her success she rebuilds Heath Hall, sending
German laborers from abroad to reconstruct it; prying neighbors find
"the foundation of the house relaid anew" (568). Hagar then returns to
the source of her identity and reconstructs her own life, which, like the
house, rests on a new foundation. Now, Hagar is truly mistress of her
property, an estate where "the ruin, the desolation, was redeemed, the
wilderness reclaimed and 'bloomed and blossomed like the rose'" (570).
Finally, in her new home, Hagar herself blossoms; secure in her independence, she can finally learn the womanly arts of tears and forgiveness.

But this new woman also understands the emotional revolution her
success has engendered. In accord with the standard plot of male reformation, Raymond returns, repentant. Yet Southworth undermines this
plot even as she exploits it: As Raymond approaches Hagar's brilliantly lit
mansion, the narrator first records that Raymond's emotions were "soon
all merged in one strong feeling – a heart-burning impatience to clasp
Hagar to his bosom." In the next lines, however, she impugns Raymond's
emotional integrity, noting that he also "thought that were he about to
meet [Hagar] in poverty, ill health, and humiliation, he should embrace
her with as *much* affection and *more* self-respect." That is, Raymond is
having difficulty adjusting to the fact that Hagar has clearly gained
hegemony – moral and financial – in their relationship. In addition, the
narrator takes care to tell us that Raymond "had, before leaving the boat,
bestowed the utmost attention upon his toilet. . . . In the grand diapason
of the reconciliation was trilling this one little absurd note" (580–1).
Raymond, in other words, is still a fop, a vain silly man mired in romantic concepts of male dominance, while Hagar (whose attention to her
own toilet is not mentioned) has grown in grace, beauty, and power.

Hagar's response to her meeting with Raymond acknowledges this
change in their relationship. Although she weeps her first tears, nevertheless her joy is diminished by her recognition that "her king – *her* king
[was] discrowned before her" (583). The reference to a discrowned king
may take us back to Southworth's initial reference to Hagar's ancestors;
in discrowning her king, she has made a new American revolution. In
this New World, women are autonomous beings, able to think, fend, and
make decisions for themselves. They also recognize the emotional up-
heaval this new order entails. Hagar's tears signal her recognition that her
victory has sundered her from the ranks of submissive wives; that in
establishing her right to her house/Self she has forfeited the ability to
surrender responsibility for herself to anyone else. In the midst of her joy,

then, Hagar realizes that "though she loved him! loved him! . . . no *worship* mingled with that love!" (583); that is, for her, love for Raymond no longer entertains the notion that he is any way more fit to direct her life than she is herself. To master one's fate, then, means a lifetime of self-reliance; in Southworth's novels, women who earn their freedom do not throw it away when a man comes home to "protect" them.

E.D.E.N. Southworth's novels tend to end happily, and Hagar and Raymond create a relationship that permits their marriage to flourish and their home to become a focus for the revived community. As the story draws to a close we are told that "The Heath is now [a] . . . fertile and productive plantation . . . the seat of elegant hospitality . . . [and Hagar] now in the meridian of her life, and of her well preserved beauty . . ." (585). Significantly, the story closes not on Hagar, but on Emily, owner of Grove Cottage, who is now married to another minister. While Hagar has grown to meet the demands of her life, has become the open-hearted, self-reliant, courageous mistress of a fine mansion, "Emily . . . is still mistress of Grove Cottage, and her husband . . . still pastor of the Church . . ." (586). Unimaginative women are not villains in Southworth's novels, but they remain among the lower orders of humankind. The heroine challenges her fate, conquers herself, creates and controls her world.

Though Southworth caters to the demand that a happy ending entail marriage or reconciliation, *The Deserted Wife* obeys only the letter of that law. The real core of the novel explores women's capacity to grow through their adversities and to use their experiences to mold the world around them. *The Deserted Wife* then, does not take back the subjectivity its heroine earns; rather, though it does not overtly admit as much, it sees her through a Romantic fascination with the fortunate fall. Not many novels about women dared admit they shared that particular Romantic ethos. *The Morgesons,* by Elizabeth Drew Stoddard, is one that does: It, too, features a protagonist who learns from her experiences rather than repudiating them. Though this heroine also marries at the end, and though her previous "adventures" remain wholly within the domestic sphere, she achieves a subjectivity so intense that she may best be seen as an Emersonian consciousness that recognizes its responsibility not only to create itself but to create and maintain its own world.

6

PROJECTING THE "I"/CONOCLAST: FIRST-PERSON NARRATION IN THE MORGESONS

Elizabeth Stoddard's *The Morgesons* (1862) has come in for some extremely respectful attention of late, more notably from Sandra Zagarell and Lawrence Buell, who edited *The Morgesons and Other Writings,* and from Sybil Weir, in an article entitled "*The Morgesons*: A Neglected Feminist *Bildungsroman.*"[1] These critics have pointed out the novel's anomalous position in nineteenth-century women's fiction, especially in its open presentation of female sexuality, its affirmation of a heroine who constantly flouts social rules, and its interest in the isolated consciousness. *The Morgesons* is quite possibly the most radical women's novel to appear in the mid-nineteenth century, and yet it expresses its heresies without ever moving its protagonist, Cassandra Morgeson, out of the domestic sphere. Although her father, too, "fails," she is never left "unprotected," and consequently never has the stimulus to write for publication, start a business, become a singer, or run a farm. Rather, Cassandra's movement of maturation is into the feminine sphere; initially unskilled in *any* art, she is forced by the family crisis to learn how to run the household. What radical possibilities *The Morgesons* offers, then, occur in the psychological rather than the professional aspects of Cassandra's development.

Another marked difference between *The Morgesons* and the other texts we have considered is that the former is narrated in the first person. There is, then, no chance for an omniscient narrator to guide and control readers' interpretations of the heroine's adventures. Given the text's at times extreme thematic radicalism, however, the first-person narration may reflect Stoddard's awareness of how isolated the text's values really were. The narrators of all the other books we have examined could assume that they echoed the value systems of some part of their readership, that they spoke *for* some social body as well as *to* elements of a specific reading community. For example, the narrator of *A New-England Tale* spoke for the liberal branch of nineteenth-century Congregationalist New England, the narrator of *Charlotte Temple* spoke for parents who wanted to see their daughters instructed in filial piety, and the narrator of *St. Elmo* spoke for those people who believed that gifted women should use their talents to help their husbands rather than to gain fame for themselves. Similarly, the narrator of *Queechy* spoke for the religious community that valued the life to come over the temporal life, the narrator of *Ruth Hall* for injured women, and the narrator of *The Deserted Wife* for deserted wives. In contrast to these, the narrator of *The Morgesons* may speak for no one but herself. Seeing through Cassandra's eyes, we evaluate according to her lights, and Cassandra's lights are patently iconoclastic. In writing her own story, however, and taking her readers through the mental exercises necessary to grasp her often oblique prose, Cassandra may also create a new set of values for women's novels and a new kind of narratee to receive them.

The *Morgesons* lacks the narrative irony of *Huckleberry Finn,* but it does feature a considerable amount of narrative ambiguity. There is an indirection to Cassandra's language that has reminded many readers of Emily Dickinson's poetry and has confused them accordingly. In their introduction to the University of Pennsylvania Press edition of *The Morgesons,* Lawrence Buell and Sandra A. Zagarell rightly claim Stoddard's work as an important predecessor of twentieth-century narrative experiments, noting that she "anticipates modern fiction in using a severely limiting mode, with minimal narrative clues (eliminating the 'she said's' as much as possible), minimal transitions, and dramatic, imagistic, and aphoristic impact."[2] As with Dickinson's poetry and Henry James's late novels, newcomers to *The Morgesons* feel that something crucial has been left out; that the dialogue and narrative have not fulfilled expectations the text has created by the fragments of standard plot devices Stoddard employs. We work hard to understand *The Morgesons,* and, as Sybil Weir has shown, in the process discover that beneath the cover story of a girl's movement from undisciplined immaturity to responsible adulthood, from rebellious daughter to virtuous wife, lies an exploration into the nature of female sexuality and the process of self-creation that has not hitherto been undertaken by any female American writer.[3]

Cassandra's first-person narration is intrinsic to this exploration because she is reporting her own experiences in her own voice and from her own heretical point of view. This may be the basis for reviewers' almost instinctive hostility to the book; although most admitted that its writing was "terse," its description "vivid," and "that there [is] freshness and originality in almost every chapter," yet with *Peterson's* reviewer they also complained that "'The Morgesons' . . . belongs to a bad school. Why is it that things which so many reverence are almost continually sneered at?" "If writers cannot introduce tragic interest into their works, without making girls fall in love with other people's husbands, or men desire to marry their own daughters, . . . then it is high time that books without tragic interest had the field to themselves."[4] Readers generally ignored the book – unlike the other novels we have examined, *The Morgesons* did not sell well.[5] Nevertheless, it apparently lingered in some readers' minds: In 1875 Constance Fenimore Woolson, also an American poet and short story writer, wrote that she had been searching for Stoddard's novels, vowing that though they were hard to find "I shall not give up the chase however. I remember them – but wish to re-read them."[6] The late twentieth century is now busy retrieving and rereading *The Morgesons* along with its contemporaries, and finding a new perspective on nineteenth-century women in Cassandra's frank sexuality. The heresies the other texts strive to hide or to devalue, *The Morgesons* takes as its central ideas.

Briefly, the plot is as follows. Cassandra (called Cassy by her family; Cass by others) and her younger sister Veronica live with their parents, Locke and Mary Morgeson, in Surrey, a New England village on a large bay. Both girls are lawless and essentially unschooled; they differ, however, in that Veronica is sickly and inwardly directed, while Cassandra is vibrantly healthy and oriented toward the world. Shortly after the story opens Cass's mother – who wants Cass to understand how her girlhood differs from her mother's – sends her to spend a year with her maternal grandfather, a dour old Puritan tailor, and her Aunt Mercy, a fun-loving but repressed spinster. These two live together in Barmouth, the inland town where Mary Morgeson was reared. Here Cass passes a miserable probation, caught between Grandfather Warren's rigid piety and the taunts of the wealthy girls in the school she attends, who suggest (but never illustrate) that her mother's sexual life had not been unblemished before her marriage.

The dialogue communicating this information is a good example of the indeterminateness of Stoddard's text as well as of its protagonist's wildness. Here, Cass suddenly responds to the cruel snobbery of her new classmates, rising from her seat:

> "I am angry," I said in a low tone, and rising, "and have borne enough."
> "Who are *you* that you should be angry? We have heard about your mother, when she was in love, poor thing."
> I struck her so violent a blow in the face that she staggered backward.
> "You are a liar," I said, "and you must let me alone" (40–1).

Although Cassandra responds as if to a concrete insult, in fact it is never clear what her mother's problem was. Later, Cass's aunt tells her that perhaps her mother will explain some time; for the reader, she never does. The passage serves as a hint, a suggestion only, that Cass's later sexual adventures exhibit a disposition inherited from the female line, much as Jane Elton's virtue was said to be inherited from her mother. But in *The Morgesons,* the connection is never made, leaving readers with the choice of spelling it out themselves or letting it go, a choice, clearly, that will be determined by the particular schema each reader brings to the text.

Certainly a blossoming sexuality accompanies Cass home from Barmouth. Soon after she returns, a distant cousin, Charles Morgeson, appears. He and Cass are instantly attracted to one another, as, in fact, Cass's mother is also to him. He persuades Cass's parents to let her come for a year of "finishing" at the academy in his home town, Rosville. There Cass lives in his house with him, his wife, Alice, and their three children. Through the year she spends with them, sexual tensions between Cass and Charles mount. During this time, Cass also meets Ben Somers, a Harvard student sent to "rusticate" in Rosville for fighting; he originally courts her but, simultaneously becoming aware of the facts that she and Charles are in love with each other and that she has a more passive sister at home, he soon switches his attentions to Veronica. Charles is killed in a carriage accident on the night when their affair would probably have been consummated; Cass, riding with him, is badly wounded and left with facial scars.

Cass returns home. Her mother's health is declining. Nevertheless Cass soon leaves for a third time, going to Belem, Ben Somers's home, to help him plead his suit for Veronica with the Somer-Pickersgills, his proud, wealthy family who disapprove of Cass and her family entirely. There, Cass meets Desmond, Ben's older brother, who – like Ben – is an alcoholic, a disease apparently hereditary in the family. Cass and Desmond are attracted to one another, in part because they share a common history of sexual transgression. However, Desmond refuses to court Cass until he has cured himself of alcoholism, and banishes himself to Spain to accomplish that reform. Meanwhile, on Cass's return home she finds her mother dead, sitting upright in her parlor chair. Shortly after, her father fails, servants are dismissed, and Cass finally realizes that she must take responsibility for the domestic side of the family. In the course of the following year, Ben and Veronica marry; Locke Morgeson's fortunes improve; and Locke marries Alice, Charles's widow, a move Cass considers incestuous. Locke moves to Rosville, Ben and Veronica move to a house of their own, and Cass convinces her father to give her the Morgeson house, where she lives with one servant. Ben's drinking worsens. After two years Des returns, cured, and he and Cass marry. Ben dies of delirium tremens. Veronica has a baby who is apparently an idiot. In the last scene Cass, Veronica, the baby, and Aunt Mercy are in Cass's old room, where Cass looks out at the sea and writes, while the others, their lives ruined, let time drift over them.

Cass and Desmond's marriage, of course, is the most conventional part of this novel, prompting one earlier critic to call it "contrived."[7] It is actually rather less "contrived" than most of the others we have examined; the kind of independence Cass pursues is not antithetical to the kind of life she will lead with Des, whose respect for her strength prompts him to "earn" her by his own efforts, who likes her in part because she is independent and sexually adventurous, and who shows no sign of wanting to run her life for her. Sandra Zagarell has commented on the qualitative differences between Cass's relationship with Charles and her relationship with Desmond, as well as on the difference between Cass's degree of sexual maturity and that of other nineteenth-century heroines of women's fiction.[8] Certainly *The Morgesons* does not use the convention of the marriage ending to retract or deny its protagonist's growth. Even Southworth bowed to the culture's demand for resolution and integration by having her heroine reunite with a man far less worthy than she. In contrast, the marriage that closes *The Morgesons* suggests an almost existentialist response to the world of shifting fortunes and disintegrating families. While the overt stories of the other texts seek to impose, or reimpose, a social–moral–spiritual order that would reverse the movement toward disintegration, *The Morgesons* uses the conventional closure to explore the capacities of individuals to take responsibility for their own lives, outside of any given social framework, and provide their own bulwark against disintegration.

One way Stoddard goes about this is to situate her protagonist within a geographical location that she knows will evoke a specific set of references – a symbolic code – for her American readers, then to proceed to subvert that code. *The Morgesons* is set in New England, a region Southworth characterized as the home of the "Pilgrim Fathers," who came to the New World seeking "spiritual liberty" and whose descendants "reached the highest seats in the temples of Fame and Fortune" (31). But the New Englanders portrayed in *The Morgesons* do not reflect this proud history. The men are merchants and factory owners intent on material profits, not spiritual ones. And the Morgeson family does not trace itself back to any proud ancestor: "The family recipes for curing herbs and hams, and making cordials, were in better preservation than the memory of their makers," Cassandra notes.[9] "They had no knowledge of that treasure which so many of our New England families are boastful of – the Ancestor who came over in the Mayflower. . . . they had no portrait, nor curious chair, nor rusty weapon – no old Bible, nor drinking cup, nor remnant of brocade"(8).

Moreover, the Morgeson family is unreflective as well as rootless: Cass's great-grandfather, "the first noticeable man of the name," was a crusty entrepreneur who bequeathed to his descendants his money and eccentricities but not the consciousness of power underlying most New England dynasties: "Comprehension of life, and comprehension of self, came too late for him to make either of value. . . . the most that could be said of him was that he had the rudiments of a Founder" (9). Cassandra's maternal grandfather is a Calvinist, but one who, as we shall see, illustrates the decline rather than the glory of New England's religious grandeur; moreover, he is also a tailor, a point that, though other girls make her suffer for it during her year in Barmouth, Cass later takes care to mention whenever snobs question her about her antecedents. Cass's portrait shows the Morgesons to be a New England anomaly, a family that does not feel a connection with a past that would root it in time. As with Hagar, this dearth of a proud family history leaves Cass with few guidelines for behavior, isolating her by depriving her of family models. Her lack of historical sensibility serves to cast her morally adrift in a region self-consciously – almost narcissistically – proud of its antecedents.[10]

It was within the permissible boundaries of iconoclasm to satirize local history in mid–nineteenth-century American novels. Devaluing religion was a more serious matter. Both Cassandra and the author evince a lack of religious sensibility that strips *The Morgesons* of conventional morality and is only leavened by the opportunity it provides Cass for displaying her considerable sense of humor. *The Morgesons* exploits its readerships' presumed acquaintance with American religious codes by satirizing the remnants of New England Puritanism extant in the environment in which Cassandra lives. First, religion is at best dysfunctional for Cass and her generation; at worst, as Richard Foster notes, it is repressive.[11] Ignored except as a social obligation by the male line, it has an empty centrality for the female. Cassandra's mother spends hours discussing "the difference between sprinkling and immersion," but Cassandra's opinion of the question is suggested by her names for the disputants: "Brother Thaddeus Turner, pastor of the Congregational Church of Hyena," and "Bother Boanerges of Andover" (6). Her maternal grandfather represents the Calvinism that Cass flatly rejects: A "Puritan, without gentleness or tenderness" (28), he is best remembered for the harsh treatment of his daughters when they were young, and for his coldness toward Cass during the year she spends with him. His house in Barmouth (in Stoddard's biographical life Fairhaven, Massachusetts, but clearly, in this novel, an analogue for Plymouth),[12] the foundation of which rests on a "great rock" (37), reminds Cass of "the casket which imprisoned the Genii" (28), and his religion is as meaningless to her as the long graces he pronounces, during which "not a word . . . was heard; for his teeth were gone, and he prayed in his throat" (30). Calvinism for Cassandra is as Western civilization would be for Ezra Pound sixty years later: old, impotent, "gone in the teeth." Rather than confront it, Cass endeavors to circumvent it; when she hears her Aunt Mercy suggest that she is too young to understand the Law of Transgression, "an acute perception that it was in my power to escape a moral penalty, by willful ignorance, was revealed to me, that I could continue the privilege of sinning with impunity" (21). For Cass, religion is a meaningless ritual having no application to her life.

By detaching Cass from local and religious histories, and by giving her an overtly secular sensibility, Stoddard creates a space around this pro-tagonist that we have seen in no other novel and that is a rarity through-out nineteenth-century American fiction. Unable to appeal beyond her-self for models – unable, that is, to assume that readers will automatically fill in elements of her character from the codes extant in contextual history – Cassandra is of necessity a self-creating protagonist, thrown back on herself to make sense of her life. The fact that she also narrates her own story compounds this necessity. Cass's telling is also her creat-ing; lacking a narrator to guide and interpret the movements of her story, she has the sole responsibility for inscribing herself into her text. Not only does she not speak *for* any segment of her readership, she does not suggest that any agent – such as God – exists to help her make sense of her experiences. Unable to appeal to outside authorities to understand what happens to her, she casts about for means to conceptualize – and therefore concretize – her own experience.

One function of Cassandra's oblique prose style is to illustrate her search for a hermeneutic code, a means of dealing with (conceptualizing, categorizing, hypothesizing, and resolving) the enigmas of her experi-ence. There is a marked difference between Cassandra's recounting of her own intense emotional experience and those of writers who can refer to authority beyond themselves. A more typical response to emotional tur-moil occurs in a letter from a young woman who has been agonizing over her sister's death. "The Captain of our salvation was made perfect through suffering, Ought not we to be willing to suffer?"[13] she con-cludes. This writer can justify her suffering through comparing herself to Christ; the appeal to external models, to someone who has gone through this before, rationalizes her experience. In contrast, Cassandra Morgeson must look *inward* for explanations; find an authority within herself. Clearly, Edna, Hagar, and Ruth also went through this experience, but Cass, because she narrates her own story, details the process far more intimately and with far less ambivalence about her femininity.

At first the effort to develop her own guidelines divides Cassandra, fragmenting rather than integrating her personality. For instance, after she returns home from Rosville, that is, after her near-affair has ended with Charles's death and her physical and psychological scars, she dramatizes her dilemma as a little dialogue with her conscience, a scene that might remind modern readers of Huck Finn's struggle with *his* "sivilized" conscience: "There was a specter," Cass reports, that "I determined to drag . . . up and face. . . ."

> It uncovered, and asked:
> "Do you feel remorse and repentance?"
> "Neither!"
> "Why suffer then?"
> "I do not know why."
> "You confess ignorance. Can you confess that you are selfish, self-seeking – devilish?"
> "Are you my devil?"
> No answer.
> "Am I cowardly, or a liar?"
> It laughed a faint, sarcastic laugh.
> "At all events," I continued, "are not my actions better than my thoughts?"
> "Which makes the sinner, and which the saint?"
> "Can I decide?"
> "Why not?"
> "My teachers and myself are so far apart! I have found a counterpart; but, specter, you were born of the union" (131–2).

Unlike Huck Finn, Cassandra knows that a radical difference exists between her "sivilized" conscience and her heart; when she faces not just her "sin" but her lack of repentance, she recognizes the immense gap between the person who seems to conform to society's mores and the person who secretly questions them. Break the bonds between acts and social judgments, and the individual must learn to judge herself for herself alone. In this first stage of her maturation, Cassandra finds herself broken into a public and private personality, a sneering "conscience" and a seeking self. But from the conflict comes a third "person" – a specter conscience – Cassandra's new awareness of her moral independence.

Stoddard illustrates the development of Cassandra's moral independence by examining how she comes to terms with her own willfulness, one characteristic that links her to other protagonists of women's exploratory novels. Unlike Ellen Montgomery, of *The Wide, Wide World,* who must crush her own will, or Fleda, of *Queechy,* who must disguise her will in velvet gloves, Cassandra's early willfulness is, like Hagar's, projected as leading to responsible adulthood. Stoddard's thematic vehicle for this idea is embodied in the word "possession," a word that recurs regularly in the novel and whose implications range from satanic possession (Cassandra is an imp) to self-possession (Cassandra can determine her own life patterns). Beneath this umbrella concept Stoddard subsumes many of the themes and cultural codes prominent in other exploratory novels: the question of willfulness, the Byronic male, the inheritance of a family history, the assumption of adult responsibility. The several variations on the idea of "possession" enable Stoddard to invert and subvert established codes within the apparent boundaries of a peculiarly New England phenomenon.

In traditional New England history, of course, to be possessed means, finally, to be on the devil's side, to be a party to the principle of disorder. As a child, Cassandra seems to *be* the principle of disorder, living for herself only, "Moved and governed by my sensations" (14). Cassandra introduces this theme in the novel's first line: " 'That child,' said my aunt Mercy, looking at me with indigo-colored eyes, 'is possessed' " (5). By introducing herself through another person's eyes rather than through her own Cass suggests how other people see her: Mercy's referring to her by using an adjective and a common noun rather than her name serves to make her an object rather than a person. The line also suggests that Cass perceives her aunt's displeasure: She characterizes Mercy's eyes as indigo, not the expected blue, dark, quite likely with anger. Still, Cass (here ten years old) is undaunted: She finishes clambering up a bureau by its knobs (the act that occasioned Mercy's rebuke), fetches *The Northern Regions,* and comments on the starving explorers' diets while her elders are discussing church doctrine; pesters her great-grandparents by asking "did Ruth love Boaz dreadfully much," wears her new shoes out into the road "wishing that some acquaintance with poor shoes could see me" (6–7), and leaps off the gate post into the arms of an outraged adult. In her opening self-portrait, then, Cass projects herself as strong-willed, determined, and impetuous.

But Cass's childhood disorderliness is a sign of her developing self-possession. In her early teens she reminds her aunt that "you have always said I was possessed" when Mercy remonstrates with her for flippancy to a minister who had tried to determine the state of her soul. By this time, Cassandra has learned that to be charged with "possession" generally means that she has been either too impetuous, too candid, or both. That her possession is actually self-preservation becomes clear much later, when Ben, who turns his attention to Veronica because he fears Cassandra's strength, charges that she had "almost unsexed" herself in her self-reliance: "unlike most women," he accuses, "you understood your instincts . . . dared to define them, and were impious enough to follow them" (226). Not until Cassandra proves the only character capable of holding the household together after her mother's death and her father's business failures does anyone appreciate her self-assertion. Then Aunt Mercy

> looked at me penitentially. "I wish I could say," she said, "what I used to say to you, – that you were 'possessed' " Now that there is no occasion

for me to comprehend people, I begin to. My education began wrong end foremost" (237).

It has taken Mercy twenty-five years to realize that Cassandra has been right in refusing to be the passive, pious female the culture claims to value.

In the meantime, Cass has learned to see herself, not just as others see her, but through her own emerging sense of self. Experimenting with the effects of her will on the world around her, she discovers that world and with it, her independence. At ten, she records, she has the blind subjectivity of the child, engaged in the moment and oblivious to her environment.

> . . . wherever I was, or whatever I did, no feeling of beauty ever stole into my mind. I never turned my face up to the sky to watch the passing of a cloud, or mused before the undulating space of sea, or looked down upon the earth with the curiosity of thought, or spiritual aspiration. I was moved and governed by my sensations, which continually changed, and passed away – to come again, and deposit vague ideas which ignorantly haunted me (14–15)

Her year in Barmouth teaches her to react and to confront – to be unhappy – but not yet how to creatively control.

> Though the days flew by, days filled with the busy nothings of prosperity, they bore no meaning. I shifted the hours, as one shifts the kaleidoscope, with an eye only to their movement. Neither the remembrance of yesterday nor the hope of to-morrow stimulated me. The mere fact of breathing had ceased to be a happiness, since the day I entered Miss Black's school. But I was not yet thoughtful. As for my position, I was loved and I was hated, and it pleased me as much to be hated as to be loved. My acquaintances were kind enough to let me know that I was generally thought proud, exacting, ill-natured, and apt to expect the best of everything. But one thing I know of myself then – that I concealed nothing; the desires and emotions which are usually kept as a private fund I displayed and exhausted. My audacity shocked those who possessed this fund. My candour was called anything but truthfulness; they named it sarcasm, cunning, coarseness, or tact, as those were constituted who came in contact with me.

Finally, after her near-affair with Charles and her mother's death, when circumstances close about her and it becomes clear that she must take over the family's domestic responsibilities, she has an experience amounting to a vision, "called" by a seaborn "spirit" who awakens her first to herself, then to beauty, and finally to a realization that she can consciously construct her environment as well as blindly confront it.

> One day I went to walk by the shore, for the first time since my return. . . . Picking my way over the beach . . . I reached the point

between our house and the lighthouse and turned toward the sea. . . .
Little pools meshed from the sea by the numberless rocks round me
engrossed my attention. . . . [One] pool showed me the motionless
shadow of my face again, on which I pondered, till I suddenly became
aware of a slow, internal oscillation, which increased till I felt in a
strange tumult. I put my hand in the pool and troubled its surface.
   "Hail, Cassandra! Hail!"
   I sprang up the highest rock on the point, and looked seaward, to
catch a glimpse of the flying Spirit who had touched me. My soul was
brought in poise and quickened with the beauty before me! The wide,
shimmering plain of sea – with its aerial blue, stretching beyond the
limits of my vision in one direction, upbearing transverse, cloud-like
islands in another, varied and shadowed by shore and sky – mingled its
essence with mine. . . .
   "Have then at life!" my senses cried. "We will possess its longing
silence, rifle its waiting beauty. We will rise up in its light and warmth,
and cry, 'Come, for we wait.' Its roar, its beauty, its madness – we will
have – *all.*" I turned and walked swiftly homeward, treading the ridges
of white sand, the black drifts of seaweed, as if they had been a smooth
floor. (214–5)

Directly after this experience, Cass assumes responsibility for the household, "giving up" herself as soon as she has discovered it. Nevertheless,
now that she knows what she has, she understands what she is expected
to do.

   In Cass's "sacrifice," Stoddard takes the opportunity to undercut one
more cultural icon – the self-abnegating woman. Cass's considerable
sense of humor facilitates this; for the first time, we see a protagonist who
can poke fun at herself. "You may depend on me," she tells her Aunt
Mercy as soon as she arrives home from the beach. "I will reign, and
serve also."

> "Oh, Cassandra, *can* you give up *yourself?*"
> "I must, I suppose. Confound the spray; it is flying against the
> windows."
> "Come in; your hair is wet, and your shawl is wringing. Now for a
> cold."
> "I never shall have any more colds, Aunt Merce; never mean to have
> anything to myself – entirely; you know."
> "You do me good, you dear girl; I love you"; and she began to cry.
> "There's nothing but cold ham and boiled rice for your dinner."
> "What time is it?"
> "Near three."
> I opened the door of the dining-room; the table was laid, and I walked
> round it, on a tour of inspection.
> "I thought you might as well have your dinner, all at once," said
> Fanny, by the window, with her feet tucked up on the rounds of her
> chair. "Here it is."

"I perceive. Who arranged it?"
"Me and Paddy Margaret."
"How many tablecloths have we?"
"Plenty. I thought as you didn't seem to care about any regular hour
for dinner, and made us all wait, *I* needn't be particular; besides, I am
not the waiter, you know."
She had set on the dishes used in the kitchen. I pulled off cloth and all
– the dishes crashed, of course – and sat down on the floor, picking out
the remains for my repast.

In establishing her "reign" Cass also establishes her mode; Fanny is an
impertinent young servant/ward, and Cass's action is calculated to put an
end to her impudence by confronting her with an even greater breach of
conventions. Cass has not only come to see herself, she accepts herself.
Like Hagar, she determines to use her willful nature for her own ends
rather than to try to change it.

But it is Cassandra's sexual life that shows this novel's greatest departure from other American women's novels of the period. Here, the use of
a first-person narrator may have been a necessity for Stoddard's purposes;
in telling her own story, Cass can avoid the censuring of her activities that
would be mandatory in a third-person narration. Since it has already been
established that she rejects most of her culture's codes for interpreting
individual experiences, she is forced to develop her own code for explaining her sexual adventures. As Zagarell notes,[14] Cassandra's resolution is
remarkable in that instead of seeing herself as a victim, a passive recipient
of male passions, she both recognizes her own passions and takes responsibility for her own sexual acts.

The Morgesons features not one but two Byronic heroes, Charles Morgeson and Desmond Somers. The first, dominating and irredeemable,
dies. The second reforms and lives. But the function of the first is to
awaken Cass's sexuality and to make her face her own responsibility for
it. Cass is almost alone in mid–nineteenth-century American women's
fiction in conducting an illicit affair (consummated or not) and not being
censured for it. While Charles gets *his* just desserts by being killed,
Cassandra escapes with physical and emotional scars. Sybil Weir sees
Cassandra's scars as signifying "her victory over a society which proclaimed women sexual imbeciles and which would automatically condemn Cassandra for loving adulterously."[15] Not only does Stoddard give
Cassandra the victory over her society, her scars ultimately aid rather
than hinder her in finding a husband and signify her discovery of her own
capabilities.

Certainly Charles exhibits the masterful personality attending the typical Byronic male; he also exudes a sexuality that attracts not only Cass
but her mother as well. When Charles first appears at the Morgeson
home, Cass watches her mother watch Charles and expresses her obser-

vations in an objective correlative: "I whispered, 'Mother, your eyes are as blue as the sea yonder, and I love you.' She glanced toward it; it was murmuring softly, creeping along the shore, licking the rocks and sand as if recognizing a master. And I saw and felt its steady, resistless heaving, insidious and terrible" (63). In fact mother's and daughter's attractions to a man who is, after all, a cousin continues the whole semi-incestuous relationship between the Rosville and Surrey Morgesons; a relationship Cassandra will recognize later when she refuses to sanction her father's marriage to Charles's widow.[16] Meanwhile, though Charles is responsible for awakening her sexuality, he is not the figure who will enjoy it. Like the other female protagonists we have seen, Cass needs time and space away from a masterful male. Charles would forbid that – as, in fact, is evident in his marriage to Alice, who plays the role of the perfect housekeeper and socialite as long as they live together. Only after his death do Alice's own real talents emerge: She takes over his mills and becomes a wealthy capitalist in her own right.

Some readers of *The Morgesons* see incest as one of its primary motifs. The contemporary reviewer of *Peterson's Magazine* referred to "men [who] desire to marry their own daughters" (231) for instance, while Sybil Weir feels that when Locke Morgeson marries Alice "the father assumes the role of the former lover" (437). It is certainly possible to read Charles and Locke Morgeson as doubles and Cass and Fanny (the servant/ward who adores Locke and seeks to marry him herself) also as doubles. In this reading, Charles's and Cass's attraction would be incestuous, and the tension between Cass and her mother would point to sexual rivalry. But I confess that I see little to support this reading, especially prior to Cass's open confrontation with Locke when he announces his second marriage. Neither father nor daughter indicate desire for each other, and Cass's tensions with her mother involve the mother's ambivalence about Cass's freedom – a freedom never possible for women in her own generation. Quarrels between Cass and her mother, in other words, concern the definition of women's place, not the father's body. Moreover, when Locke comes to discuss his marriage to Alice with his daughter, Cass's protest suggests that she rejects Locke's stepping into Charles's place. In possessing Charles's wife, Locke would symbolically possess Charles's near-mistress, too; Cass implies as much when she tries to dissuade her father from his plans, telling him, for the first time, about her relations with Charles. Unbeknowst to Cass, however, the marriage has already occurred, and Locke, shocked and angered at this revelation of Charles's perfidy, cannot reverse his actions. The incestuous moves existing in the novel, then, originate with Locke, not, as Weir suggests, with Cass; they are in addition oblique, unpremeditated, distanced, and ineffectual. When Cass fails to dissuade her father, her relationship with

Locke essentially comes to an end. She is left – significantly, in this literature – alone, forced to define herself and the shape of her own life without the mediation of any dominating male character.

A more fruitful reading of these doubles and tensions, I suggest, lies in their representation of the New England sexual and economic patriarchy that Stoddard's text continually critiques. With the decayed Calvinism of Gran'ther Warren, Locke (the New England capitalist) and Charles (both capitalist and sexual tyrant) form the patriarchal background against which Cassandra must struggle to realize her Selfhood. Both men are destroyed. Charles is killed, leaving Cass free to marry a man capable of envisioning her as a Subject in her own right; Locke is ruined financially, forcing Cass to recognize her own capabilities. Though Locke recovers part of his fortune, his loss of potency is signaled by his removal from Surrey, his loss of face among his relatives and neighbors, his marriage to Alice (at least in part motivated by her money), and his surrender of the Morgeson house to Cass – on Cass's demand. Rather than becoming her own parents, as Weir suggests (437), when Cass assumes sole possession of her parents' house, she – like Southworth's heroines–becomes truly her Self. While Cass's mother, who is rarely seen outside of her house and never outside domestic arrangements, dies of her years of domestic definition, Cass, freed from sexual and economic domination, can make her own rules, live her own life, possess her house/Self. Her sexual liberation is central to her personal realization; the oblique references to incest point to the sexual/economic domination of patriarchal New England society, rather than to a family "romance."

Rather than foregrounding incest (thereby focusing, as did the contemporary reviewer, on the antisocial aspects of the novel), Stoddard foregrounds Cass's burgeoning sexuality. Cass's sexual awakening is important because it is a central aspect of her emerging self-awareness; as she deals with her attraction to Charles, she becomes aware of her responsibility for her actions. Cass's sexual education is the most dramatic element in her development toward responsibility. Alfred Habegger has explored the centrality of sexuality in nineteenth-century women's writing, pointing out that the words "I love you" were linguistic representations for the act of copulation. All of the novels we have looked at have recorded their heroines' sexual awakenings; but all have done so under linguistic disguises and have cast sexual attraction as a simple magnetism, a force emanating from the male that the female has the choice either to resist or to accept. In defiance of this obliterating magnetism, many heroines fight to establish a counterforce of their own, manifested by their success in the world beyond the home. The Morgesons does not set up this counterforce. Rather, it explores the nature of female sexuality, showing it to be far more complex than a need to yield to male magnetism. What makes Stoddard's novel different is its honest portrayal of women's sexuality and its insistence that, among women's many responsibilities, responsibility for their sexual lives had to be confronted and accepted.

Cassandra comes to realize her complicity in her affair with Charles by means of a trivial incident. Having been warned by a doctor not to drink coffee, she begs Alice not to "tempt" her by offering it. "Tempted!" Charles responds, it seems irrelevantly. "Cassandra is never tempted. What she does, she does because she will" (98). Cass, understanding that he is not referring to coffee, instantly sees that he means to implicate her in their impending affair: " 'Because I will,' I repeated." And she recognizes that she does, in fact, want to sleep with him; like the other unorthodox impulses that have "possessed" her, consciousness of her sexual desires confronts her as an imperative for which she must assume responsibility: "A nervous foreboding possessed me . . ." (99), she records, as she enters her room; the next morning she finds evidence that Charles has watched her as she slept. After Charles is killed, Cass continues to share blame for their relationship. As she bitterly remarks when she later tells her mother of the affair, "our experiences are not foretold by law. We may be righteous by rule, we do not sin that way. There was no beginning, no end, to mine" (133). That is, Cassandra's experience encompassed a series of individual choices each contingent on the circumstances of the moment, rather than a single incident in which the role of moral law could be brought to bear on one decision. Moreover, even in her bitterness Cassandra realizes that this affair may serve her well in the future, that it may contribute to the code that she is developing to explain her life to herself. "Wait," she tells her appalled mother, "what is bad this year may be good the next. You blame yourself, because you believe your ignorance has brought me into danger. Wait, mother" (133).

Desmond Somers is Cass's second lover, earned through her painful experiences with Charles and her own period of domestic trial. While Charles resembles St. Elmo in his arrogant passions, Desmond has overcome his own dissolute and arrogant past to become a new kind of lover, one who respects the heroine's self-sufficiency and insists on coming to her as an equal rather than as a master. As Cass had resisted her society's efforts to mold her, so Des defies his family's efforts to define the shape of his life; he subjects himself to a rigorous two-year course of abstinence to rid himself of the alcoholism that his family regards as inescapable. He chooses to do so because he sees Cass's suffering over Charles as heroic and wants to be worthy of her before they marry. Like Charles, he is dark, moody, and passionate; unlike Charles, he wants to come to Cassandra unencumbered. Like *Queechy*'s Guy Carleton, Des asks his lady to trust him when he returns from his travels, but his request bears very different implications from Carleton's. While Carleton wants Fleda to trust him to run her life for her, offering certainty and security in exchange for submission, Des asks Cass to risk marrying a man who lives on the edge of the abyss, knowing that he risks relapse. "Spare, . . . brown, . . . grey" from his ordeal, he tells Cass that "You see what battle *I* have had since I saw you. It took me so long to break my cursed habits. I was afraid of myself, afraid to come; but I have tried myself to the utmost, and hope I am worthy of you. Will you trust me?" (250).

Certainly, Cassandra's influence has helped Desmond's reform, and in this she reflects the cultural code of feminine influence that marked Edna Earl and Fleda Ringgan's effects on their men. Nineteenth-century reforms were, like St. Elmo's, largely religious; cures of diseases of the will, like alcoholism, were seen as spiritual problems, to be effected through the victim's submission of self and will to God. In contrast, Desmond's reform is secular and tentative. Like Cass, he knows that security is tenuous and that he alone can account for his own life. Unlike the gilded chain that binds Fleda to her lord, bright with religious hopefulness, "the chain between us," Cass recognizes, "was corroded, for it was forged out of his and my substance" (227). This hero and heroine do not have God to help them; rather, they are linked by their shared understanding of guilt, complicity, and accountability.

With her subversion of familial and religious conventions and her inversion of the code mandating that good women abnegate their own desires, Stoddard also subverts the image of the ideal Victorian woman. Veronica, Cassandra's sister, is also Cass's opposite: frail, delicately featured, adept at the piano, and home loving. Stoddard's variation on the True Woman of nineteenth-century fantasy, she is also decidedly strange – sickly, introverted, and self-absorbed. Like Cass, Verry begins life wild:

> too strange-looking for ordinary people to call her pretty, and so odd in her behavior, so full of tricks, that I did not love her. She was a silent child, and liked to be alone. But whoever had the charge of her must be watchful. She tasted everything, and burnt everything, within her reach. A blazing fire was too strong a temptation to be resisted. . . . She had a habit of frightening us by hiding, and appearing from places where no one had thought of looking for her. People shook their heads when they observed her. . . . (13).

But Veronica is prey to mysterious bouts of illness, which confine her to her room for months and succeed in "educating" her to her womanly role:

> We did not perceive the process, but Verry was educated by sickness; her mind fed and grew on pain, and at last mastered it. The darkness in her nature broke; by slow degrees she gained health, though never much

strength. Upon each recovery a change was visible; a spiritual dawn had risen in her soul; moral activity blending with her ideality made her life beautiful, even in the humblest sense. Veronica! You were endowed with genius; but while its rays penetrated you, we did not see them. How could we profit by what you saw and heard, when we were blind and deaf?

As Zagarell notes,[17] the implication here is that while Cass's adolescence is passed honing her will by battling with others, Veronica's is passed learning to subordinate hers to her physical limitations; a discipline that, from the point of view of the dominant cultural values, lifts her above ordinary mortals, but in Stoddard's view so distorts her natural character that, for all practical purposes, she becomes dysfunctional. Like Rebecca Lloyd, from *A New-England Tale,* or the young Edna Earl or Fleda Ringgan, Veronica learns to establish that harmony with nature that marks the ideal nineteenth-century woman as close to God; like Edna, she educates herself, like Fleda, she occupies herself in doing for others. Cass records her sister's evolution into Victorian womankind in a passage that stops just short of parody:

> . . . when I went to Rosville she was reading "Paradise Lost," and writing her opinions upon it in a large blank book. She was also devising a plan for raising trees and flowers in the garret, so that she might realize a picture of a tropical wilderness. Her tastes were so contradictory that time never hung heavy with her; though she had as little practical talent as any person I ever knew, she was a help to both sick and well. She remembered people's ill turns, and what was done for them; and for the well she remembered dates and suggested agreeable occupations – gave them happy ideas. Besides being a calendar of domestic traditions, she was weather-wise, and prognosticated gales, meteors, high tides, and rains.
> Home, father said, was her sphere (60).

Dysfunctional in any useful occupation, inside or outside the home, Veronica's "talents" nevertheless fulfill the prescription for ideal upper-class womanhood. Certainly she fulfills Ben Somers's dream: After his first sight of Veronica, he tells Cass, her sister "has never been out of my mind a moment since" (114).

But Ben, like other "readers" of the codes that enshrine Veronica, actually knows little of the girl he thinks he loves. Sybil Weir finds Veronica's actions sadomasochistic,[18] but seen through Cassandra's eyes, ideal Veronica is, simply, inadequate. Despite her gentle domesticity, Veronica is ill equipped to grapple with adult responsibilities. As in *Moby-Dick,* Stoddard uses the sea and the land to represent the differences between passionate questers and home lovers. While Cass is continually associated with the sea, reading its moods as objective correlatives for her life, Veronica is associated with the land. Shortly before Ben and Veronica marry, he and Cass walk along the shore, and he is surprised when Cass tells him how much her sister "detests the sea." Trying to warn him, Cass remarks that he knows "few of [Veronica's] tastes or habits" (159), but Ben refuses to believe that the woman he has courted is anything but the beautiful, self-abnegating creature he perceives. Nevertheless Veronica, though she seems the Victorian ideal of the good woman, is actually incapable of helping anyone else: "I know that my instincts are fine only in a self-centering direction," she tells Cass. "Yours are different" (233).

Delicate, eccentric, self-centered, Verry is the wrong wife for Ben because she cannot help him wean himself from the family affliction and, unlike Des, Ben is not strong enough to stop himself from drinking. When he comes home "reeling slightly," for instance, Verry

> nodded kindly to him, shut her book, and slipped out, without approaching him.
> "That's *her* way," [Ben] said, staring hard at [Cass], "She always says in the same unmoved voice, 'Why do you drink brandy?'" (244).

For Ben, Verry's inability to face his drinking is a sign of coldness; having married the ideal image she represented, without understanding how she fears any demands that she act for others, he cannot fathom the extent of her self-centeredness. Through Veronica, Stoddard shows where her own values lie; this ideal woman is an image only; incapable of reaching beyond herself or of meeting the challenges of independence.

Having subverted the code of the ideal woman, however, Stoddard shows her alternative. Cass, too, insists on the limits of her responsibilities to others, but from strength, not from weakness. Though she takes over the household when she must, she refuses to take over the moral life of anyone else. When Ben realizes that Verry will not help him, he turns to Cass. "You have a great power, tall enchantress," he tries to persuade her. But Cass will not accept the responsibility he wants to give her. "Veronica will probably not understand you," she warns him, "but you must manage for yourself" (160). Ben, however, does not manage for himself. When Des returns, Ben tries to prevent his and Cass's marriage by laying the burden for his survival on her; referring to his dipsomania, he declares that "the jaws of hell are open. If you are satisfied with the end, I must be" (252). Refusing to be his alter ego, Cass marries Desmond, and Ben dies of delirium tremens. The marriage between the ideal couple has failed; the marriage between the two "sinners" succeeds. Like Hagar Churchill, Cass and Desmond are individuals who have confronted and controlled their passions and learned how to use their wills to control their world. Their marriage succeeds because they have summoned the strength to recognize their own imperatives.

At the end of this novel, Cass and Des have been married more than two years, Ben has been dead for six months, and Veronica is left with a "year-old baby" that "smiles continually, but never cries, never moves, except when it is moved," Stoddard's ironic inversion of the sunny offspring of the ideal Victorian couple (252). This description of Veronica's child not only reflects contemporary theories that alcoholics engender retarded children, but also suggests that the progeny of those too weak to control themselves will be even more dependent than their parents. It also reflects Stoddard's vision of the abyss, a world that continues to threaten the existence even of those who defy it. Although Desmond calls on God the night Ben "sprang from his bed, staggered backwards, and fell dead" (269–70), his plea is a cry of anguish rather than an affirmation of belief, and the "mad world" that he calls God to rule has already crushed those who could not summon strength to withstand it. Those who do, tread cautiously through a universe that promises neither love nor pity. Looking out at the "blue summer sea," Cass records that "its eternal monotone expresses no pity, no compassion" (252).

Although Cass and Desmond's marriage bring *The Morgesons* to a conventional closure, it does not end "happily," with reintegration of all the principals and a landscape blooming and redeemed. Rather, the end of *The Morgesons* suggests that survival is the only "happy" outcome for the descendants of the Puritans. Cassandra's narrative is the record of her survival through self-knowledge, through recognizing her own nature and its imperatives. Her final image of the sea illustrates her progress – whereas she had previously projected the sea as a reflection of her moods, now she describes it as simply a natural element, without relevance to her life or to the lives of others. Far from being in touch with nature and nature's God, Cass recognizes that no supernatural force can reintegrate her "mad world." But determined personalities can impose provisional order on it, possess it through their own self-possession. And, in writing her own story, inscribing her Self as a controlling force in that world, Cassandra Morgeson breaks through the restrictions on nineteenth-century women's voices, insisting that women can control their environment, take responsibility for their own sexuality, and negotiate the loneliness of a decadent culture whose members are increasingly isolated.

PART IV

THE LATER DIDACTIC NOVEL

7

NARRATIVE CONTROL AND THEMATIC RADICALISM IN WORK AND THE SILENT PARTNER

Just as the exploratory novel did not spring into being in a specific year, with a single, identifiable text, so it did not abruptly disappear. Rather, the form, with its cover text and the language conventions, codes, and values associated with it, continued, ultimately merging with the realist novel that dominated early twentieth-century fiction. Nevertheless, from a distance it is possible to see that the exploratory novel's ascendency only lasted about two decades, roughly from 1850 to 1870. Its decline during the 1870s was accompanied by a new phenomenon, a type of women's novel thematically descended from exploratory novels but formally related to early didactic texts. This late didactic novel is structurally regressive but thematically progressive; its often indeterminate form illustrates authors' struggles to embody emerging new ideas about women. Narratively, it reflects the didactic mission of earlier texts, featuring an engaging narrator who reaches out to a specific class of readers; consequently, for late didactic works, unlike for exploratory novels, the concept of narrator–narratee relationships becomes a useful analytical tool once more.

In addition, the late didactic novel once more reasserts the dominance of ideas over action, actively and consciously teaching – and preaching – as it tells its tales. Yet those tales show how far the literary inscription of women had come. The novels examined in this chapter do not call for expanded professional opportunities for women. They do, however, lay the groundwork for such demands. Overtly and enthusiastically, late-didactic novels valorize women who reach beyond marriage for self-definition and gratification, and who question the restrictions the marriage relation imposes on their freedom to do and be all they can. In this chapter, I will examine two of these novels, showing their relationship to the didactic and exploratory novel forms preceding them and suggesting that they mark a new era in the history of American women's fiction. Both Louisa May Alcott's *Work: A Story of Experience* and Elizabeth

Stuart Phelps's *The Silent Partner* show that women who live without men are capable of deeply enriched and rewarding lives and suggest that marriage itself constitutes a barrier to women's full development.

Like all the other novels we have examined, Louisa May Alcott's *Work: A Story of Experience* (1873) has a narrative design. Unlike in exploratory novels, however, the overplot is not undermined by either narrative, thematic, or rhetorical elements. Rather, like *Charlotte Temple* and *A New-England Tale,* all its structural elements work in tandem. But *Work's* thematic mission is radically different from the goals of early women's didactic novels. Where they preach submission to external authority, *Work* valorizes self-trust; where they advocated female passivity, *Work* advocates feminist activism. In 1875 Louisa May Alcott noted that a discussion she had attended on Conformity and NonConformity "was very lively; and being called upon, I piped up, and went in for nonconformity when principle was concerned. . . ."[1] The spiritual history of Alcott's principled nonconformity is embodied in *Work.*

Briefly, the story is as follows. Proclaiming a "new Declaration of Independence," Christie Devon, an orphan, leaves the crusty uncle and loving aunt who have reared her and goes to the city because she seeks a broader definition of herself than her environment offers: "I'm sick of this dull town, where the one idea is eat, drink, and get rich,"[2] she tells Aunt Betsy. Chapters 2–6 chronicle her experiences as, successively, servant, actress, governess, companion, and seamstress, experiences that enrich both her skills and her consciousness of herself, her world, and her capabilities. Chapter 7 records her nadir: months of solitude, search, and poverty. After this she ascends, but her subsequent experiences focus less on successive jobs and more on Christie's discovery and adoption of a communitarian ethos, presented through her religious, sexual, and sororal relationships.

At the end of Chapter 7 ("Through the Mist") Christie is saved from suicide by Rachel, a fallen woman whom she had befriended, and sent as a charity girl first to a working woman whose home offers her spiritual and physical respite, then to the country, where she works in the house and greenhouses of the Sterlings, a mother–son couple whose own daughter/sister had been lost through sexual error. Christie eventually marries David Sterling, after they discover that the Rachel she had befriended is actually "Letty," the family's lost daughter. But the marriage takes place on the eve of the Civil War, and David and Christie both join the Union forces, he as soldier, she as nurse. He dies, and she returns to his home, bears his daughter, tends the greenhouses, and becomes the focus of a women's community that includes women from all walks of postbellum American life. In the last chapter, Christie determines to become a liaison between working and leisured women, a position for which her experiences have uniquely fitted her. The last scene presents her female community, including her daughter, seated in a circle, hands joined, pledging to "know and help, love and educate one another . . . a loving league of sisters, old and young, black and white, rich and poor, each ready to do her part to hasten the coming of the happy end" (442).

From beginning to end, then, *Work* is a novel that openly explores and advocates women's self-development and cooperation. Despite its title, it focuses less on expanding women's professional opportunities, or re-defining female nature, than on expanding women's opportunities for psychological and spiritual development; the jobs Christie performs, es-pecially those she undertakes before her marriage, remain within the realm of traditional women's work, and her nature is essentially generous and nurturing, both qualities high on the value hierarchy of nineteenth-century True Womanhood. The truly radical emphasis of the novel lies in its advocacy of women's freedom to explore the world and to determine the shape of their own lives. Rather than fighting for open job markets, in *Work* Alcott is trying to redefine women's possibilities and to lay the foundation for a society based on cooperation rather than competition, nurturance rather than manipulation.[3] As Jane Tompkins has noted, sim-ilar values underscore Harriet Beecher Stowe's presentation of her ideal society in *Uncle Tom's Cabin,* where Rachel Halliday's Quaker kitchen signals a matriarchal society founded on cooperative love.[4] The difference between Alcott and earlier writers lay not in her highlighting a women's community, but in foregrounding it, in making it the specific vehicle for the reconstitution of American society. Moreover, her special contribu-tion to this movement lay in her perception that individuals must free themselves from the self-images society imposes on them before they can realize their mutual strengths. Throughout *Work: A Story of Experience,* Alcott's emphasis is on experience, in all its ramifications. Consequently, she frames her story with references to the American Revolution, the episode that represented new beginnings for nineteenth-century Ameri-cans. Like *Queechy, Work* begins with an evocation of the Founding Fa-thers. Unlike *Queechy,* its overt intention is to feminize everything they represented. When Christie proclaims a "new Declaration of Indepen-dence" she is referring to her freedom to determine the shape of her own life; when the narrator valorizes girls who want to "escape," "break loose," and "go out into the world," she is referring to a new ideology of American womanhood.

As in early didactic novels, the narrator in *Work* continually monitors her narratee's interpretations, holding Christie up as a positive exemplary character. The modeling of Christie after Christiana, the female exemplar in *Pilgrim's Progress,* signals the novel's didactic intent. But Christie's

Heavenly City is defined not externally but internally, not as obedience to heavenly authority but as obedience to her own imperatives. Alcott's transcendentalist background is nowhere more evident than in her creation of this Emersonian heroine.

> Christie was one of that large class of women who, moderately endowed with talents, earnest and truehearted, are driven by necessity, temperament, or principle out into the world to find support, happiness, and homes for themselves. Many turn back discouraged; more accept shadow for substance, and discover their mistake too late; the weakest lose their purpose and themselves; but the strongest struggle on, and, after danger and defeat, earn at last the best success this world can give us, the possession of a brave and cheerful spirit, rich in self-knowledge, self-control, self-help. This was the real desire of Christie's heart; this was to be her lesson and reward, and to this happy end she was slowly yet surely brought by the long discipline of life and labor (11).

This passage focuses on the effect of work experience on the protagonist's self-perception, introducing the story to follow by suggesting that the reader broadly interpret Christie's ambitions. In fact this passage lays out the interpretive strategies for the entire novel and suggests the kind of reader it addresses: "that large class of women" who are unexceptional (an anti-Romantic description calculated to appeal to readers who may not identify with exceptional heroines) but who long for emotional and/or financial independence. By moving out from the specific figure to the general category, Alcott's narrator defines the class that constitutes her dominant narratee; women seeking experience, trying to escape the confines of women's sphere, and willing to reevaluate their own ontological definition – like seventeen-year-old Virginia Benton, who, still camping out while her family searched for a ranch, passed one Sunday rereading *Work*.[5] For readers such as Benton – who became a strong female force in the community affairs of early twentieth-century Wyoming – Christie's adventures are to be seen as apprenticeships for a life of feminist activism.[6]

The broad definition of work implied in this passage not only contributes to the creation of the dominant narratee but also to the overall message of the book. More than physical or mental labor, here "work" signifies the individual's control of the world around her. Combining comparatives with parallel clauses ("Many," "More," "the weakest," "the strongest") the narrator elevates her protagonist's adventures into an almost metaphysical realm, marking the passage rhythmically in order to highlight her message. In moving from the specific to the general and back again to the specific, she signals her narratee as she explicates her character, casting a net wide enough to catch those women who want to try their wings as Christie does, but who fear the consequences of taking their freedom. As in *Charlotte Temple* and *A New-England Tale,* the passage outlines its hypothetical reader's character and circumstances, then warns of the difficulties facing her. Unlike in the earlier novels, however, this narratee is not projected as an individual suffering from a specific problem, but rather as a group of individuals whose entire moral, philosophical, and spiritual lives need to be restructured. The identifiable "problem" in *Work* is far more complex than in the earlier novels: It is the problem of patriarchy, of women's definition by a culture that forbids them "self-knowledge," "self-control," "self-help." Consequently the narrator's function is to teach her narratee how to transform the foundations of her life – her image of herself, her capabilities, and, fully as important, her image of other women and their capabilities.

One indication of her effect on readers was recorded by Alcott herself. In the early summer of 1873 Alcott recorded that they had settled their "servant problem" "by getting a neat American woman to cook and help me with the housework. Peace fell upon our troubled souls and all went well. Good meals, tidy house, cheerful service, and in the P.M. an intelligent young person to read and sew with us." She continues.

> It was curious how she came to us. She had taught and sewed, and was tired, and wanted something else; decided to try for a housekeeper's place, but happened to read "Work," and thought she'd do as Christie did, – take anything that came.
>
> I was the first who answered her advertisement, and when she found I wrote the book, she said, "I'll go and see if Miss A. practises what she preaches."
>
> She found I did, and we had a good time together.[7]

This reader responds to Christie's adventurousness by imitating her and launching her career into unknown realms; as a reward, she finds a good berth and sisterly companionship. Alcott's text provided her with the stimulus to test herself and her possibilities; in return, by Alcott's account, she entered a household that could only expand her horizons.

Interestingly, few contemporary American reviewers interpreted *Work* in these terms. British reviewers seem to have perceived its Emersonian impulse most clearly: "Miss Alcott's New Novel is a plea for independence as preferable to a life of dependence. Work is wealth, and occupation is a surer promoter of health and happiness than money."[8] Another reviewer more accurately pinpointed Alcott's central theme: "In all [of Alcott's fiction] underlying the main story . . . burns the one great keynote of success, *self-reliance,* and clustered around it are purity, kindness, faith, and endeavor."[9] In contrast, American reviewers focused either on the professional aspects of the novel or on its appeal to traditional definitions of women's role. *Godey's* saw its central message through the text's introductory epigram: "An endless significance lies in work, in idleness alone is there perpetual despair."[10] *Harper's* suggested that it was less a novel than "a serious didactic essay on the subject of women's work."[11] Henry Ward Beecher, who had commissioned it for serialization in his *Christian Union,* apparently advertised it as a novel appealing to domestic virtues,[12] and others praised it for its "earnest Philanthropy and good Principles."[13] Yet *Work* expends little of its energies depicting the actualities – the minute particulars – of work skills. It is not an employment manual; it is a study of the soul's journey toward redemption. Intertextually framed by *Pilgrim's Progress,* it implicitly refers to a society that is morally inadequate and from which its protagonists must struggle to free themselves.

The backdrop to Christie's struggle, and to the struggles of the other women Christie encounters, can be seen in both economic and feminist terms. In her introduction to the Schocken reprint of *Work,* Sarah Elbert notes that Alcott juxtaposes a noncompetitive, feminist work ethic against the capitalist ethic articulated by Christie's Uncle Enos and most of the other men featured in the novel (*xxxiii*). This is most forcefully evident near the novel's conclusion, when Enos queries Christie about the women's community in which she is living. When Christie tells him that "we work for one another and share every thing together," Enos "grumbles": "So like women!" (419). But Enos's role as representative of an insensitive patriarchy is evident in the first chapter as well, when he denigrates Christie's ambitions and orders his wife – who has "a most old-fashioned and dutiful awe of her lord and master" – into bed (10). Similarly, Aunt Betsy's role is to represent the mother generation that has obeyed cultural mandates to marry, and has compromised her life in the process: When Christie asks her if she never had "discontented fits" as a girl, Aunt Betsy replies "Shouldn't wonder ef I did; but Enos came along, and I forgot 'em" (8). Reflecting on both, at the end of the first chapter Christie realizes that the social network into which she has been born offers her few options:

> . . . either marry Joe Butterfield in sheer desperation, and become a farmer's household drudge; settle down into a sour spinster, content to make butter, gossip, and lay up money all her days; or do what poor Matty Stone had done, try to crush and curb her needs and aspirations till the struggle grew too hard, and then in a fit of despair end her life, and leave a tragic story to haunt their quiet river (12).

The social network against which Christie rebels is also evident in the backgrounds of the women she meets on her journey. All are enmeshed in the sexual and economic fabric which defines and limits them. The wealthy married women, almost all presented as either foolish or unhappy, are trapped in an economic system that defines them as indices to their husbands' pecuniary abilities; the effect of their illusory comforts is to make them vain, frivolous, superficial, and ultimately ludicrous: "Mrs. Stuart possessed some beauty and chose to think herself a queen of society. She assumed majestic manners in public and could not entirely divest herself of them in private, which often produced comic effects. Zenobia troubled about fish-sauce, or Aspasia indignant at the price of eggs will give some idea of this lady when she condescended to the cares of housekeeping" (19).

Christie's next wealthy mistress shows even more tragically how wealth caused leisured women to waste their lives: "Mrs. Saltonstall's mission appeared to be the illustration of each new fashion as it came, and she performed it with a devotion worthy of a better cause. . . . Her time was spent in dressing, driving, dining, and dancing; in skimming novels, and embroidering muslin; going to church with a velvet prayer-book and a new bonnet; and writing to her husband when she wanted money, for she had a husband somewhere abroad, who so happily combined business with pleasure that he never found time to come home" (65).

Finally, Helen Carrol, suffering from hereditary insanity passed down through the male line, ironically blames her mother, who had married even though she knew "the sad history of my father's family. He was rich, she poor and proud. . ." (109). Like Aunt Betsy, Helen's mother married because she had been taught that that was her only avenue to economic security. Both are trapped by their marriages, their relationships, and their need to defend their "choices." The society that produced these women is morally inadequate because it drains them of the will to question themselves and the roles that have been prescribed for them. It is a society that seems to offer no release except through death: Helen Carrol's suicide is figuratively as much an escape from the future her status prescribes as from the madness her father has bequeathed her.

In contrast to these, Hepsy Johnson, Cynthy Wilkins, Rachel/Letty Sterling, and Bella Carrol are women who have seized control of their own lives and turned them to uncommon ends. An escaped slave, Hepsy Johnson has made the most extreme choice, and slavery is the most intense form of oppression suggested in *Work*. Yet it sets the stage for the novel's demonstration of the strategies women can use to free themselves from their various gender-based entrapments. As the women's movement grew out of the antislavery movement, reflecting white women's acknowledgment of a common oppressor, so Hepsy's story initiates Christie's discovery of women's implicit, as well as explicit, oppressions.

Cynthy Wilkins's story differs from Hepsy's in that she had to recognize her own complicity in her troubles. Married to a man she professes to love even though he offers her little in the way of support or companionship, Cynthy's spiritual growth took place as she came to realize that she could create a viable and happy life for herself and her family if she refused to be a pawn in other people's power plays. When Christie meets her, Cynthy has grown from a narrow, confused young mother to a matriarch, generous of body and soul. Leader of her family and her neighborhood, member of Mr. Power's liberal Christian church, Cynthy's motherly care encourages Christie to seek a new kind of environment for her talents; her appearance signals an ideological turning point in the text. Rachel/Letty, victim of the sexual double standard, also seizes control of her own life, transforming herself from victim to savior. Bella Carrol, forbidden to marry lest she pass down her father's insanity, determines to make Christie's mission her own. With Hepsy and Cynthy, they exemplify women who determine to create new conditions for other women's self-realization.

Many of the themes we have seen recurring in exploratory novels also occur in *Work*. As in *Ruth Hall* and *Queechy*, the language of flowers is central to one portion of this text. As in *Queechy, The Deserted Wife,* and *The Morgesons*, references to the American context form an ideological backdrop for the heroine's adventures. Here too, the central male disappears from the scene, and a lower-class woman serves as a model for self-reliance for the protagonist. Here too, favored characters lust for education. As in *St. Elmo*, the text rejects the idea that women must sacrifice themselves to redeem a man. As in *Queechy*, Portia's speech articulates the relationship of the protagonist to one of the male characters. As with most of the novels we have examined, the protagonist goes out into the world unprotected.

Unlike exploratory novels, however, *Work* uses these conventions for explicitly feminist ends. Where exploratory novels refuse to pursue the implications of these themes, subordinating and ultimately perverting them to make way for the closures mandated by their conservative narrative designs, *Work* uses them as the matrix for a new ideology of womanhood, as a means of dramatizing the feminist ideology most exploratory novels seek to hide. Where the loneliness of the heroines in most exploratory novels results from their friends and protectors dying or deserting them, for instance, in *Work* Christie Devon's loneliness is a result of her choice to leave the relatives who have cared for her, reject the worthy farmer who has sued for her hand, and launch herself upon the world.

Christie's single declaration of dependence upon a man, rendered in a scene where she quotes Portia's speech ending in the lines that "her willing spirit / Commits itself to yours to be directed, / As from her lord, her governor, her king" (274) is directed not to her future husband, as in *Queechy*, but to Mr. Power, whose liberal brand of Christian activism she has adopted. Moreover, her relationship with David Sterling, whom she does marry, is conducted on egalitarian principles, and their courtship is conducted along lines not of compelling male to passive female but of individuals who bring to their relationship their past histories of struggle. When they use flowers as a means of communication, they define the blossoms' meanings themselves, instead of accepting a priori definitions. Refusing to refer to guidebooks, Christie and David establish a relationship of equals. Their courtship follows Christie's refusal of an earlier suitor who would have expected her to nurse him physically and redeem him morally; significantly, during that earlier episode Christie had criticized *Jane Eyre* because the ideal of womanly self-sacrifice its conclusion embodies does not appear to her "a fair bargain" (80–1).

Additionally, David's "disappearance" is strategically placed so as to reveal the strengths of a woman whose prenuptial life has prepared her for independence. While the leitmotif of the disappearing male allowed authors of exploratory novels the freedom to develop their protagonists' talents, his reappearance contributed to the conventional closures both of the novels and of their heroines' ambitions. In contrast, David's death permits Alcott to show Christie's talents flowering. Christie's brief union suggests the possibilities of companionate marriage, but her widowhood demonstrates the strengths of independent women cooperating in a female community.[14] In *Work* Christie's marriage is structurally placed as another "experience," not as the crowning event of her life.[15]

Finally, the quest for education, though less central to this text than to many others, also functions to bolster the characters' image of their power over their own lives. This is most evident in Hepsy's desire to learn to read and cipher quickly because when she goes South to steal her family out of slavery "I must know little 'bout readin' and countin' up, else I'll get lost and cheated" (30). Hepsy's need for education is basic, pragmatic; its import lies in the fact that she will use it to subvert her society's oppressions. Thematically, then, *Work* appropriates the conventions of exploratory novels only to use them to illuminate rather than to disguise its ends.

As Nina Auerbach notes,[16] *Work*'s chronicling of Christie's journey through the fields of labor available to women contains elements of the picaresque. But the structuring of *Work* also permits Alcott to extend the implications of Christie's experiences far more openly than the overplot of exploratory novels permits. This apparently disturbed contemporary reviewers, who had, perhaps, become accustomed to the intense plotting of exploratory texts; Zehr records that the book was criticized as "disjointed" and "without the semblance of a plot."[17] *Work is* episodic, but it is not disjointed; rather it is held together by a determined narrative design. That design, however, is manifested by its narrator rather than its characters, appearing in its constant narratorial monitoring. As a didactic novel, *Work* focuses on theme rather than plot, the narrator's interpretations rather than the characters' adventures.

For instance, although its opening pages are rendered through dialogue – a technique focusing on character development – the narrator remains close, continually commenting on the significance of what the reader is seeing and hearing. During her opening conversation with her aunt, Christie kneads the bread and helps with the pies; throughout the novel her domestic efficiency, nurturing abilities, and feminine modesty remain constant. But the visual evidence of Christie's conformity to cultural mandates is accompanied by running narrative commentary interpreting Christie as a woman who is both feminine and adventurous, qualities the narrator in no way sees as antithetical. As Christie tells her aunt that she wants to leave home, for example, she is preparing bread, a task closely associated with domestic accomplishments. The narrator, however, interprets her actions in terms of her protagonist's quest for freedom: Christie was kneading the dough "as if it was her destiny, and she was shaping it to suit herself" (2).

By the second half of Chapter 1, the narrator's voice has come to predominate, advancing her thesis in order to ensure that her reader understands that true women have the right – even the obligation – to discover their talents and realize their possibilities. Christie leaves home, the *character* claims, because she wants to find "work," to "travel away into the world and seek my fortune" (2). Where the narrator of an early didactic novel would find this reprehensible, this narrator applauds Christie's adventurousness, explaining that it demonstrates that Christie has the "instincts of a strong nature for light and freedom" (9). In the passage introducing Christie and suggesting her significance within "that large class of women" (11), the narrator distances herself from her character's more limited view, establishing an omniscience that provides her with the distance she needs to explicate the significance of Christie's development. As character, Christie cannot see the full implications of her choice; the narrator, however, can, and her interpretation of Christie's impending journey guides her narratee into expecting a story about a woman's inner, as well as outer, development. After this initial chapter, the narrator increasingly takes over dramatic and ideological movements, becoming the "Providence" to whom she attributes Christie's adventures. By the end of the second chapter, when she prepares for a change of scene by simply announcing that "Providence had other lessons for Christie, and when this one was well learned she was sent away to learn another phase of woman's life and labor" (31), she has established herself as the novel's mover and shaker, fashioning a character whose function is to explicate her creator's thesis.

That thesis is the redefinition of women's potential, regardless of color or class. To this end new voices, predominantly female, are added to *Work* as Christie moves through the experiences that shape her. Each step explores different types of American womanhood: at times – as with Christie's wealthy employers – simply to dismiss them, to write them off, with a sidelong glance at the reader who may conform to the image; at other times, to use them to illustrate exemplary qualities. These latter form the chorus of women's voices Alcott employs to explicate her themes: most notably among them, Hepsy, whom Alcott uses to teach the narratee racial tolerance and respect; Cynthy Wilkins, a clear-starcher, "a large woman . . . with fuzzy red hair, no front teeth, and a plump clean face" (165), who illustrates the strengths of women who have always had to provide their own protection; and Rachel/Letty, the fallen woman, whom Alcott uses to undermine the society's sexual double standard. These women first encourage Christie in her search for "work," then join her in her project to bring rich and poor women together to fight for their common goals.

Of themselves, these are not unusual characters in women's fiction; as we have seen, the lower-class woman often stands as an unsung model for middle-class heroines, and escaped slaves and fallen women were also common in midcentury fiction, generally functioning to illuminate some social ill. What is unusual about these characters is the legitimacy of their voices. Unlike most of the other novels, *Work* accords these characters a status beyond their representation of their problems; their errors are seen as parts of the complex whole of women's oppression, and their liberation as contributing to women's freedom. The figure of Rachel, for instance, evokes Charlotte Temple; her fall came when she was persuaded to run away with a suitor. But rather than dying on foreign shores, as Charlotte did, or being destined for perpetual servitude, as is Maggie, the rescued magdalen in Stowe's *We and Our Neighbors* (also 1873), Rachel returns to America, takes up her life, and lives, to help others and ultimately to return to the bosom of her family. In other words Rachel remains an integral character even after she is redeemed – an unusual event in nineteenth-century American novels. At no point does the narrator censure Rachel's past; rather, she presents her as a character who has gained control over her future. Like Cassandra, of *The Morgesons*, Rachel's sexual transgressions contribute to her eventual discovery of her own power; rejecting "Magdalen Asylums" as "penitentiaries" (139), Rachel sets herself the task of helping other fallen women. In doing so, she discovers her own strength: "with every one I helped my power increased" (161). Similarly, Hepsy and Cynthy, both dialect speakers, are credited for their full life experiences; both are held up as representative of working women who have found dignity, love, and self-worth through their personal suffering and their efforts for others. The female voices that surround Christie, then, articulate the fullness of women's experiences regardless of race, class, or social status.

In addition, Alcott's narrator at times uses her protagonist to articulate some of the authorial values that contribute to Alcott's project to change the ideological basis on which American women construct their lives. The most notable of these issues is color prejudice, an attack Alcott mounts not just on slavery but on whites who are repelled by black skins; and which in this novel she uses to insist on the need for female solidarity, transcending differences of race as well as of class.[18] Here, the distance maintained between the author and her character collapses, much as it collapses in the Colonel Sherbourne episode in *Adventures of Huckleberry Finn*. When Christie tells Hepsy Johnson, who serves as cook in the household where Christie serves as housemaid, that she (unlike the Irish housemaid who had preceded her) is happy to sit down to supper with the black woman, the author's animus against color prejudice appears as a subtheme that bolsters her argument for a universal solidarity among women.

> . . . I suppose Katy thought her white skin gave her a right to be disrespectful to a woman old enough to be her mother just because she was black. I don't; and while I'm here, there must be no difference made. If we can work together, we can eat together; and because you have been a slave is all the more reason I should be good to you now (24).

Though it may sound condescending to our ears, Christie's speech was militantly liberal for the nineteenth century. Moreover, in many ways, this is the sharpest of Alcott's thrusts: In attempting to abolish the color line, she is attacking the most fundamental barrier Americans place to the realization of equality. But this is integral to her overall design: to create a society in which women can fulfill their full human potential. Here Christie penetrates the color barrier by recognizing the commonality of womanhood. Alcott's narrator makes this commonality her central goal throughout the novel, guiding her readers' interpretations through her own explicit pronouncements. When she informs us that Christie "suffered a sort of poverty which is even more difficult to bear than actual want. . . . Her heart was empty and she could not fill it; her soul was hungry and she could not feed it" (146), she is referring to the lack of communal, not sexual, love: "It is not always want, insanity, or sin that drives women to desperate deaths; often it is a dreadful loneliness of heart, a hunger for home and friends" (150).

Christie finds succor through the agency of Rachel, Cynthy, and Mr. Power, the clergyman who was, according to Ednah D. Cheney, modeled on Theodore Parker, one of Boston's most radical Unitarian ministers.[19] Cynthy introduces her to Mr. Power, and through him Christie first feels the stirrings of a genuine religious fervor. But Power's religion is communitarian, predicated on the principle of benevolence, and it is not until long after their initial encounter, after Christie has experienced wifehood and widowhood and is about to experience motherhood, that she fully understands what Power means, finding genuine religion "where she least expected it, in herself" (411). That self is em/powered through its relationships with others, especially women seeking to restructure American society. By the last chapter, when Christie speaks to a meeting of working and leisured women, she has gained the power to help others find themselves and each other:

> more impressive than any thing she said was the subtle magnetism of character, for that has a universal language which all can understand. They saw and felt that a genuine woman stood down there among them like a sister, ready with head, heart, and hand to help them help themselves; not offering pity as an alms, but justice as a right. Hardship and sorrow, long effort and late-won reward had been hers they knew; wifehood, motherhood, and widowhood brought her very near to them; and behind her was the background of an earnest life, against which this figure with health on the cheeks, hope in the eyes, courage on the lips, and the ardor of a wide benevolence warming the whole countenance stood out full of unconscious dignity and beauty; an example to comfort, touch, and inspire them (429).

The narrator interprets the closing scene, in which Christie's community of women join hands in fellowship, as "a hopeful omen" which promises that "the coming generation of women will not only receive but deserve their liberty" (443). To deserve liberty, according to Alcott's schema of values, is to have had experience: of life, of others, of oneself. In *Work: A Story of Experience* she takes the thematic conventions of exploratory novels, extends them, and combines them with a didactic narrative structure. Rather than a "disjointed" or plotless story, she produced a genuinely radical critique of her society, one of the first fictional texts to openly advocate women's freedom to realize their fullest possibilities.

Their possibilities, but not their actualities. For all its transcendentalist optimism, *Work* does not attempt to test its theories in the public, male-dominated sphere: the nineteenth-century world of capital and labor. Seen from the viewpoint of its contemporaries, *Work* presents a genuinely radical transformation in women's perceptions of themselves – the starting point for any revolution. The next problem lies in the area of women's performance – what self-realized women can actually do in the public, as well as the private, sphere. The answer, for most writers of the late nineteenth century, seems to be – very little. As soon as they attempt to move their protagonists out of the domestic sphere, women writers come up against an almost impenetrable barrier: men. Male hegemony appears complete in all areas: in marriage, in business, in politics, in the language of power. While exploratory novels exerted considerable ingenuity devising plots that avoided confronting these questions, late didactic novels, intent on encouraging women to seek effective work beyond the home, could not avoid them. For women writers of the late nineteenth century (and well into the twentieth) the central problem becomes how to escape male dominance.

Elizabeth Stuart Phelps's *The Silent Partner* (1871) is one of the first novels to dramatize this problem, treating its exploration of the relations between men and women in tandem with its condemnation of the relations between labor and capital. Thematically linked – workers' oppressions are associated with women's restrictions, and the chief culprits are men – both plots' closures seem inadequate to the issues that have been raised, making the novel look, structurally, more like *St. Elmo* than like *Work*. Narratively, however, *The Silent Partner* is openly didactic: Its strong narrative voice seeks its narratee, consciously controlling her attitude toward both capitalist and sexist inequities and urging that both systems be changed. Although it is possible to see *The Silent Partner* as a hybrid form, spanning the gap between exploratory and late didactic texts, I am treating it as a didactic novel because its narrative presence is so strong, its ideological intentions so clear, and the issues it raises so central to both labor and gender politics. Although it inadequately resolves the labor and gender problems on which it focuses, it does not try to disguise them; rather, it forcefully articulates them. Its significance as a didactic women's text lies in its exposure of the issues – especially its confrontation of male dominance in private relations – rather than in its call for specific action.

The Silent Partner tells the stories of Perley Kelso and Sip Garth, two young women from opposing classes. Whereas Perley is the daughter of a mill owner, Sip is the daughter of a mill worker; whereas Perley is indolent, lethargic, and thoughtless, Sip is active, feisty, and analytical. Here, the lowerclass woman whose function is to provide a model of self-reliance for the heroine achieves the status of a full-fledged protagonist. As in the other novels we have examined, both girls lose their "protection," in this case their fathers, shortly after they meet. But Sip's father was an abusive drunkard, and Perley's, merely a paternal presence; neither offspring's emotional life is significantly changed by her loss. The impact of paternal death is more significant for Perley, since she inherits her father's share of the mill. But she inherits in name only; in fact, the other partners, her fiancé Maverick Hayley and his father, Hayley Senior, refuse to let her become an active partner. Increasingly concerned for the plight of the workers, Perley educates herself in the life of the mill town, breaking her engagement when she discovers the extent of Maverick's complicity in the workers' oppression, and losing her lethargy as she becomes a ministering angel to the town. Whereas Perley climbs on Phelps's moral scale, Sip remains constant; her function is not so much to change herself as to effect change in Perley by articulating the workers' problems. Sip does, however, soften; she loses her brittle cynicism and becomes a leader of her own class. During the course of the novel both young women refuse to marry. By its end Perley has established a life of philanthropy for herself, and Sip has become a street preacher, urging the workers to put their faith in Christ.

Overtly, *The Silent Partner*'s intent is guided by its author's prefacing note, which claims that "Had Christian ingenuity been generally synonymous with the conduct of manufacturing corporations, I should have found no occasion for the writing of this book" and that "I believe that a wide-spread ignorance exists among us regarding the abuses of our factory system, more especially, but not exclusively, as exhibited in many of the country mills."[20] In terms of the novel's heteroglossia – the multiplicity of languages and verbal–ideological belief systems represented by the play of different voices[21] – many of the characters speak to this issue. The chapter entitled "A Troublesome Character," for instance, focuses on the tragedy of Bijah Mudge, an old man blacklisted for having testified to the state legislature in support of the ten-hour day. Similarly, the chapter "Bub Mell," which focuses on the abuses of child labor, contains author's footnotes to the effect that some of the characters' histories were culled directly from testimonies to the Massachusetts legislature. In addition, hymns and references to Christian texts scattered throughout the novel stress the responsibility Christians must take for the laborers they hire.

The background voices to Sip and Perley's stories, then, articulate an ideology of Christian reform; they are calculated to speak to a narratee who can be roused to sympathy – and action – on behalf of the working class. For instance one appropriate reader for *The Silent Partner* would be nineteen-year-old Mary Willard (sister of Frances Willard, founder of the WCTU), who, reading the serialization of Rebecca Harding Davis's *Life in the Iron Mills* – another strongly didactic novel criticizing the factory system – wrote in 1862 that

> It seemed as though each sentence of [Davis's] strong and passionate writing were a wrench drawing up the lax strings of my being into harmony with those of the wretched people whose miseries she describes. "The cry of the human" is very distinct in this woman's voice; and it will be heard and heeded, I am sure. She makes me feel more like helping those who need help than ever before.[22]

This member of the reading community responded to Davis's *Life in the Iron Mills* as the narrator of Phelps's novel wishes her reader to respond to her.

In addition to the strong ideologies displayed by the novel's many voices, Phelps's narrator positions herself as the arbiter of her reader's point of view. As Mari Jo Buhle and Florence Howe note (373), Phelps, too, had read Davis's *Life in the Iron Mills,* and *The Silent Partner* reflects its influence, not only in its depiction of mill life, but also in its strong, controlling narrative voice. Both Davis and Phelps work with striking linguistic designs; both use the aesthetic potential of language to reinforce their didactic intents. Phelps wrote poetry as well as fiction, and her interest in language is evident in her extraordinary parallelisms and her extended synecdochic descriptions. Her wording is precise and pointed; she uses it to highlight her subjects, especially Perley and the life of the mill workers; to signal, rhythmically and imagistically, exactly what attitudes her reader is expected to take.

For instance, in her introductory description of mill life, Phelps uses synecdoche to indicate the psychological effect on a mill girl of her ontological status as, simply, a pair of "hands":

> If you are one of "the hands" in the Hayle and Kelso Mills – and again, in Hayle and Kelso, – you are so dully used to this classification, "the hands," that you were never known to cultivate an objection to it, are scarcely found to notice its use or disuse. Being surely neither head nor heart, what else remains? Conscious scarcely, from bell to bell, from sleep to sleep, from day to dark, of either head or heart, there seems even a singular appropriateness in the chance of the word with which you are dimly struck. Hayle and Kelso label you. There you are. The world thinks, aspires, creates, enjoys. There you are. You are the fingers of the world. You take your patient place. The world may have need of you, but only that it may think, aspire, create, enjoy. It needs your patience as well as your place. You take both, and you are used to both, and the world is used to both, and so, having put the label on for safety's sake, lest you be mistaken for a thinking, aspiring, creating, enjoying compound, and so some one be poisoned, shoves you into your place upon its shelf, and shuts its cupboard door upon you.

The double-directedness of this passage is complicated by its second-person address, a narrative ploy directed not to worker/readers but to a hypothetical narratee who spans class categories. The "you" being addressed here needs educating in the actualities of mill life, which a worker/reader would not; additionally, she needs to be made conscious not just of work conditions, but their effect on workers' psyches. The narratee addressed here is, then, middle class and female (a later reference is made to "hanging up your shawl and crinoline"), the reader encouraged to identify with the worker along gender lines. This narratee is capable of discerning the narrator's ironies, of understanding the dissociation of sensibility created by being treated only in functional terms. Implicated in the description by the second-person pronoun, drawn into the semi-conscious psyche of a mill girl through the narrative rhythms, stripped of her sense of physical and mental wholeness through being regarded only in functional terms – in terms of her usefulness to someone else, isolated by a sense of herself as a pair of hands as opposed to the rest of creation, the narratee here is transformed into her working double. Unlike Davis's description of her mills, this passage is calculated to impress on the reader not so much the physical horror as the mental horror of mill life, the bludgeoning indifference that blights workers' minds and hearts – their abilities to see themselves as capable of being anything beyond simply "hands."

But Phelps's prose rhythms also associate the bludgeoning effect of mill work with the stultifying effect of wealth; and both, finally, with the stultifying effect of being treated as a woman. The binary categories (primarily inside/outside, us/them, I/other) her narrator uses to characterize both Perley's and the workers' relationships to the world beyond their immediate purview also associate Perley's and the workers' situations. Both are trapped, one by wealth – or, as Perley says later, by "a dream" (127); one by poverty; both by gender. Ultimately, they are linked by limited perceptions and limited options, both class and gender induced. The narrator stands ever ready to point out this linkage.

Perley, too, lives in an I/other world, but her self-absorption, her propensity to see everything beyond herself in purely aesthetic terms, is a product of her wealth and privilege, privilege that finally signals lack of experience. In this novel aestheticism – the classification of perceptions in terms of harmony, color, line – signals poverty of imagination; aesthetic perceptions are limited to people who have no other way of knowing the world, of empathizing with other people's experiences. Thus for instance Perley, seated in her scented carriage, "languidly smiled" at the spectacle of pedestrians in a storm because "She was apt to be amused by the world outside of her carriage. It conceived such original ways of holding its hands, and wearing its hats, and carrying its bundles. It had such a taste in colors, such disregard of clean linen, and was always in such a hurry. This last especially interested her; Miss Kelso had never been in a hurry in her life" (17–18). She has also never been exposed to a winter storm in her life. She can be entertained by the forms and colors of the world beyond her window because her education has only given her that means of conceptualizing what she sees.

When the narrator first introduces Perley, who has passed a dismal January afternoon lounging in the library, she uses alliteration and color and sound imagery to highlight her protagonist's passivity, then parallelism to emphasize the contrast between outside and inside that characterizes Perley's relation to everything beyond her immediate existence.

> [Perley] had noticed in an idle way, swathed to the brain in her folds of heat and color, that the chromatic run of drops upon a window, duly deadened by drawn damask, and adapted nicely to certain conditions of a cannel blaze, had a pleasant sound. Accurately, she had not found herself to be the possessor of another thought since dinner; she had dined at three.
>
> It had been a long storm, but Miss Kelso had found no occasion to dampen the sole of her delicate sandals in the little puddles that dotted the freestone steps and drained pavement. It had been a cold storm, but the library held, as a library should, the tints and scents of June. It had been a dismal storm; but what of that? Miss Kelso was young, well, in love, and – Miss Kelso. Given the problem, Be miserable, she would have folded her hands there by her fire, like a puzzled snow-flake in a gorgeous poppy, and sighed, "But I do not understand!" (11–12)

Here the narrator uses her omniscience to denigrate her protagonist, taking advantage of her ability to know all to render simultaneously Perley's point of view and to characterize Perley's thoughts as "idle." Perley's aesthetic observation – which the narrator highlights through consonance and fusion of sound and color imagery – is not only the one thought she had had in several hours, it is also a cover for her sense (it could hardly called a thought) that her comfort is a function of the cold outside. The parallelism of the second paragraph reinforces the difference between Perley and the cold world beyond her closed and privileged life.

In Bakhtinian terms, the above passage also demonstrates one of the text's double-voiced strategies: hybrid constructions, simultaneously exhibiting the narrator's and Perley's antithetical points of view – "the library held, *as a library should,* the tints and scents of June." In this sentence the subordinate clause reflects Perley's patrician expectation that a well-dressed library should have fresh flowers; at the same time the clause's placement conveys the narrator's intimation of doubt, a clause calculated to suggest that a library should hold books, not flowers, and that perhaps a young woman possessed of enough leisure to spend an afternoon there should be reading, not gazing blankly into the fire. The narrator builds her picture of Perley through such ironic structures, rendering both the girl's and her own value systems through the interactions of antithetical points of view embedded in dominant and subordinate clauses. Through her careful linguistic structuring, the narrator economically and forcefully presents a character whose unreflective indolence marks her as a negative exemplar.

In the linguistic strategies she uses both in reference to Perley and to the mill workers, the narrator establishes a contract with her narratee that assumes the reader shares her animus against lethargy, ignorance, and functional definitions of human beings. In addition, the contract assumes that activity, the conscious effort to "escape," "break loose," and "go out

into the world," as Alcott's narrator would express it, are positive characteristics. When Perley realizes that she has been living in a "dream," for
instance, she attempts to expand and control her life, seeking partnership
in the mills and involvement in her workers' lives. Her move out of her
class perceptions, her effort to assume the experiences of others, is com-
municated by a narrator whose attitude toward her changes as the character expands, shifting from hostility to sympathy. Perley's recognition
that her perceptions, even her conceptions, had been controlled by her
class status constitutes the most violent breaking loose in the novel; the
shift transforms her from a negative to a positive exemplar, and signals
the kind of action the narrator most values, the reaching out of self into
the minds and conditions of others.

But Perley's move out of class restrictions only highlights her gender
restrictions. Now, her limitations are explicitly linked to being female: to
her lack of business experience and to the social barriers to gaining it.
Aware, suddenly, of the world beyond her windows, able and willing to
empathize with her laborers, Perley determines to take her father's place
as a partner in the mills, with the expectation that she will learn the
business and that a position of power will enable her to improve working
conditions; in other words, to take part in the world's work. But Maverick and his father refuse to let her become a partner, offering her at best a
"silent partnership."

Perley's confrontation with her father's partners is rendered through
linguistic structures similar to those that had controlled readers' attitudes
toward Perley's privilege and the workers' lack of it; language that in this
case is calculated to awaken the female reader's resentment of Perley's
subordinate female status. Entitled "A Game of Chess," this chapter uses
the Renaissance convention of chess as sexual metaphor to display the
politics of gender.[23] In it, Perley, her fiancé, and his father ("the Senior")
argue from opposite sides of an inlaid chess table – at various times she
and her lover move fingers and pencils about on the board in various
feints and retreats. Throughout, the men react scornfully to her proposals, alternately bullying and teasing her until "For the first time in her
life [Perley] was inclined to feel ashamed of being a woman" (59). The
chapter concludes by bringing the argument (with its rhetoric of polite
but adamant refusal) and the imagery of the game together, in a closure
of apparent – but only apparent – amicability.

> "What's the use of talking business to a woman?" said Maverick, with
> such unusual animation that he said it almost impatiently.
> "I understand, then" said Perley . . . "that my application to look
> after my mills in an official capacity is refused?"
> "Is refused."
> "In any official capacity?"

> "In any official capacity."
> "It is quite impossible to gratify me in this respect?" pursued Perley, with her bent head inclined a little to the Senior.
> "Quite impossible," replied the Junior.
> "So, out of the question?"
> "And so, out of the question."
> The finger-touch brought the pencil-mark abruptly to a stop upon a helpless square of green.
> "Checkmate?" asked the young man, smiling.
> "Checkmate," said the young lady, smiling too.
> She closed the pencil-case with a snap, tossed the little glazed black-book into the fire, and rang for luncheon, which the three ate upon the chess-table – smiling" (68–9).

There is a studied terseness to the rhythms here, a taut attention to parallel clauses that should alert readers not only to the narrator's anger, but also encourage them to share it. Similar tensions underscore a subsequent scene, in which Maverick treats Perley as an aesthetic object in much the same way as she had treated pedestrians on the stormy night. While she expostulates with him over the workers' living conditions, he

> entertained himself by draping Perley in the shawl from the *tête-à-tête,* as if she had been a lay-figure for some crude and gorgeous design which he failed to grasp. Now he made a Sibyl of her, now a Deborah, now a Maid of Orleans, a priestess, a princess, a Juno; after some reflection, a Grace Darling; after more, a prophetess at prayer (133).

Whereas Perley's objectification of the Other signaled her lack of experience, Maverick's objectification of her signals his refusal to take her seriously – to see her, any more than he sees the mill hands, as a complicated being, not just a useful one. Her only means of retaliation is to reject him, to break their engagement, telling him that she has discovered that "it is only that part of me which gets tired, and has the blues, and minds an easterly storm, and has a toothache, and wants to be amused, and wants excitement, and – somebody on the other side of a silver teapot – which loves you. *I* do not love you, Maverick Hayle!" (164).

Following Perley's discovery of her subordinate female status, these words initiate the novel's most radical theme. As in *Work,* Perley is indicating her emergence into self-consciousness, into awareness of personal integrity. Perley's hitherto passive, passionless ego has discovered itself in relation to others, glories in its discovery, and refuses to relinquish the freedom it gives her. Moreover, while it is not unusual for heroines to break their engagements once they discover their fiancés' moral inadequacies – in *A New-England Tale* Jane Elkins does exactly that – Perley's rejection of marriage altogether is a new element in women's fiction. In *A New-England Tale* Jane marries the "right" man when she finds him, but

in *The Silent Partner* Perley refuses him. "I do not need you now," Perley
tells Stephen Garrick, the man who seems ideally suited for her:

> ". . . Women talk of loneliness. I am not lonely. They are sick and
> homeless. I am neither. They are miserable. I am happy. They grow old.
> I am not afraid of growing old. They have nothing to do. If I had ten
> lives, I could fill them! No, I do not need you, Stephen Garrick."
>
> "Besides," she added, half smiling, half sighing, "I believe that I have
> been a silent partner long enough. If I married you, sir, I should invest
> in life, and you would conduct it. I suspect that I have a preference for a
> business of my own. Perhaps that is part of the trouble" (262).

Similarly, Sip Garth refuses the man who proposes marriage, not because she does not need him, but because she refuses to reproduce her
situation: "I'll never marry anybody, Dirk. I'll never bring a child into the
world to work the mills. . . . I won't be the mother of a child to go and
live my life over again. I'll never marry anybody" (287–8). Sip, the
narrator is careful to state, "was neither a heroine, nor a saint, nor a
fanatic"; she loves Dirk, and she laments her need to make this decision:
"'I don't see why I couldn't have had *that,* leastways,' she cried. . . . 'I
haven't ever had much else. I don't see why *that* should go too.' But she
did see." The next chapter begins "She saw clearly enough in time to be a
very happy woman," introducing a temporal flash forward to show Sip
an itinerant street-preacher, a woman who has achieved happiness
through discovering a public voice. Sip's "life" has combined the oppressions of gender and class; marriage, she recognizes, would perpetuate
them. Celibacy is her way of refusing to keep the system going.

In rejecting marriage, then, Perley and Sip reject male dominance,
seeking their own sources of power. But the novel demonstrates how
limited that power is. *The Silent Partner* identifies the major barrier to
effective women's work as male, men defined – as women are – through
their society's prescriptions, which give them near-absolute power and
encourage them to abuse it. Perley may become a ministering angel to the
workers, but she never becomes an active partner in the mill's administra-
tion. Moreover, her work is meliorist, not radical; her social evenings,
libraries, mission schools, and hospital facilities help polish the edges of
the workers' lives, but they do not effect a change in the twelve-hour day.
Similarly, Sip's plea for "a poor folks' religion," "the religion of Jesus
Christ the Son of God Almighty" (296), which she herself declares is a
"patient way," "a long way and a winding way" (300), preaches patience
rather than immediate change.

But *The Silent Partner* exhibits a more complex problem than its recourse to meliorism, and that concerns the failure of Perley's voice to
maintain its hard-won independence from the men of her class. If we feel
uncomfortable with Perley's and Sip's careers, we need to remind our-

selves that we are reading anachronistically. Phelps, herself a committed Christian, intended *The Silent Partner* as a suggestion for ways to "expend . . . Christian ingenuity . . . in ameliorating the condition of factory operatives" (7). Melioration, then, is part of the novel's didactic intent, a logical outgrowth of its author's convictions. The more complicated problem of the text occurs in conjunction with Phelps's exploration of the verbal–political sources of power. Judith Fetterley has studied *The Silent Partner* from the viewpoint of language, claiming that "At the heart of the book lies the issue of what constitutes a significant act of communication in a world where power depends on verbal dishonesty,"[24] and showing how Phelps associates the silencing of women with the silencing of the mill workers by the male mill owners. Fetterley's discomfort focuses on a chapter near the novel's conclusion, when Perley, who has gained the workers' confidence, quells an incipient strike and convinces the workers to accept the wage cut the "other" partners insist is imperative. In doing so, Perley, in Fetterley's words, "once herself a flood, . . . is now simply another boundary."[25] Fetterley sees this as Phelps's fantasy; rather than continuing to struggle to redefine women's voices, Phelps gives in to the temptation to grant her heroine "power as traditionally conceived – the opportunity to stand out, to impress oneself on others, to cause and direct their motion."[26] "Action," Fetterley shows, is male identified, and Perley's assumption of the voice and ideologies of the men of her class indicates Phelps's failure to find a female voice capable of speaking with as much authority as a man's.

An additional approach to this episode may help put its import into literary–historical perspective. As noted earlier, structurally, *The Silent Partner* looks like an exploratory novel, even though, narratively, it is clearly didactic. If we join our analysis of its didactic narrator–narratee relationship to the Iserean model of the reading process that has underlain our examination of exploratory texts, we will be able to examine the novel in terms of the expectations it has set up, the narrator–narratee contracts it has established, and the possible results of its failure to fulfill its contracts. We have seen how Mary Willard responded to Davis's text, answering its call to action. The long-term significance of *The Silent Partner* may lie in the way it deflects the radical impulses that it, like *Life in the Iron Mills,* has previously awakened. According to Wolfgang Iser, "the more a text . . . confirms an expectation it has initially aroused, the more aware we become of its didactic purpose, so that at best we can only accept or reject the thesis forced upon us."[27] Through their repetitions, their emphases, and their "messages," didactic texts force us to confront each explicit thesis and chose whether or not to accept it. In addition, in his analysis of the reading process Iser discusses readers' identification with the text as one strategy for stimulating their attitudes; that is, he suggests that the preconceptions readers bring to a specific text will influence their interpretations. If the reader's preconceptions are similar to the text's implicit ideology, then she or he will be its ideal interpreter, in harmony with it at all points. Any *disruption* of that harmony would cause a discomfort that would force the reader either to reject or to rationalize – to hide – the disruptive element.

This process helps explain what happens to feminist readers of *The Silent Partner* when its heroine suddenly starts to sound like a male capitalist. Readers who come to *The Silent Partner* prepared to question women's subordinate status, their roles as "silent" partners in a world owned and operated by men, might – like Fetterley – find the disruption of Perley's voice a politicizing experience. Having been led to sympathize with Perley's revolt against male hegemony, they may have responded much as Fetterley responds. In other words, the real impact of *The Silent Partner* may lie in exactly what fueled Fetterley's own discomfort – its power to make readers reject or ignore the actual politics of Perley's "success" in this scene. As we have already seen, nineteenth-century readers freely criticized all aspects of the novels they read, including their logical development. Just before *The Silent Partner* was published, for instance, Katharine Johnson criticized the plot of Mrs. Gaskill's *Wives and Daughters* because "I think Roger's rapid transfer of his affections from Cynthia to Mollie was inconsistent with his slow serious character and a decided mistake [on the author's part],"[28] and remarked apropos of Dickens's *The Mystery of Edwin Drood* that "after all perhaps it is better that the book was never finished for the dénouement might have been as absurd as that of 'Our Mutual Friend,' 'Martin Chuzzlewit,' etc. As it is we can finish it to suit ourselves."[29]

As with the novels whose structural inconsistencies Johnson criticizes, readers can also finish *The Silent Partner* to suit themselves, reading it as they had learned to read exploratory novels, that is, rejecting Perley's change of tone and instead foregrounding her declaration of independence. Fetterley notes that the chapter recording Perley's speech to the strikers is predominantly told by voices other than the narrator's, a distancing technique that indicates Phelps's discomfort with the chapter's implications. Seen within the context of other women's novels of the period, the uneasiness indicated here – both Phelps's and Fetterley's – functions as part of the text's narrative strategy. Unlike Phelps's recourse to Christian meliorism, Perley's assumption of male capitalist discourse is a logical flaw in the text. Certainly the voice that claimed female independence is not the same voice that bids the strikers trust their boss. But, for readers familiar with the interpretive strategies needed to uncover the subversive themes of exploratory texts, the impulse is simply not to "hear" it, to reject its actual implications and to interpret it only through the connotations – the schemata – established by Perley's rejection of male hegemony: that is, to read this scene as Perley's demonstration that she is superior to the male capitalists. This reading processes the text through its feminist plot rather than through its concerns for labor, foregrounding the protagonist's public triumph rather than her reactionary politics. In Iser's terms, the text, its own strong narrative presence springing out of its intertextual context, teaches readers how to complete its feminist mission.

While the class–political voice Perley actually achieves in her freedom does not fulfill the immediate promise inherent in her assumption of a leadership position among the workers, then, the gender–political voice that she achieves does fulfill its didactic mission. The feminist significance of *The Silent Partner* lies in the fact that, in rejecting marriage for her protagonists, Phelps opens up a new arena for women's fiction, making explicit what all the earlier novels sought to hide. Her didacticism is most effective in the arena of heterosexual relationships: Perley and Sip are the first protagonists we have examined to resist openly and successfully the sexual magnetism of the male, creating and maintaining viable, interesting, and rewarding lives for themselves. But this is only apparent from the perspective of literary history, seen within the struggle for voice and self-realization demonstrated by so much of mid–nineteenth-century women's fiction.

Together, *Work* and *The Silent Partner* demonstrate the next step in the fictional liberation of women from ascribed roles, a step in which confrontation with male power was inevitable. Among the exploratory novels examined in this study, only *Ruth Hall* shows a woman freed from marriage and fully successful in finding her own voice. But *Ruth Hall* limits its protagonist's effective work to the apolitical realm. *Work* posits a cooperative women's community with the potential for political action; ending on that note, its optimism is hypothetical. *The Silent Partner* tries to go beyond this; to examine the effectiveness of women's voices in the political world, the world of undiminished, absolute, male power. In the process it shows just how difficult both access and alternatives to that world would be.

PART V

CONCLUSIONS AND IMPLICATIONS

8

ANOMALIES AND ANXIETIES: THE STORY OF AVIS, A COUNTRY DOCTOR, THE AWAKENING, O PIONEERS!

This study has proposed new interpretive strategies for mid–nineteenth-century American women's fiction, taking into account shared responses among the community of nineteenth-century women to the materials they read, and suggesting that the novels offered possibilities for multiple interpretations. In searching out continuities of theme and form, it has also demonstrated that American women's fiction has a shape, a history, a process of evolution that can be traced over time. In "Literary History as a Challenge to Literary Theory" reception-theorist Hans Robert Jauss has written of literature's power to change social expectations. By leading readers to assume that the story they are reading is one whose basic outline they already know – that is, by situating a literary work within a specific literary tradition – and then disappointing those anticipations, texts can help alter readers' literary, and ultimately social, horizons.[1] The thematic evolution of American women's novels from what I have called the early didactic novel to the late didactic novel demonstrates precisely this kind of shift. Over a roughly eighty-year span, women's fiction documents a radical turnabout in attitudes toward women's duties and possibilities. Exploratory novels, with their conventional overplots and their unconventional subthemes, mark a watershed in the literary inscription of American women.

The horizons delineated by each type of novel illustrate the possibilities for female action to which authors could expect their readers to respond. Formally, early nineteenth-century women's texts are closely related to the eighteenth-century English novel; their significance for a study of American women's literature lies in their *exclusion* of possibility: first, in their thematic insistence on women's submission to justified authority and, second, in their formal restriction of readers' interpretations, their refusal to countenance alternative points of view. Didactic in intention and design, they focus on exemplary characters – often created in sets of binary opposites – and feature engaging narrators (generally women) who identify their narratees (also generally women), speaking to them openly and frequently. The dominant contract struck between the narrator and her narratee is predicated on the narratee's weakness, her potential for error; the narrator's function is to teach her how to maintain her virtue. Because these texts are so tightly focused, they contain a high level of internal coherence, employing traditional rhetorical devices such as parallelism and repetition to reinforce their points, and classical imagery and allusions to establish standards for conduct. Overall, their assumption is that virtue in a woman consists of passivity, obedience to legitimate external authority, and self-abnegation. Apolitical, they do not question their society's power structures; rather, they teach their readers how to accommodate themselves to the status quo.

Exploratory novels undermine cultural ideologies, expanding readers' horizons of acceptable female behavior as they posit alternatives to conventional female roles. Often employing distancing narrators, they tend to refrain from overt monitoring of their narratees' interpretive strategies, leaving them with far more freedom to construe stories according to their own personal experience and ideological categories. In addition, the multiple rhetorical and cultural codes on which exploratory novels are built create much more open hermeneutic possibilities than do didactic texts. Although most conform to an overplot that valorizes marriage as the ultimate goal of a woman's life, most also "write beyond the romantic ending," as Rachel Blau DuPlessis expresses it,[2] containing subthemes that deflect readers' attention from those goals. Between their initial "abandonment" by those appointed to protect them and their ultimate "rescue" by the men they will marry, heroines of exploratory novels learn how to fend for themselves in a society that denigrates women's capabilities and restricts their access to power in the world beyond the home. In the process, the novels expose the biases that rationalize women's restrictions: as the protagonists become successful writers, farmers, or performers, they prove to themselves – and most importantly to their readers – that in fact they are capable of achievement beyond the home. For readers already predisposed toward women's movement out of the domestic sphere, they provide a strong incentive to explore alternative possibilities.

Late didactic novels show the influence of the thematic forays of the exploratory strain. Formally reverting to a more tightly controlled narrative structure – engaged narrators interpreting the story for their narratees – thematically they present an ideology antithetical to early didactic texts. Building on exploratory novels' experiments in possibility, they emphasize women's adventures beyond the home, advocating increased

worldly experience and challenging the hierarchical structure of traditional marriage. They also reach out into the political realm, associating
women's restrictions with racial and wage slavery, and placing women in
the forefront of social reform. Instead of seeking to cure a specific problem latent in a class of atomized narratees, they seek to restructure the
ideologies that define – that give meaning to – women's lives. Seen
historically, that is, within the development of nineteenth-century American women's fiction, they illustrate a genuinely radical change in wom-
en's attitudes toward themselves and their personal and political capabilities. By the mid-1870s, the passive, self-abnegating female of early
didactic novels had been transformed into an active, self-possessed, and
politically conscious woman. The subversive effect of exploratory novels
was to expand horizons, to redefine women's possibilities within the
dominant culture.

The next step required exploration of how those possibilities could be
realized. We have already seen how Elizabeth Stuart Phelps struggled to
create a protagonist who becomes conscious of her possibilities, who
rejects marriage in order to maintain her autonomy, but whose work is
limited by her lack of effective power, and her leadership of the workers
compromised by capitalist exigencies. Later novels address these and
related issues with increasing anxiety. The literary history this study has
traced also provides a context for these later novels; well-known works
like Kate Chopin's *The Awakening* (1899), Sara Orne Jewett's *A Country
Doctor* (1884), and Willa Cather's *O Pioneers!* (1913) build on the tradi-
tions delineated through the course of nineteenth-century American
women's novels. Neither didactic nor exploratory, these later works can
and have been seen as forerunners of modern fiction; formally, they are
material for a study of twentieth-century American women's novels. But
because their themes evolve out of nineteenth-century women's concerns, it is useful to look briefly at them as examples of texts that both
culminate that tradition and articulate new concerns. With Phelps's lesser-
known *The Story of Avis* (1877), they take as their problematic the two
themes most often addressed in exploratory novels (covertly) and late
didactic novels (overtly): the moral and psychological problem of effective nondomestic work for women, and the sexual problem of male
dominance, especially within the marriage relation. Self-gratification becomes a related issue, and, with that, the nature of women. None of the
heroines of these texts are self-abnegating women, and their creators'
varying treatments of them on this score demonstrate an evolving redefinition of women's nature.

Work becomes the central goal for the protagonists of late nineteenth-
and early twentieth-century women's novels, work overtly defined as
occupation other than domesticity. Only nondomestic work comes to be

seen as the avenue to genuine self-reliance. In many, there is a moment of epiphany, often occurring in a solitary natural setting, during which the protagonists recognize their identities and their missions. The Words-worthian moment of self-realization is here appropriated for a specifically feminist purpose.

> Avis climbed down from the apple-tree . . . with eyes in which a proud young purpose hid. It had come to her now – it had all come to her very plainly – why she was alive; what God meant by making her; what he meant by her being Avis Dobell, and reading just that thing [i.e., *Aurora Leigh*] that morning in the apple-boughs, with the breath of June upon her. . . .
>
> She went straight to her father's knee, and, standing with her straw hat hanging by the strings between her crossed hands, said as simply as if she had been asking for a kiss, –
>
> "Papa, I should like to be an artist, if you please."[3]

Avis is not reading *Aurora Leigh* by chance; as we have seen, women's diaries and letters amply testify to their admiration for Browning, and her story of a woman poet figures as an inspirational text in American women's novels through much of the nineteenth century. Here Phelps uses it to signal Avis's awakening to her own talents. The conjunction of precursive text and natural setting form the matrix for Avis's discovery of her own identity; Phelps is drawing on an established tradition in women's fiction.

Nan Prince, of Jewett's *A Country Doctor,* also discovers her vocation in a solitary natural setting, during the long, unhappy summer following her completion of formal schooling, when she rambles through the woods and fields, feeling that "This was no life at all, this fretful idleness" (123); "for her part it was not enough to be waited upon and made comfortable, she wanted something more, to be really of use in the world, and to do work which the world needed" (124). Unknowingly lying on the spot where her unhappy mother had almost drowned them both, Nan realizes that she wants to study medicine – a childhood ambition that her school years had almost made her forget.

> The thought entirely possessed her, and the flow of excitement and enthusiasm made her spring from the ceder boughs and laugh aloud. Her whole heart went out to this work, and she wondered why she had ever lost sight of it. She was sure this was the way in which she could find most happiness. God had directed her at last, and though the opening of her sealed orders had been long delayed, the suspense had only made her surer that she must hold fast this unspeakably great motive: something to work for with all her might as long as she lived.[4]

In both these scenes, the authors draw on the nineteenth-century asso-ciation of good women with nature and nature's God; here, however, they are turning the association to new uses, extending the scenic background – the code – to suggest that God may have intended good women for purposes other than domesticity. Both Avis and Nan are breaking new ground, choosing careers that reject the primacy of domesticity. In doing so, they seek a worldly authority that, if successful, would go far toward changing the ontological status of all women. Thirty years later, Cather's O Pioneers! shows the influence of that search. Alexandra Bergson, Cather's protagonist, also has an epiphanic moment when she recognizes her kinship to the land. After forcing her reluctant brothers to take advantage of a drought by buying up their failed neighbors' lands, she finds that, in leadership, she has defined herself:

> That night she had a new consciousness of the country, felt almost a new relation to it. . . . She had never known before how much the country meant to her. The chirping of the insects down in the long grass had been like the sweetest music. She had felt as if her heart were hiding down there, somewhere, with the quail and the plover and all the little wild things that crooned or buzzed in the sun. Under the long shaggy ridges, she felt the future stirring.[5]

In this as in the other moments of realization, the heroine identifies herself with her mission; significantly, in Cather's novel Alexandra's epiphany comes after she has imposed her will on the male members of her family and assumed the authoritative voice. Unlike Fleda Ringgan, Alexandra has no ambivalence about becoming a leader.

In some of these novels, protagonists' ambitions are projected as inheritances from frustrated mothers – the search for nondomestic careers is seen as a biological as well as a spiritual inheritance. In fact, this phenomenon becomes a new code, elaborated in the first novels, referred to in succeeding ones. In Work, Christie's Aunt Betsy confesses to having had "restless fits" before she married. In The Story of Avis the connection is more explicit: Avis Dobell's mother had wanted to be an actress but had married instead Hegel Dobell, professor of philosophy. When Avis later asks him whether her mother "in all those years, shut up in this quiet house . . . ever knew a restless longing in that – in those – in such directions?" her father responds, "superbly," "Your mother was my wife. . . . and my wife loved me" (25). Still, Avis remembers that when she had asked her mother if marriage had fully satisfied her ambitions, her mother had wept, clutching the child and calling her "my little woman" (24). The novel hints that the mother died from her frustrations; she "had been ailing, ill: none knew exactly why. It was quite certain that she had no disease; only the waxing and waning and wasting of a fine, feverish excitement, for which there seemed to be neither cause nor remedy" (25). In A Country Doctor the association between mother's and daughter's ambitions is less elaborated, but it draws on prior texts that associated women's frustrations with their limited options. Here Nan Prince's mother is merely said to have had a "restless, impatient, miserable sort of longing for The Great Something Else" which had ruined her marriage and led to her premature death.

The biological justification suggested in both novels supports authorial contentions that not only women's career expectations but their very natures were changing; each text occasionally speaks directly to this point. While latter-day women's novels contain few narrative addresses to the reader (*The Awakening* and *O Pioneers!* have none), the narrators, when they speak, generally do so to highlight their contention that a major redefinition of women's nature and function is imminent. The narrator of Jewett's *A Country Doctor,* for instance, culminates her story of a girl's struggle to realize her ambition to study medicine by announcing that "The preservation of the race is no longer the only important question; the welfare of the individual will be considered more and more. The simple fact that there is a majority of women in any centre of civilization means that some are set apart by nature for other uses and conditions than marriage" (248). Equally militant is Phelps's summarizing homily, in which her narrator culminates her story of a talented artist whose career has been destroyed by marriage and motherhood by announcing that

> We have been told that it takes three generations to make a gentleman; we may believe that it will take as much, or more, to make A WOMAN. A being of radiant physique; the heiress of ancestral health on the maternal side; a creature forever more of nerve than of muscle, and therefore trained to the energy of the muscle and the repose of the nerve; physically educated by mothers of her own fibre and by physicians of her own sex, – such a woman alone is fitted to acquire the drilled brain, the calmed imagination, and sustained aim, which constitute intellectual command.
>
> A creature capable of this command, in whom emotion intensifies reflection, and passion strengthens purpose, and self-poise is substituted for self-extravagance, – such a creature only is competent to the terrible task of adjusting the sacred individuality of her life to her supreme capacity of love and the supreme burden and perils which it imposes upon her (246).

These narrators' remarks nicely delimit the problems their novels address: Nan Prince, Jewett's protagonist, achieves her goal but renounces the possibility of marriage in order to do so; Avis Dobell, Phelps's protagonist, fails because she is unable to find a way to combine her career with her domestic duties. Whereas Jewett's novel ends with Nan glorying in her own future, Phelps's concludes with Avis reading the story of Sir Galahad's inheritance of the quest for the Holy Grail to her daughter, significantly named "Wait." Both novels affirm nondomestic careers; neither, however, can envision a way to combine them with marriage.

These affirmations of work, of a particular mission in life, seem antithetical to Edna Pontillier's awakening, in Kate Chopin's *The Awakening*. Here, music is the vehicle for the protagonist's self-consciousness. Another woman, a pianist who has renounced human relationships in favor of her work, first arouses Edna's emotions. Listening to her, ". . . the very passions themselves were aroused within [Edna's] soul, swaying it, lashing it, as the waves daily beat upon her splendid body. She trembled, she was choking, and the tears blinded her."[6] Unlike Nan, Avis, or Alexandra, however, Edna has no specific purpose. Conscious of her restricted life, she nevertheless drifts, rebelling against her limitations but unable to formulate concrete goals.

Yet Edna's awakening is significant within this literature – first, because it highlights the circumstances of women for whom marriage spells an end to possibility, and second, because it portrays female sexuality *without* recourse to a magnetic male. Partly in rebellion against her family, partly because she thought that marriage would make her "take her place with a certain dignity in the world of reality, closing the portals forever behind her upon the realm of romance and dreams" (47), Edna had married a wealthy Creole after a girlhood preoccupied with romantic fantasies. Once she realizes that her husband does not satisfy her sexually and that marriage and motherhood bore her, she searches for a way to gratify herself, in part confusing her search for selfhood with her late-burgeoning sexuality. In this, Edna is unique among the protagonists we have seen; none of the others, not even Cassandra Morgeson, confused self and sex. Rather, they resisted sex in the interest of self; as we have seen, one function of the Byronic male in women's literature consists in being a force to be resisted. But unlike Edna Earl, Edna Pontillier is not brought to consciousness by a St. Elmo; she is awakened by a combination of music, sun, ocean, and a very pliable young man. Without a concrete force against which to define herself, her self-discovery is confused and aimless: Although "she was becoming herself and daily casting aside that fictitious self which we assume like a garment with which to appear before the world" (148), her burgeoning self has nowhere to go, no object upon which to spend itself. Playing with art, playing with financial independence, playing with various young men, Edna comes to realize that she will never find fulfillment.

> Despondency had come upon her there in the wakeful night, and had never lifted. There was no one thing in the world that she desired. There was no human being whom she wanted near her except Robert; and she even realized that the day would come when he, too, and the thought of

him would melt out of her existence, leaving her alone. The children appeared before her like antagonists who had overcome her; who had overpowered and sought to drag her into the soul's slavery for the rest of her days. But she knew a way to elude them. She was not thinking of these things when she walked down to the beach (300).

Edna's predicament is the underside of Nan Prince's, Avis Dobell's, and Alexandra Bergson's; like them, unable to define herself as wife and mother (the text is careful to tell us that she is not a "mother-woman"), but lacking the talent or courage to develop a professional mantle, she is unable to formulate a viable selfhood. Although Rachel Blau DuPlessis regards Edna's suicide as a rejection of "the binary, either/or convention of love versus vocation,"[7] in fact Edna's condition never achieves the definition of either/or. In the course of her awakening Edna learns how to regard herself as a sexual being – a necessary aspect of her burgeoning awareness of selfhood – but, unlike the misanthropic woman artist whose music arouses her, she never transcends that self-image, formulating an ego that sees itself divorced from intimate relationships. Her problem is not that she wants a vocation that her society forbids, but that she cannot – or will not – define herself in opposition to private relationships. Her suicide is a means of "eluding" – frustrating – forces, including herself, that insist on defining her as mother, lover, or wife. No promise of future change emerges at the end of this book; *The Awakening* exposes a problem without suggesting that it can be resolved. In contrast, although Avis Dobell's own goals are destroyed, she at least looks forward to the time when her daughter will take over her mission: "It would be easier for her daughter to be alive; and be a woman, than it had been for her; so much as this, she understood; more than this she felt herself too spent to question" (247). Edna, goalless, daughterless, not understanding how to manifest herself outside of the sexually delineated sphere, escapes a future that she sees as only further enslaving her.

For all these protagonists, marriage is antithetical to self-realization. Where exploratory novels circumvented the issue of male dominance, removing heroes in order to give their protagonists time and space to realize themselves (a theme I have come to think of as "the phenomenon of the disappearing male"), later novels confront the problem of male dominance directly. We have seen how Phelps rejects marriage for her protagonists in *The Silent Partner;* in *The Story of Avis* she shows what happens to a talented woman who attempts it. Believing that "success, for a woman, means absolute surrender, in whatever direction" (69), Phelps shapes the novel to demonstrate what happens to a woman who tries to divide her energies. Almost naturalistic in its determinist imagery, *The Story of Avis* is the story of inevitable failure. Avis, of course, is

Latin for bird, and dead bird symbols abound in the novel, from the birds who are killed flying into the harbor light to the wounded bird Avis's lover inadvertently smothers when he is supposed to be keeping it warm. In addition the text is shaped by quest myths: It opens referring to Spenser and closes quoting the story of Sir Galahad. All of these references illuminate Avis's own failed mission. In Florence, studying art, young Avis had worked "with . . . patient service of her possibility" (38), knowing that "My ideals of art are those with which marriage is perfectly incompatible" (69). Once persuaded to marry Philip Ostrander, however, domestic and maternal cares destroy her. The burden of sleepless nights with fretful children, laundry-days, unexpected guests, a self-centered and unsympathetic husband, and the host of other interruptions slowly eat away at her possibilities.

Phelps's feminist determinism has offended some twentieth-century readers who would not, one suspects, bring similar complaints to their reading of, say, Stephen Crane or Theodore Dreiser. Alfred Habegger, for instance, has claimed that "the basic defect in *Avis* . . . is that it was too feminine . . . written for women, in defense of women's interests and in support of women's myths and values . . . It was not an exploration of the bitter antagonism between men and women; it was itself bitterly antagonistic."[8] Critical remarks like this need to be considered within the entire context of writing that challenges the dominant power group by portraying that group as it looks to those outside: Few critics would dare to claim that a novel written by a man is "too male . . . written for men, in defense of men's interests," though most books written by men are precisely that. There is a tendency among white male critics, however, to fault women's writing for being antagonistic to men, and to fault minority writing – especially Black writing – for being antagonistic to the white power structure. These critics miss the heart of the works they censure: What they see as defects are in fact the lifeblood of protest literature, portraits of power relationships from the point of view of the subordinate member.

Such portraits produce a shock of recognition from those readers who find their own experience mirrored in the text. For example, although Habegger objects to Avis's "'maternal' endurance" of her ailing, self-centered husband, Philip Ostrander (Ostrander develops tuberculosis, from which he eventually dies),[9] contemporary readers would have found him familiar both from their own experience and from their reading. Victims of tuberculosis are noted for their irritability, as Martha Farnsworth learned when tending the ailing husband she had dutifully followed out to Colorado and California in 1891.[10] Not only did Farnsworth endure her husband's vicious temper, she nursed him through his last illness despite having lost all affection for him. Like Avis, she listened to him maunder on his deathbed, recording that he told her that "when he gets well . . . he will be a better man and be good to me, and do many things for me."[11] Farnsworth believed him no more than Avis believes Philip.

Readers would also understand Avis's maternal relationship to Philip intertextually, through other novels that portrayed women's strategy of coping with an unhappy marriage by assuming a maternal relationship to their husbands, as Sophie Churchill does to John Huss Withers, in *The Deserted Wife*. What Habegger – and Helen Papashvily before him – reads as a reduction, or maiming, of the male to infantile or invalid status is in fact a code describing a major strategy American women use to maintain themselves and their marriages when they discover that their husbands are not equal to them. In a society in which divorce was shameful, a viable way to cope with a man who could not or would not rise to his wife's level of intelligence, morality, or courage was for her to assume a stance that admitted intimacy but at the same time preserved distance and respect; that is, to act as his mother. The quality of Avis that Habegger sees as too feminine is in fact an extremely effective portrayal of a woman's coping strategy from a woman's point of view. Or, as Phelps commented about her own response to this novel, " 'The Story of Avis' is a woman's book; and an author would care for it in proportion as she cared for her own sex."[12]

Phelps does blame the demands of domesticity for women's failures, using examples familiar to middle-class women who have chosen the "normal" life of marriage, childbearing, and domesticity but who harbor personal aspirations as well. In one of her rare interruptions into the text, the narrator situates Avis – hitherto presented as exceptional – within the ordinary world of women whose ambitions are daily frustrated:

> Women understand – only women altogether – what a dreary will-o-the-wisp is this old, common, I had almost said commonplace, experience, "When the fall sewing is done," "When the baby can walk," "When the house-cleaning is over," "When the company has gone," "When we have got through with the whooping-cough," "When I am a little stronger," then I will write the poem, or learn the language, or study the great charity, or master the symphony, then I will act, dare, dream, become. Merciful is the fate that hides from any soul the prophecy of its still-born aspirations (149).

Avis – like Edna Pontillier a bird that wants to fly – is destroyed by the inessential, the incessant, trivial demands that constitute most women's lives.

Surprisingly, in this text Phelps is not ideologically opposed to marriage, only to its arrangements. By the end of the story, when Avis, bereft of husband and first-born child, realizes that she will never again paint a great picture, she does not regret having loved, only the way conventional marriage forbids women from realizing any other ambition.

> Avis stretched out her arms into the empty air. She did not know how to express distinctly, even to her own consciousness, her conviction that she might have painted better pictures – not worse – for loving Philip and the children; that this was what God meant for her, for all of them, once, long ago. She had not done it. It was too late now (244).

Singleminded dedication to her work and understanding that it cannot be combined with marriage also characterize Jewett's Nan Prince. This text contains much discussion of work and its function in human life. "Christ's glory was his usefulness and gift for helping others" (85) one character remarks, and medicine is seen as a way to live a genuinely Christian life. In the novel, this provides a rationale for Nan's profession; unlike Dr. Zay, in Phelps's 1882 novel of that name, in A Country Doctor Jewett feels the need to finesse Nan's livelihood. In giving her heroine's life to a service profession, she eludes the accusation that Nan is an unnatural woman. Nan's choice to practice medicine is projected as an almost holy decision; "Nan was no idler; she had come to her work as Christ came to his, not to be ministered unto but to minister" (251).

Nevertheless Jewett, too, projects her protagonist's career in opposition to marriage and domesticity. Nan's mentor sees that "Nan is not the sort of girl who will be likely to marry. When a man or woman has that sort of self-dependence and unnatural self-reliance, it shows itself very early. I believe that it is a mistake for such a woman to marry. . . . the law of her nature is that she must live alone and work alone, I shall help her to keep it instead of break it, by providing something else than the business of housekeeping and what is called a woman's natural work, for her activity and capacity to spend itself upon" (103). Similarly, when Nan rejects the young man who seeks to marry her, she tells him that "something tells me all the time that I could not marry the whole of myself as most women can; there is a great share of my life which could not have its way, and could only hide itself and be sorry. I know better and better that most women are made for another sort of existence, but by and by I must do my part in my own way to make many homes happy instead of one . . ." (242). Like Avis, Nan recognizes that she can only dedicate herself to one great work; unlike Avis, she does not try to divide her energies. Returning to her mentor, Nan finishes her medical studies and prepares to take over his practice. The novel concludes with her thanking God "for my future" (259).

Finally, in O Pioneers! Alexandra Bergson does not marry until she has achieved her purpose, creating a fertile farmland out of the rough prairie. Projected as the strongest woman – even the strongest person – on the

Divide, Alexandra is an emblem of the land itself; as such, no real man can be her equal. Only her fantasy lover, "a man . . . like no man she knew; he was much larger and stronger and swifter, and he carried her as easily as if she were a sheaf of wheat" (206) is a fit mate for a woman of her stature; the man she finally marries, Carl Lindstrum, is much weaker than she. Moreover, the marriage comes at the end of the novel, when Alexandra is over forty and her work is essentially accomplished. It is clear that she is the dominant character in their relationship, and it is unlikely that she will have children. Alexandra's purpose in life was to tame the prairie; that accomplished, marriage for her is tantamount to retirement.

Late nineteenth- and early twentieth-century American women's novels, then, begin to confront the issues – ultimately power issues – that midcentury novels could only treat covertly. In all, struggle is evident; no single author resolves the problem of combining work, self-reliance, self-gratification, sexuality, and marriage. In all, awareness of heroines' anomalous positions is evinced through minor characters' disapproval; even Alexandra suffers from her companions' assumption that her self-reliance renders her incapable of giving or receiving romantic love. In addition, most of the heroines suffer internal conflicts when they discover that domestic life – especially motherhood – is not in itself fulfilling; they fear they may not be natural women. All the novels posit marriage as the foremost barrier to women's freedom to harvest their own talents. Married women in these novels not only carry the burden of domestic responsibilities, they also suffer the onus of second-class status, constantly being required to defer their own gratification in response to their families' immediate needs. Significantly, they resent it. Those like Edna, who rebel, find themselves adrift; those like Avis, who yield, find their own creativity eroded. In these novels women achieve meaningful and effective work that defines them in nondomestic terms only when they remove themselves from the heterosexual arena.

American women writers ushered in the new century by inscribing a woman who was actively seeking to be defined in terms of the world and her own ambitions. That they could write as openly as they did indicates that a major shift in readers' horizons of expectation had already occurred. The exploratory novel of the mid-nineteenth century was in part responsible for that; in inscribing women's adventures beyond the private sphere, it created a literary history that valorized women's experience, encouraged readers to consider alternative possibilities, and ultimately altered the social framework within which women's ambitions could be received.

NOTES

INTRODUCTION
1. Nathaniel Hawthorne to George Ticknor, 1:78, quoted in Joyce W. Warren, ed., *Ruth Hall and Other Writings by Fanny Fern* (New Jersey: Rutgers University Press, 1986), *xxxv*.
2. Fred Lewis Pattee, *The Feminine Fifties* (New York: D. Appleton-Century Company, Inc., 1940), 118, 120.
3. Judith Fetterley, ed., *Provisions: A Reader from 19th-Century American Women* (Bloomington: Indiana University Press, 1985), 22.
4. For a discussion of cultural associations of women with excessive speech see Dale Spender, *Man Made Language* (London: Routledge and Kegan Paul, 1980). Reviewing some recent studies comparing the actual amount men and women speak, Spender concludes that the standard for the traditional assumption that women talk most is not men but silence – that is, the desirable state for women, unlike for men, is silence, and therefore that any female speech is seen as excessive (42–3). More recent contributions to the study of gender differences in oral discourse include Sally McConnell-Ginet, "Intonation in a Man's World," in *Language, Gender, and Society,* Barrie Thorne, Cheris Kramarae, and Nancy Henley, eds., 1983, 69–88; Candace West and Don H. Zimmerman, "Small Insults: A Study of Interruptions in Cross-Sex Conversations between Unacquainted Persons," ibid., 102–17; and Audre Lorde, "The Transformation of Silence into Language and Action," *Sister Outsider: Essays and Speeches by Audre Lorde* (Trumansburg, New York: The Crossing Press, 1984), 40–4.
5. Herbert Ross Brown, *The Sentimental Novel in America, 1789–1860* (Durham, NC: Duke University Press, 1940).
6. Mrs. Mary Ann (Coit) Parker, Diary, 1849–50; entry for March 26, 1850. New York Historical Society, Manuscripts Division.
7. Fred Kaplan, *Sacred Tears: Sentimentality in Victorian Literature* (Princeton, NJ: Princeton University Press, 1987).
8. Fred Kaplan, *Sacred Tears*, 6.
9. Helen Waite Papashvily, *All the Happy Endings: A Study of the Domestic Novel in America, the Women Who Wrote It, the Women Who Read It, in the Nineteenth Century* (New York: Harper and Bros., 1956).

211

10. Ann Douglas, *The Feminization of American Culture* (New York: Avon Books, 1977).
11. Recent articles by Jane Tompkins, Joanne Dobson, and Mary P. Hiatt undertake just such explorations. See Tompkins's afterword to *The Wide, Wide World*, by Susan Warner (New York: The Feminist Press, 1987), 584–608; Dobson's "The Hidden Hand: Subversion of Cultural Ideology in Three Mid–Nineteenth-Century Women's Novels," *AQ*, Vol. 38, No. 2 (Summer 1986), 223–42; and Hiatt's "Susan Warner's Subtext: The Other Side of Piety," *Journal of Evolutionary Psychology*, Vol. 8, Nos. 3 & 4 (August, 1987), 250–61.
12. Nina Baym, *Woman's Fiction: A Guide to Novels by and about Women in America, 1820–1870* (Ithaca: Cornell University Press, 1978).
13. Nina Baym, "Melodramas of Beset Manhood: How Theories of American Fiction Exclude Women Authors." Reprinted in Elaine Showalter (ed.) *The New Feminist Criticism: Essays on Women, Literature, Theory* (New York: Pantheon Books, 1985), 63–80.
14. Mary Kelley, *Private Woman, Public Stage: Literary Domesticity in Nineteenth-Century America* (New York: Oxford University Press, 1984).
15. John Tebbel, *A History of Book Publishing in the United States: The Creation of an Industry, 1630–1865* (New York: R. R. Bowker Co., 1972).
16. Frank Luther Mott, *Golden Multitudes: The Story of Best Sellers in the United States* (New York: The Macmillan Company, 1947).
17. Alfred Habbegger, *Gender, Fantasy, and Realism in American Literature* (New York: Columbia University Press, 1982).
18. Annette Kolodny, *The Land before Her: Fantasy and Experience of the American Frontiers, 1630–1860* (Chapel Hill, NC: University of North Carolina Press, 1984).
19. Nina Baym, *Novels, Readers, and Reviewers: Responses to Fiction in Antebellum America* (Ithaca: Cornell University Press, 1984).
20. Jane Tompkins, *Sensational Designs: The Cultural Work of American Fiction, 1790–1860* (New York: Oxford University Press, 1985).
21. David S. Reynolds, *Beneath the American Renaissance: The Subversive Imagination in the Age of Emerson and Melville* (New York: Alfred A. Knopf, 1988).
22. Elizabeth Ammons, ed., *Critical Essays on Harriet Beecher Stowe* (Boston: G. K. Hall, 1980).
23. Eric J. Sundquist, ed., *New Essays on* Uncle Tom's Cabin (Cambridge, England: Cambridge University Press, 1986).
24. Ann D. Wood, "The 'Scribbling Women' and Fanny Fern: Why Women Wrote,'" *AQ*, Vol. 23, No. 1 (Spring 1971), 3–24.
25. Jane Tompkins, "Sentimental Power: *Uncle Tom's Cabin* and the Politics of Literary History," *Glyph*, 8 (1981); republished in *Sensational Designs: The Cultural Work of American Fiction, 1790–1860*, 122–46.
26. Annette Kolodny, "Dancing through the Minefield: Some Observations on the Theory, Practice, and Politics of a Feminist Literary Criticism." First published in *Feminist Studies*, Vol. 6, No. 1 (Spring 1980), 1–25; reprinted in Elaine Showalter, ed., *The New Feminist Criticism*, 144–67.

27. Alfred Habegger, "A Well-Hidden Hand," *Novel: A Forum on Fiction*, Vol. 14, No. 3 (Spring 1981), 197–212.

28. Annette Kolodny, "A Map for Misreading: Or, Gender and the Interpretation of Literary Texts." First published in *New Literary History*, Vol. 11, No. 3 (Spring 1980), 451–68; reprinted in Showalter, ed., *The New Feminist Criticism*, 46–62.

29. Joanne Dobson, "The Hidden Hand: Subversion of Cultural Ideology in Three Mid–Nineteenth-Century Women's Novels."

30. Judith Fetterley, " 'Checkmate': Elizabeth Stuart Phelps's *The Silent Partner*," *Legacy: A Journal of Nineteenth-Century American Women Writers*, Vol. 3, No. 2 (Fall 1986), 17–30.

31. Roland Barthes, "Structural Analysis of Narratives," in *A Barthes Reader*, Susan Sontag, ed. (New York: Hill and Wang, 1982), 293.

32. Hans Robert Jauss, *Toward an Aesthetic of Reception*, translated by Timothy Bahti (Minneapolis: University of Minnesota Press, 1982), 40–1.

33. Steven Mailloux, *Interpretive Conventions: The Reader in the Study of American Fiction* (Ithaca: Cornell University Press, 1982), 169–70.

34. Julia Newberry, *Diary*, Introduction by Margaret Ayer Barnes and Janet Ayer Fairbank. (New York: Norton & Co., Inc., 1933), 75.

35. *The North American Review*, Vol. 76, No. 158 (January, 1853), 113.

36. Catharine E. Beecher, *Woman Suffrage and Woman's Profession* (Hartford: Brown and Gross, 1871).

37. Kathryn Kish Sklar, *Catharine Beecher: A Study in American Domesticity* (New York: W. W. Norton & Co., 1976; first published, 1973, by Yale University), 193.

38. Nina Baym, *Woman's Fiction*, 294.

39. Rachel Blau DuPlessis, *Writing beyond the Ending: Narrative Strategies of Twentieth-Century Women Writers* (Bloomington: Indiana University Press, 1985).

40. Lydia Maria Child Letters, 1845–1880, American Antiquarian Society Manuscripts Department, Worcester, Massachusetts. Reprinted in Milton Meltzer and Patricia G. Hollands, eds., *Lydia Maria Child: Selected Letters, 1817–1880* (Amherst: University of Massachusetts Press, 1982), 238–9.

41. Nina Baym, *Novels, Readers, and Reviewers*, esp. 173–95.

42. Herman Melville, *Moby Dick* (New York: W. W. Norton and Company, Inc., 1967), 349.

43. Nina Baym, *Novels, Readers, and Reviewers*, 257.

44. Harriet Beecher Stowe to Lady Byron, April 9, 1859. Beecher-Stowe Collection, Folder A-102-302, the Arthur and Elizabeth Schlesinger Library on the History of Women in America, Radcliffe College, Cambridge, Massachuetts (hereafter abbreviated to Schlesinger Library). The entire Beecher-Stowe Collection is owned by the Stowe-Day Foundation, Hartford, Connecticut.

45. Harriet Beecher Stowe to Calvin Stowe, August, 1844. Beecher-Stowe Collection, Folder 67-93, Schlesinger Library.

46. E.D.E.N. Southworth, *The Deserted Wife* (Philadelphia: T. B. Peterson, 1855), 372. First published in 1850.

47. Nathaniel Hawthorne to George Ticknor, 1:78, quoted in Joyce W. Warren, ed., *Ruth Hall and Other Writings by Fanny Fern*, *xxxv*.

48. Roland Barthes, "Structural Analysis of Narratives," in Susan Sontag, ed., *A Barthes Reader*, 254.
49. Ibid, 269.
50. Mary Crawford and Roger Chaffin, "The Reader's Construction of Meaning: Cognitive Research on Gender and Comprehension," in Elizabeth A. Flynn and Patrocinio P. Schweickart, eds., *Gender and Reading: Essays on Readers, Texts, and Contexts* (Baltimore: The Johns Hopkins University Press, 1986), 4. Other literary scholars have been working with similar reader-response investigations into current women's reading behavior, most notably Janice A. Radway in *Reading the Romance: Women, Patriarchy, and Popular Literature* (Chapel Hill: University of North Carolina Press, 1984), and Elizabeth Long, in "Women, Reading, and Cultural Authority," *American Quarterly*, Vol. 38, No. 4 (Fall 1986), 591–612.
51. Mary Crawford and Roger Chaffin, "The Reader's Construction of Meaning," 15.
52. Hannah Davis Gale's Journal "A" is in the Gale Family Papers at the American Antiquarian Society (hereafter abbreviated to AAS). Although the journal itself covers the period between late 1837 and 1838, there is no indication of Gale's date of birth. Margaret Fuller taught for a time with Hiram Fuller (no relation) at the Greene Street School in Providence. Gale may be the "Anna" Gale also quoted in Bell Gale Chevigny's *The Woman and the Myth: Margaret Fuller's Life and Writings* (New York: The Feminist Press, 1976), 151 and 159–60.
53. Julia Newberry, *Diary*, 75.
54. Ada R. Parker, *Letters of Ada R. Parker* (Boston: Crosby and Nichols, 1863), 154.
55. Julia A. Parker Dyson, *Life and Thought: Or, Cherished Memorials of the late Julia A. Parker Dyson*, edited by Miss E. Latimer, 2nd edition (Philadelphia: Claxton, Remsen, Hafflefinger and Co., 1871), 59.
56. Ibid., 60.
57. Ibid., 60.
58. Ibid., 62.
59. Catharine Merrill, *Catharine Merrill, Life and Letters*, collected and arranged by Katharine Merrill Graydon (Greenfield, IN: The Mitchell Company, 1934), 38.
60. Hannah Davis Gale, *Diary*, 116.
61. Ibid., 131.
62. Frances E. Willard, *Nineteen Beautiful Years; Or, Sketches of a Girl's Life* (Chicago: Women's Temperance Publications Association, 1886), 179.
63. Ada R. Parker, *Letters*, 154.
64. Julia Newberry, *Diary*, 153–5.
65. Celia Thaxter, *Letters of Celia Thaxter* (Boston: Houghton Mifflin and Co., 1895), 8.
66. In the last two decades historians have most intensely studied nineteenth-century women's efforts to improve their educational opportunities, revealing just how concerted a movement it was. Foremost among the now many books and articles taking this issue into account are Nancy Cott's *The Bonds of Womanhood: "Woman's Sphere" in New England, 1780–1835* (New Haven:

Yale University Press, 1977); Kathryn Kish Sklar's *Catharine Beecher;* Cathy N. Davidson's *Revolution and the Word: The Rise of the Novel in America* (New York: Oxford University Press, 1986); and Mary Kelley's *Private Woman, Public Stage.*

67. Julia Newberry, *Diary,* 32.
68. Samuel Gilman to Louisa Gilman, Feb. 3, 1810. Samuel and Caroline Howard Gilman Papers, 1809–58, AAS.
69. Samuel Gilman to Louisa Gilman, April 8, 1821.
70. Ibid.
71. Mary Guion, *Diary,* New York Historical Society Manuscripts Collection (hereafter abbreviated as NYHS), typescript, 25–6.
72. Cathy N. Davidson, *Revolution and the Word, 98ff.*
73. Samuel Gilman to Louisa Gilman, April 8, 1821.
74. Mary Guion, *Diary,* typescript, 76.
75. Mary Guion, *Diary,* 203.
76. Mary Guion, *Diary,* 242. The passage of *Paradise Lost* to which she refers occurs in Book IX, lines 895–989.
77. Mary Guion, *Diary,* 244.
78. Mary Guion, *Diary,* 159.
79. Mary Guion, *Diary,* 194.
80. In "Archimedes and the Paradox of Feminist Criticism," Myra Jehlen addresses the problem of devising a method of research that includes women's perspectives, and Section 2 of her essay applies some of her ideas to American women's novels of the mid-nineteenth century. But Jehlen begins that section by stating that "most of the women's writing [of the period] is awful" (201), and proceeds to investigate the reasons for its dreadfulness by examining the genre's relationship to *Pamela* and *Clarissa.* Having been intrigued by the essay's first section, I have struggled – unsuccessfully – to find anything either new, feminist, or revealing about the second section. See Jehlen in *Feminist Theory: A Critique of Ideology,* edited by Nannerl O. Keohane, Michelle Z. Rosaldo, and Barbara C. Gelpi (Chicago: The University of Chicago Press, 1982), 189–216. DuPlessis, on the other hand, while focusing on twentieth-century texts, is nevertheless sensitive to the "repressed element" in nineteenth-century texts that struggles against set narrative closures. DuPlessis, *Writing beyond the Ending,* 6–7.
81. Roland Barthes, introduction to *S/Z: An Essay,* translated by Richard Miller (New York: Hill and Wang, 1974), 3–11 and throughout; also see Jonathan Culler, *Structuralist Poetics: Structuralism, Linguistics, and the Study of Literature* (Ithaca: Cornell University Press, 1975), 189–238.
82. Hans Robert Jauss, *Toward an Aesthetic of Reception,* 25.
83. Roland Barthes, *S/Z,* 5–16; see also Barbara Johnson, "The Critical Difference: BarthesS/BalZac," in *Contemporary Literary Criticism: Modernism through Poststructuralism,* edited by Robert Con Davis (New York: Longman, Inc., 1982), 439–46.
84. Jacques Derrida, "Structure, Sign, and Play in the Discourse of the Human Sciences," in Davis, ed., *Contemporary Literary Criticism,* 480–98; also see Jonathan Culler, *Structuralist Poetics,* 133.
85. Roland Barthes, *Writing Degree Zero,* translated by Annette Lavers and Colin

Smith (New York: Hill and Wang, 1967); also see Culler, *Structuralist Poetics*, 134.

86. Jonathan Culler, *Structuralist Poetics*, 134.

87. Gerald Prince, "Introduction to the Study of the Narratee," reprinted in *Reader-Response Criticism: From Formalism to Post-Structuralism*, edited by Jane P. Tompkins (Baltimore: The Johns Hopkins University Press, 1980), 7–25.

88. Ann Douglas Wood, "The 'Scribbling Women' and Fanny Fern: Why Women Wrote," 13.

CHAPTER 1

1. Mary Guion Diary, NYHS; typescript, 201–2.

2. Cathy N. Davidson, *Revolution and the Word*, especially Chapter 4, "Literacy, Education, and the Reader" (New York: Oxford University Press, 1984).

3. For many of the analytic concepts included here I am indebted to Susan Rubin Suleiman's exploration of the didactic nature of the French *roman à thèse* in *Authoritarian Fictions: The Ideological Novel as a Literary Genre* (New York: Columbia University Press, 1983), 54.

4. See especially, Leslie A. Fiedler, *Love and Death in the American Novel* (New York: Dell Publishing Company, 1960); Myra Jehlen, "Archimedes and the Paradox of Feminist Criticism," in *Feminist Theory: A Critique of Ideology*, Keohane, Rosaldo, and Gelpi, eds. (Chicago: The University of Chicago Press, 1982) 189–216, and Cathy N. Davidson, *Revolution and the Word*.

5. Susanna Rowson, *Charlotte Temple: A Tale of Truth*, with an Introduction by Cathy N. Davidson (New York: Oxford University Press, 1986). *Charlotte Temple* was first published in England in 1791; in America in 1794.

6. Suleiman breaks down narrative repetitions (redundancies), charting and codifying them. While I am not concerned to perform a similar codification of my materials, I do refer to her chart with gratitude and admiration. See *Authoritarian Fictions*, 159–70.

7. In her discussion of negative and positive apprenticeships in *Authoritarian Fictions*, Susan Suleiman notes that "the function of the fable . . . is to allow us to live vicariously" (53). Suleiman builds on George Lukács's discussion of authentic (positive) versus inauthentic (negative) exemplary apprenticeships for her own analysis of the French *roman à thèse* of the 1930s. Briefly, for Kukács, "a 'positive exemplary' apprenticeship leads the hero to the values propounded by the doctrine that founds the novel; a 'negative exemplary' apprenticeship leads him to opposite values, or simply to a space where the positive values are not recognized as such" (67). Suleiman amends Lukács's analysis by noting that the *roman à thèse* "invests these categories with nonproblematic meanings" (67). Her amendment is useful for our investigation because it also holds true for early nineteenth-century American didactic novels. There, the narrator presents the narratee with heroines (and some heroes) about whom there is little or no ambiguity; they either take the right path (right according to the narrator's values) or the wrong one. Accordingly, the protagonists are proffered either as positive or negative exemplary apprentices.

8. Mary Guion, *Diary*, 191.

9. Ibid.

10. Ibid., 152.
11. Ibid., 156–7.
12. Davidson, *Revolution and the Word*, 137.
13. Catharine M. Sedgwick, *A New-England Tale, and Miscellanies* (New York: George P. Putman and Co., 1852), unnumbered dedication page; hereafter referred to as the 1852 edition. In this edition, the dedication is broken into poetic lines and printed with four different typefaces.
14. Catharine Maria Sedgwick, *A New-England Tale* (New York: E. Bliss and E. White, 1822), *vii–viii;* hereafter referred to as the 1822 edition. Internal citations are from this edition.
15. *The North American Review,* Vol. *xv,* New Series Vol. *vi,* No. 1 (July, 1822), 279.
16. Richard Henry Dana, Senior, letter to the Honorable Gulian C. Verplanck, August 11, 1822. NYHS, Verplanck Collection.
17. *A New-England Tale* did incur criticism for its apparent attack on New Englanders. On May 25, 1822, Sedgwick's brother Harry wrote to her about the progress of the book on the marketplace, first noting that though "its sale was dull at first, . . . now it was going off very rapidly . . ." but also reporting that "the only difficulty with the book is the unfavorable representation of the New England character. . . ." *Life and Letters of Catharine M. Sedgwick,* edited by Mary E. Dewey (New York: Harper and Bros., Pubs., 1871), 152. A review of two of Sedgwick's later novels, *The Poor Rich Man, and the Rich Poor Man* and *Live and Let Live; Or, Domestic Service Illustrated,* stresses Sedgwick's talent for the didactic and notes that her intentions directly influence her style: ". . . it is to be said to her great praise, that her mind, in order to put forth its full strength, needs to be excited by the sense of having undertaken to impress some weighty doctrine of practical philanthropy; and all experience speaks against the attempt to enforce a single moral of any kind by a fiction extended to any great length." *North American Review,* Vol. 45, No. 97 (October, 1837), 475.
18. Mikhail M. Bakhtin, *The Dialogic Imagination: Four Essays,* translated by Caryl Emerson and Michael Holquist (Austin: University of Texas Press, 1981), 316.

CHAPTER 2
1. Mary Kelley, *Private Woman, Public Stage* (New York: Oxford University Press, 1984), 25.
2. William Perry Fidler, *Augusta Evans Wilson, 1835–1909: A Biography* (University, AL: University of Alabama Press, 1951), 142–4. According to Fidler, the play, first produced in 1909, was a standard offering in stock repertories for years. A movie version was produced in 1914 and again in 1923.
3. Ibid., 131–5.
4. Ibid., 131–5.
5. Ibid., 132.
6. Julia A. Parker Dyson, *Life and Thought: Or, Cherished Memorials of the late Julia A. Parker Dyson,* ed. by Miss B. Latimer, 2nd edition (Philadelphia: Claxton, Remsen, Hafflefinger & Co., 1871).

7. William Perry Fidler, *Augusta Evans Wilson*, 131.
8. Fred Lewis Pattee, *The Feminine Fifties* (New York: D. Appleton-Century Co., Inc., 1940), 125.
9. Augusta J. Evans (Wilson), *St. Elmo* (Chicago: M. A. Donohue & Company, n.d.).
10. William Perry Fidler, *Augusta Evans Wilson*, 134.
11. Nina Baym, *Woman's Fiction* (Ithaca: Cornell University Press, 1978), 290.
12. Alfred Habegger, *Gender, Fantasy, and Realism in American Literature* (New York: Columbia University Press, 1982), 18.
13. Nina Baym, *Woman's Fiction*, 290–1.
14. Gerald Graff, *Professing Literature: An Institutional History* (Chicago: The University of Chicago Press), 1987.
15. David Simpson, ed., *German Aesthetic and Literary Criticism: Kant, Fichte, Schelling, Schopenhauer, Hegel* (New York: Cambridge University Press, 1984), 204.
16. Gerald Graff, *Professing Literature*, Footnote 30, p. 267, points out that Hegel called for synthesis but that few "educated" men were able to go beyond the grammar and etymologies they had been taught.
17. Ibid., 20.
18. Mary Kelley, *Private Woman, Public Stage*, 191.
19. Nina Baym, *Woman's Fiction*, 290.
20. Mrs. Mary Ann (Coit) Parker, Diary, 1849–50, NYHS.
21. A clue to the way exploratory novels develop may lie in Caroline Gilman's description of her mode of writing fiction. "It is a curious thing in my narratives," she wrote in 1838,

> that when I sit down to write a chapter, I have no more idea of the result than my readers. It cannot be the right way I am certain, and I wish I could discipline myself into a regular story. My object in Ruth Raymond [a didactic novel for girls then in progress] is to show how much of what is called love, depends on mere accident, – and after a long series of changes, which as almost every girl has felt, to develop the true sentiments – which withstand change and triumph over temptation. In this course I shall have an opportunity of wandering out of the track, and developing many of the incidents and feelings which occur to the young.

June 5, 1838, Caroline Howard Gilman Papers, Box 2, Folder 5, AAS. Gilman's novels are not exploratory, but her method of "developing many of the incidents and feelings which occur to the young" suggests that she may have produced a text whose incidental development – its middle – appealed to young readers more than did its final moral.
22. Robyn Warhol has expanded Prince's discussion to consider the differences between engaging and distancing narrators and their function in nineteenth-century women's novels. Robyn R. Warhol, "Toward a Theory of the Engaging Narrator: Earnest Interventions in Gaskell, Stowe, and Eliot," *PMLA*, Vol. 101, No. 5 (October, 1986), 811–17.
23. Maud Rittenhouse, *Maud*, edited by Richard Lee Strout (New York: The Macmillan Co., 1939), 26.

24. Willaim Perry Fidler, 132.
25. Nina Baym has also commented on this in *Woman's Fiction*, 293.
26. Wolfgang Iser, "The Reading Process," in *The Implied Reader: Patterns of Communication in Prose Fiction from Bunyan to Beckett* (Baltimore: The Johns Hopkins University Press, 1974), 279.
27. Nina Baym, *Woman's Fiction*, Introduction and Chapter 2, "Form and Ideology."

CHAPTER 3

1. Wayne C. Booth, *The Rhetoric of Fiction* (Chicago: University of Chicago Press, 1961), 153.
2. Jonathan Culler, *On Deconstruction: Theory and Criticism after Structuralism* (Ithaca: Cornell University Press, 1982), 45.
3. In *The Feminization of American Culture* (New York: Avon Books, 1977), Ann Douglas attributes the destruction of American Calvinism to the development of "'feminizing' sentimental forces" that developed as a backlash to the patriarchal limitations of the earlier religious creed (12–13). Douglas sees these new forces as an inadequate replacement, contributing to the development of a mass culture that did not gain a "comprehensive feminism" or a useful modern religious sensibility. In the course of demonstrating these developments, Douglas documents the privileging of piety and sentimentality in American popular culture.
4. Susan Warner, *Queechy* (Philadelphia: J. B. Lippincott & Co., 1852), 106. Subsequent quotations will be documented internally.
5. Sarah Josepha Hale, *Flora's Interpreter; Or, The American Book of Flowers and Sentiments* (Boston: Marsh, Capen and Lyon, 1832). Fourteenth edition published by Thomas H. Webb and Co., Boston, no date.
6. Ibid., 142.
7. Anna's letters speak of flowers frequently and lovingly. She also later published a book on gardening. Olivia Egleston Phelps Stokes, *Letters and Memories of Susan and Anna Bartlett Warner* (New York: G. P. Putnam's Sons, 1925). Anna's book was entitled *Gardening by Myself* (New York: A. D. F. Randolph and Co., 1872).
8. In *S/Z*, Roland Barthes lists five codes under which he groups textual signifiers: hermeneutic, semes (or linguistic), symbolic, proairetic, and cultural. See *S/Z: An Essay*, Richard Miller, trans. (New York: Hillard Wang, 1974), 18–20. In *Narratology*, Gerald Prince explicates the codes, showing how they work and what kinds of questions they answer. Prince, *Narratology: The Form and Functioning of Narrative* (Berlin: Mouton Publishers, 1982), Chapter 4, "Reading Narrative." In my analysis of *Queechy* I will not attempt to deal with either the linguistic or the proairetic codes, but am concerned to see how far the concepts of cultural, symbolic, and hermeneutic codes will take us in determining how this novel communicates its several messages.
9. An exceptionally clear portrait of this type appears in the portrait of the father in Susan Warner's (Elizabeth Wetherell, pseud.), *The Red Wall-Flower* (New York: Robert Carter and Brothers, 1884).
10. As Josephine Donovan has shown, this latter term has been used to denigrate women writers – who flocked to the patriotic call and consistently starred in

the production of literature reflective of the American scene – and to marginalize the particularly female concerns of the texts. Josephine Donovan, *New England Local Color Literature* (New York: Frederick Ungar Publishing Co., 1983).

11. *Queechy*, by Elizabeth Wetherell, in *Peterson's Magazine*, Vol. 22, No. 1, (January, 1852), 71.

12. *The North American Review*, Vol. 76, No. 158 (January, 1853), 104–23.

13. Ibid., 115.

14. Elizabeth Barrett Browning, *Elizabeth Barrett Browning's Letters to Mrs. David Ogilvy* (New York: Quadrangle/The New York Times Book Co., and The Browning Institute, 1973), 107.

15. Linda K. Kerber, *Women of the Republic: Intellect and Ideology in Revolutionary America* (Chapel Hill: University of North Carolina Press, 1980), especially Chapter 9, "The Republican Mother: Female Political Imagination in the Early Republic."

16. A sizable secondary literature now exists investigating the concept of the redeemer nation and its ramifications for American history and literature. See, among others, Ernest Lee Tuveson, *Redeemer Nation: The Idea of America's Millennial Role* (Chicago: The University of Chicago Press, 1968); Cushing Strout, *The New Heavens and New Earth: Political Religion in America* (New York: Harper and Row, Publishers, 1974); and Sacvan Bercovitch, *The Puritan Origins of the American Self* (New Haven: Yale University Press, 1975).

17. *The North American Review*, Vol 76, No. 158 (January, 1853), 122.

18. Susan Strasser, *Never Done: A History of American Housework* (New York: Pantheon Books, 1982), 35.

19. John Jacob Astor left $400,000 for a reference library in 1848; it was chartered in 1849 and opened to the public in 1854, so it would have been in process while Warner was writing *Queechy*.

20. Constance Rourke, *American Humor: A Study of the National Character* (New York: Harcourt, Brace and Company, Inc., 1931).

21. *The North American Review*, Vol. 76, No. 158 (January, 1853), 119.

22. *Peterson's Magazine*, Vol. 22, No. 1 (January, 1852), 71.

23. *The New Path: Ruskin and the American Pre-Raphaelites*, The Brooklyn Museum, March 29–June 10, 1985.

24. See also Nina Baym, *Novels, Readers, and Reviewers* (Ithaca: Cornell University Press, 1985), 97–102, for analysis of reviewers' calls for "fragile, beautiful, lovable" heroines.

25. In *Queechy*, Warner accurately delineates the differences between an earlier mode of employment, the hired woman, and a later, the professional servant, often an immigrant. In the opening pages of *Queechy* another hired woman had insisted on her right to preside at the family table, even when visitors came to tea. Though Warner's portraits of these characters do not explode any contemporary prejudices, for our purposes the fact that she simply introduces them through dialogue and scene rather than through narrator's homily is significant. She trusts that her narratee knows what she is talking about and will interpret the scenes correctly.

26. Wolfgang Iser, *The Implied Reader* (Baltimore: The Johns Hopkins University

Press, 1974). For a discussion of indeterminacy see especially Chapter 11, "The Reading Process."

27. Louisa Jane Trumbull, *Diaries, 1829–34, 1834–5, 1835–6, 1836.* Trumbull Family Papers, 1773–1896, Folder 6, AAS. Quotation from diary entry for September 9, 1833, 62.

28. Ibid., 91–3.

29. Hannah Blaney Thacher Washburn, *Diaries, 1861–70*, Rare Books and Manuscripts Division, The New York Public Library, Astor, Lenox and Tilden Foundations (hereafter abbreviated NYP). This quotation is from the diary of Hannah Maria Washburn.

30. Katharine Bayard Johnson, Record of Books Read, 1868–71, NYHS.

31. Julia Newberry, *Diary,* Introduction by Margaret Ayer Barnes and Janet Ayer Fairbank (New York: Norton and Co., Inc., 1933), 32.

32. Mrs. Mary Ann (Coit) Parker, *Diary, 1849–50,* 60 and 35, NYHS.

33. Elizabeth Starling, *Noble Deeds of Woman; Or, Examples of Female Courage and Virtue,* in *Peterson's Magazine,* Vol. 17, No. 4 (April, 1850), 207.

34. Annie A. Mackay, *Commonplace Book, 1883–90,* no pagination. NYP.

35. "The Spears of Sheridan County: Diary of Virginia Belle Benton," *Annals of Wyoming,* Vol. 14, No. 2 (April, 1942), 117.

36. In *Woman's Fiction,* Nina Baym also notes that the "fairy-tale ending and continuous celebration of the heroine's perfections do not make up for *Queechy*'s mood of hopelessness. . ."; Baym, however, reads this as a deficiency in Warner's political vision: "As usual . . . Warner fails to generalize from her particular situation to some vision of social injustice." *Women's Fiction: A Guide to Novels by and about Women in America, 1820–1870* (Ithaca: Cornell University Press, 1978), 151.

37. For a study of the ideological background of death, tears, and sentiment in nineteenth-century literature see Fred Kaplan, *Sacred Tears: Sentimentality in Victorian Literature* (Princeton, N.J.: Princeton University Press, 1987).

38. *The North American Review,* Vol. 76, No. 158, (January, 1853), 121.

39. Ibid., 116.

CHAPTER 4

1. Joyce W. Warren, ed., *Ruth Hall and Other Writings by Fanny Fern,* American Women Writers Series (New Brunswick, NJ: Rutgers University Press, 1986). All citations will refer to this edition.

2. The autobiographical elements of *Ruth Hall* are discussed both by Warren and by Mary Kelley, in *Private Woman, Public Stage* (New York: Oxford University Press, 1984).

3. *Peterson's Magazine,* Vol. 27, No. 2 (February, 1855), 179.

4. *Godey's Lady's Book and Magazine,* Vol. 50–1 (February, 1855), 176. In her introduction to the Rutgers edition of *Ruth Hall,* Joyce Warren notes the controversy it engendered.

5. Nina Baym, *Novels, Readers, and Reviewers: Responses to Fiction in Antebellum America* (Ithaca: Cornell University Press, 1984), 257. In other words, writing was supposed to reflect ideal gender definitions.

6. Sarah Josepha Hale, ed., *Flora's Interpreter; Or, The American Book of Flowers*

and Sentiments (Boston: Thomas H. Webb and Co., no date). First published by Marsh, Capen and Lyon, Boston, 1832, 234.

7. Ibid., 235.

8. "Women," in F. A. Moore, ed., *The Present; or A Gift for the Times* (Manchester, NH: R. Moore, 1850), 43.

9. Fred Kaplan, *Sacred Tears* (Princeton, NJ: Princeton University Press, 1987), 5–6, 37. Chapter 1, "The Moral Sentiments," explores the history of British sentimentality.

10. *The Knickerbocker,* Vol. 45 (January, 1855), 84–6.

11. *Peterson's,* Vol. 27, No. 2 (February, 1855), 179.

12. Julia Newberry, *Diary* (New York: Norton and Co., Inc., 1933), 67.

13. *The Story: A Bundle of Letters of an Age Gone By,* copyright 1966 by Reginald Barr, 2907 W. Montebello, Phoenix, Arizona. Antiochiana Archives, Yellow Springs, Ohio. This is a collection of privately printed letters of the Sherwin family, who lived in and around Yellow Springs, 1858–60 and 1861–4, mostly as students at Antioch College.

14. Perhaps Jonathan Culler explains Barthes best, when he notes in his discussion of Barthes that "the *lisable* [readerly] is that which accords with the codes and which we know how to read, the *scriptable* [writerly] that which resists reading and can only be written." See Culler, *Theory and Criticism after Structuralism* (Ithaca: Cornell University Press, 1982), 32.

15. In *Toward an Aesthetic of Reception* (Minneapolis: University of Minnesota Press, 1982), Hans Robert Jauss defines culinary or entertainment art as "precisely fulfilling the expectations prescribed by a ruling standard of taste, in that it satisfies the desire for the reproduction of the familiarly beautiful; confirms familiar sentiments; sanctions wishful notions; makes unusual experiences enjoyable as 'sensations'; or even raises moral problems, but only to 'solve' them in an edifying manner as predecided questions" (25).

16. Augusta Evans Wilson, *St. Elmo,* 439.

17. Wolfgang Iser, "The Reading Process: A Phenomenological Approach," in *The Implied Reader* (Baltimore: The Johns Hopkins University Press, 1974), 274–94.

18. Peter J. Rabinowitz, "Truth in Fiction: A Reexamination of Audiences," *Critical Inquiry,* Vol. 4, No. 1 (Autumn 1977), 121–41.

19. M. M. Bakhtin, "Discourse in the Novel," from *The Dialogic Imagination* (Austin: University of Texas Press, 1981), 192.

20. Ibid., 324.

21. Mary Guion, *Diary*, typescript, 159, NYHS.

22. Catharine E. Beecher, *Woman's Suffrage and Woman's Profession* (Hartford: Brown and Gross, 1871).

23. Mary Austin, "The Return of Mr. Wills," in *Stories from the Country of Lost Borders,* Marjorie Pryse, ed., American Women Writers Series (New Brunswick, NJ: Rutgers University Press, 1987), 181–7.

24. Nina Baym, "Melodramas of Beset Manhood: How Theories of American Fiction Exclude Women Authors." Reprinted in Elaine Showalter (ed.) *The New Feminist Criticism* (New York: Pantheon Books, 1985), 63–80.

25. *The Knickerbocker,* Vol. 45 (January, 1855), 84–6.

CHAPTER 5

1. *The Hidden Hand or, Capitola the Madcap,"* by E.D.E.N. Southworth, edited and introduced by Joanne Dobson (New Brunswick, NJ: Rutgers University Press, American Women Writers Series, 1988), *xvii.*
2. For Southworth's publishing history, see John Trebbel, *A History of Book Publishing in the United States: The Creation of an Industry, 1630–1865* (NY: R. R. Bowker Co., 1972), and Frank Luther Mott, *Golden Multitudes: The Story of Best Sellers in the United States* (New York: The Macmillan Co., 1947). Mary Kelley's *Private Woman, Public Stage* has a wonderful chapter on the publishing history of twelve of the most prominent nineteenth-century women writers (New York: Oxford University Press, 1984).
3. John S. Hart, ed., *The Female Prose Writers of America,* third edition (Philadelphia: E. H. Butler & Co., 1857), 214.
4. Ibid., 214–15.
5. Ibid., 213.
6. Emma D.E.N. Southworth, *The Deserted Wife* (Philadelphia: T. B. Peterson, 1855), 372.
7. Joanne Dobson, ed., *The Hidden Hand,* by Southworth, *xix.*
8. E.D.E.N. Southworth, *The Deserted Wife* (Philadelphia: T. B. Peterson, 1855), 25–6.
9. John Hart, ed., *Female Prose Writers of America,* 214–15.
10. *The Literary World,* Vol. 7, No. 187 (Aug. 31, 1850), 171.
11. Nina Baym, *Novels, Readers, and Reviewers* (Ithaca: Cornell University Press, 1984).
12. Ibid., 184.
13. Mary Kelley, *Private Woman, Public Stage,* 294, and Joanne Dobson, ed., *The Hidden Hand,* by Southworth, *xiii.*
14. For a synopsis of Schiller's contribution to Romantic thought see M. H. Abrams, *Natural Supernaturalism: Tradition and Revolution in Romantic Literature* (New York: W. W. Norton and Co., Inc., 1971), 206–17.
15. *Diary* of Louisa Jane Trumbull, February, 1834, 82. Trumbull Family Papers, Folder 6, AAS.
16. Julia Newberry, *Diary* (New York: Norton and Co., Inc., 1933), 32.
17. In this, *The Deserted Wife* resembles Maria Cummins's *Mabel Vaughan* (Boston: Crosby, Nichols, and Co., 1858), whose heroine also conquers her circumstances and is last seen in her "beautiful Western home" (506).
18. Andrew Jackson Downing, *The Architecture of Country Houses* (New York: D. Appleton and Co., 1859), 259.
19. *The Mother-In-Law* was first serialized in *The National Era,* Vol. 3, No. 47 (November 19, 1849) through Vol. 4, No. 29 (July 18, 1850) as *The Mother-in-Law, A Story of the Island Estate.*
20. In *Woman's Fiction,* Nina Baym has also noted the wonderful antistereotyping of this character (Ithaca: Cornell University Press, 1978), 120.
21. Gaston Bachelard, *The Poetics of Space,* translated by Maria Jolas (Boston: Beacon Press, 1969), 5.
22. M. H. Abrams, *Natural Supernaturalism,* Chapter 4.
23. In his preface to a posthumous edition of Downing's *Villas and Cottages* (New

York: Harper and Brothers, 1864), Calvert Vaux observes that Downing "used every effort to break down the foolish barrier that ignorance had set between the artist and the moralist, and strove to make manifest in all his works the glorious truth that the really 'beautiful' and the really 'good' are one" (*xi–xii*).

One sign of Downing's success appears in his response to a parson's request that he design a house that "a poor country clergyman" – the writer's own self-description – could afford. Downing's design includes two stories with seven and a half bedrooms, parlor, study, dining room, kitchen, storage rooms, and a "rustic" exterior in the stick-and-shingle style, complete with peaked roofs, a large veranda, small porches, and arbors. To keep costs down the architect suggests that the minister add the picturesque details himself:

> The rustic veranda and rustic trellises over the windows are intended for vines – though not merely as supports for vines, but rather as thereby giving an air of rural refinement and poetry to the house without expense. . . . we do not mean these rustic trellises to be built by carpenters . . . but to be added afterwards . . . by the clergyman himself, aided by some farm hand expert with the saw and hammer. . . . By the addition of such trellis-work and a few vines, a simple rustic cottage like this may be made a most attractive object in a rural landscape.

The design was budgeted at $2,800.00 to $3,000.00. See A. J. Downing, *Victorian Cottage Residences* (New York: Dover Publications, Inc., 1981, reprint of 1873 edition), 163–8.

24. According to the *Oxford Dictionary of Saints,* edited by David Hugh Farmer (Oxford: Oxford University Press, 1987), Petronella

> belonged to the family of Domitilla, in whose catacomb she is described as a martyr. Her fictitious sixth century Acts make her a daughter of Peter. She refused marriage to a Count Flaccus; he threatened to have her killed, but she died after three days fasting. . . . St. Petronilla occurs fairly frequently in English late medieval stained glass and painted screens, and her usual emblem is a set of keys, presumably borrowed from St. Peter.

Volume 5 of *The Encyclopedia of Catholic Saints* (New York: Chilton Books, 1966) claims that St. Petronella left her family to become a servant in St. Peter's household. In *Actes and Monuments* (i.e., the *Book of Martyrs*) John Foxe mentions a Petronyll who was wife to a Walter Apelbye of Maidstone (New York Public Library Microfilm Collection, call number 2KC, pp. 1556–7) and presumably one of the "seven godly martyrs, five women and two men, burned at Maidstone for the word of truth and professing of sincere Religion of Christ" (1570).

25. Helen Waite Papashvily, *All the Happy Endings* (New York: Harper and Brothers Pubs., 1956). The phenomenon can of course be seen in the works of many women novelists; most readers will immediately recognize Mr. Rochester, from Charlotte Brontë's *Jane Eyre.*

26. Readers unfamiliar with the convention of the dark and fair ladies should see Leslie A. Fiedler's *Love and Death in the American Novel* (New York: Dell Publishing Company, 1960).

27. It is significant for a study of Southworth's women that Rosalia's protector is not a community of nuns – women who withdraw from the world – but "the Grand Duchess Maria Louisa of Parma," who rules her own domain.
28. In *Woman's Fiction* Baym rightly identifies marriage in *Queechy* as celebrating "an escape from adulthood," 155.
29. Joseph Campbell, *The Hero with a Thousand Faces* (Princeton, NJ: Bollingen Series XVII, Princeton University Press, 1968). An interesting study of female heroes is Carol Pearson and Katherine Pope, *The Female Hero in American and British Literature* (New York: R. R. Bowker Company, 1981).
30. For the myth of the Fisher King, see Jesse L. Weston, *From Ritual to Romance* (Cambridge, England: Cambridge University Press, 1920).
31. Mary Kelley, *Private Woman, Public Stage.*
32. Joanne Dobson, ed., *The Hidden Hand,* by Southworth, *xi–xx.*
33. Frances S. Osgood (1811–50) was an American poet who frequently wrote about heterosexual relationships.

CHAPTER 6

1. Sybil Weir, "*The Morgesons:* A Neglected Feminist *Bildungsroman,*" *New England Quarterly,* Vol. 49, No. 3 (September, 1976), 427–39. This path-breaking article preceded my own 1985 essay on *The Morgesons* and makes many of the points I have made, especially as regards Cassandra's sexuality and the irreligious quality of the novel.
2. Elizabeth Stoddard, *The Morgesons and Other Writings, Published and Unpublished,* edited by Lawrence Buell and Sandra A. Zagarell (Philadelphia: University of Pennsylvania Press, 1984), *xxiii.*
3. Stoddard's admiration for the Brontë sisters and for George Sand probably contributed to this venture. In a review of June 2, 1855, Stoddard spoke of *Jane Eyre* as "that leaf of heart life . . . a daring and masculine work." George Sand she wrote of as "a true prophet of what a woman can be." See "Early Journalism," in *The Morgesons and Other Writings.* In addition to Weir, Buell and Zagarell also discuss these ideas in their introduction, as does Sandra A. Zagarell, in her article "The Repossession of a Heritage: Elizabeth Stoddard's *The Morgesons,*" *SAF,* 13, No. 1 (1985), 45–56.
4. *Peterson's Magazine,* Vol. 47, No. 3 (September, 1862), 231.
5. See the introduction to *The Morgesons, xix.* Nathaniel Hawthorne did like it. See James H. Matlack, "Hawthorne and Elizabeth Drew Stoddard," *New England Quarterly,* Vol. 50, No. 2 (June, 1977), 278–302.
6. Constance Fenimore Woolson, Letter to Edmund Clarence Stedman, January 20, 1875, from St. Augustine, Florida. Edmund C. Stedman Papers, Rare Book and Manuscript Library, Columbia University.
7. See James H. Matlack's "Hawthorne and Elizabeth Barstow Stoddard," *New England Quarterly,* Vol. 50, No. 2 (June, 1977), 293. Matlack claims that "the predictable implausibility of the happy marriage at the end" is a borrowed plot convention and feels that the novel as a whole deteriorates into sentimentality and improbability.
8. Sandra A. Zagarell, "The Repossession of a Heritage," 53.
9. Elizabeth Stoddard, *The Morgesons and Other Writings, Published and Un-*

published, edited by Lawrence Buell and Sandra A. Zagarell, 8. All subsequent references to *The Morgesons* will be documented internally.

10. Bringing a different literary schema to her reading of *The Morgesons* than I bring, Sandra A. Zagarell sees the novel as thematizing the problem of female inheritance, whereas I read it as highlighting a self-creating protagonist's isolation by stripping her of historical ties that would inscribe and define her. See Zagarell, "The Repossession of a Heritage," 47.

11. Richard Foster, introduction to *The Morgesons* (New York: Johnson Reprint Corp., 1971), *xviii.*

12. Until recently, the tendency has been to give biographical readings of *The Morgesons;* Buell/Zagarell lean that way in their introduction to this volume, as does Richard Foster [who wrote the introduction to the 1971 reprint of *The Morgesons*]. Matlack also sees the novel as a kind of spiritual biography that depends heavily on biographical material. Lately, articles by Harris, in *ESQ* (Vol. 31, lst Quarter, 1985), 11–22, and Zagarell, in "The Repossession of a Heritage," have begun to revise these earlier readings.

13. 19 January, 1822. Hooker Collection, Folder #6, Letters from Almira Eaton to Weltha Brown, 1812–22. Schlesinger Library.

14. Sandra A. Zagarell, "Repossession of a Heritage," 50–1.

15. Sybil Weir, "The Morgesons: A Neglected Feminist Bildungsroman," 433.

16. For Sybil Weir, these relationships signal Stoddard's incest fantasy (436–7).

17. Sandra A. Zagarell, "The Repossession of a Heritage," 51.

18. Sybil Weir, "The Morgesons: A Neglected Feminist Bildungsroman," 429.

CHAPTER 7

1. Ednah D. Cheney, ed., *Louisa May Alcott: Her Life, Letters, and Journals* (Boston: Little, Brown, and Co., 1928; first published 1889), 231.

2. Louisa May Alcott, *Work: A Story of Experience,* with an introduction by Sarah Elbert (New York: Schocken Books, 1977, first published 1873), 2. All subsequent citations will refer to this edition.

3. Similar observations are made by Sarah Elbert in *A Hunger for Home: Louisa May Alcott and Little Women* (Philadelphia: Temple University Press, 1984), 190–7.

4. "Sentimental Power: *Uncle Tom's Cabin* and the Politics of Literary History," reprinted in Jane Tompkins, *Sensational Designs: The Cultural Work of American Fiction, 1790–1860* (New York: Oxford University Press, 1985), 122–46. The section referred to is on pp. 141–2.

5. "The Spears of Sheridan County: Diary of Virginia Belle Benton," *Annals of Wyoming,* Vol. 14, No. 2 (April, 1942), 117.

6. Ibid., 125*ff.* Virginia Benton became Mrs. Willis Spear, at various times President of the WCTU, and active in the church, the DAR, the Sheridan Women's Club, the Book Review Club, and the Music Club. During World War I she was captain of a group selling Liberty Bonds and raised money for an ambulance to be sent to France. Benton's life work was not radical, but it was activist in the sense that Alcott advocated.

7. Ednah D. Cheney, *Louisa May Alcott: Her Life, Letters, and Journals,* 225.

8. From "A London Paper, May 31, 1873; as quoted in Janet S. Zehr's "The Response of Nineteenth-Century Audiences to Louisa May Alcott's Fiction," *The American Transcendental Quarterly*, New Series 1:4 (December, 1987), 332.
9. Ibid.
10. Alma J. Payne, *Louisa May Alcott: A Reference Guide* (Boston: G. K. Hall & Co., 1980), 18.
11. Ibid.
12. Madeleine B. Stern, *Louisa May Alcott* (Norman, OK: University of Oklahoma Press, 1950), 230.
13. From the (Boston?) *Daily Journal*, quoted by Zehr, "The Response of Nineteenth-Century Audiences," 331.
14. Apparently, Christie's marriage posed a confusion for some contemporary reviewers, who, as Janet S. Zehr points out, had difficulty processing novels with multiple messages. One, open to the novel's call for female self-reliance, commented that "At first it seemed as if the author intended to show how a woman might support herself and lead a noble, honorable and happy life, without the inevitable resort to matrimony. But this intention, unfortunately, is laid aside" (Janet S. Zehr, "The Response of Nineteenth-Century Audiences," 333). Perhaps this reviewer laid the book down at the wedding; he or she does not seem aware of Christie's "noble, honorable" widowhood. Nevertheless, the review is useful for the insight it gives us into reviewers' propensities to read intertextually; this reviewer sees only the "inevitable resort to matrimony," not its careful placement as only one of the "experiences" that contribute to Christie's evolution into a figure who is, finally, as much the Christ of other women's journeys as the Christiana of her own.
15. This point is also discussed by Nina Auerbach in "Austen and Alcott on Matrimony: New Women or New Wives?," in Mark Spilka, ed., *Towards a Poetics of Fiction* (Bloomington: Indiana University Press, 1977), 266–86. Discussion of *Work* occurs on 283.
16. Nina Auerbach, *Communities of Women: An Idea in Fiction* (Cambridge: Harvard University Press, 1978), 67.
17. Janet S. Zehr, "The Response of Nineteenth-Century Audiences," 328.
18. Also see Nina Auerbach, "Austen and Alcott on Matrimony," in Spilka, *Towards a Poetics of Fiction*, 283.
19. Ednah D. Cheney, ed., *Louisa May Alcott: Her Life, Letters and Journals*, 220.
20. Elizabeth Stuart Phelps, *The Silent Partner and "The Tenth of January,"* with an afterword by Mari Jo Buhle and Florence Howe (New York: The Feminist Press, 1983), 7. All subsequent citations will refer to this edition.
21. M. M. Bakhtin, "Discourse in the Novel," in *The Dialogic Imagination* (Austin: University of Texas Press, 1981), 311.
22. Frances E. Willard, ed., *Nineteen Beautiful Years; Or, Sketches of a Girl's Life* (Chicago: Woman's Temperance Publications Association, 1886, originally published Harper and Bros., 1864), 186–7.
23. As would T. S. Eliot fifty years later, in *The Wasteland*.
24. Judith Fetterley, "'Checkmate': Elizabeth Stuart Phelps's *The Silent Partner*," *Legacy: A Journal of Nineteenth-Century American Women Writers*, Vol. 3, No. 2 (Fall 1986), 17–29.

25. Ibid., 28.
26. Ibid., 28.
27. Wolfgang Iser, "The Reading Process," in *The Implied Reader* (Baltimore: The Johns Hopkins University Press, 1974), 278.
28. Katharine Bayard Johnson, "Record of Books Read, 1868–71," NYHS, 13.
29. Ibid., 169–70.

CHAPTER 8

1. Hans Robert Jauss, *Toward an Aesthetic of Reception*, Timothy Bahti, translator (Minneapolis: University of Minnesota Press, 1982), 39–41.
2. Rachel Blau DuPlessis, *Writing beyond the Ending* (Bloomington: Indiana University Press, 1985), 4.
3. Elizabeth Stuart Phelps, *The Story of Avis* (New Brunswick, NJ: Rutgers University Press, 1985), 32–3.
4. Sarah Orne Jewett, *A Country Doctor* (New York: New American Library, 1986), 125.
5. Willa Cather, *O Pioneers!* (Boston: Houghton Mifflin Co., 1941), 71.
6. Kate Chopin, *The Awakening* (G. P. Putnam's Sons, 1964), 66.
7. Rachel Blau DuPlessis, *Writing Beyond the Ending*, 88.
8. Alfred Habegger, *Gender, Fantasy, and Realism in American Literature* (New York: Columbia University Press, 1982), 46.
9. Ibid., 49.
10. Marlene Springer and Haskell Springer, eds., *Plains Woman: The Diary of Martha Farnsworth, 1882–1922* (Bloomington: Indiana University Press, 1986), 108*ff*.
11. Ibid., 118.
12. Elizabeth Stuart Phelps, *Chapters from a Life* (Boston: Houghton, Mifflin and Co., 1896), 272.

GENERAL INDEX

Alcott, Louisa May, 174, 177
  Work: A Story of Experience, 35, 77,
    173–86, 203
All the Happy Endings: A Study of the
  Domestic Novel in America, the
  Women Who Wrote It, the Women
  Who Read It in the Nineteenth Cen-
  tury, Papashvily, 5–7, 142, 208
Ammons, Elizabeth, 11
apprenticeships, positive and nega-
  tive, 44–5, 53–5, 57, 58, 143,
  158, 190–1
  see also inscription; models
"Archimedes and the Paradox of
  Feminist Criticism," Jehlen, 215
architecture, and women, 129–30,
  137–47, 149–51, 165
The Architecture of Country Houses,
  Downing, 137
Astor Library, in *Queechy,* 90, 220
Auerbach, Nina, 6, 181
Authoritarian Fictions: The Ideological
  Novel as a Literary Genre,
  Suleiman, 77, 216–17
The Awakening, Chopin, 35, 201,
  204–6

Bakhtin, Mikhail, 116, 118–19, 124,
  187–90
Barthes, Roland, 22–3, 30–2, 115,
  219–20
Baym, Nina, 9–11, 21, 62, 69, 76,
  79, 112

Beecher, Catharine, 15–18, 113
Beneath the American Renaissance: The
  Subversive Imagination in the Age
  of Emerson and Melville,
  Reynolds, 11
The Bostonians, James, 76
Brown, Herbert Ross, 4–6
Browning, Elizabeth Barrett, 86
  Aurora Leigh, 26, 30, 202
Buell, Lawrence, 152, 156, 163, 168
Buhle, Mari Jo, 186

Cather, Willa
  O Pioneers!, 35, 84, 201, 203, 204,
    209–10
  Song of the Lark, 148
Chaffin, Roger, 23–4
Charlotte Temple, Rowson, 33, 40–52,
  54, 55, 57, 59, 78, 153, 174, 177
"'Checkmate': Elizabeth Stuart
  Phelps's *The Silent Partner,*"
  Fetterley, 12, 194–5
Cheney, Ednah D., 184
Chopin, Kate, *The Awakening,* 35,
  201, 204–6
class
  bias, in *Queechy,* 87, 91–3
  lower class women, as role models,
    92–3, 180, 183–4, 186–7
codes, hermeneutic and symbolic, for
  American women's novels, 20,
  32–3, 77–82, 95, 99, 113, 120–1,
  126–7, 167–8, 200, 208

229

INDEX TO DIARIES, LETTERS, AND REVIEWS

INDEX TO LITERARY
AND HISTORICAL
REFERENCES

235